ROYAL BOROUGH OF GRE

West Greenwich Library
Tel: 020 8858 4289

Please return by the last date shown		
~~11/18~~ 07/22 B ETTER(WORLD)		
Thank you! To renew, please contact any Royal Greenwich library or renew online or by phone www.better.org.uk/greenwichlibraries 24hr renewal line 01527 852384		

Cambridge Studies on the African Diaspora

Editor

Michael Gomez
New York University

Cambridge Studies on the African Diaspora places the experiences of African-descended communities within contexts of transnational, transregional, and transcultural exchange, united by the concept of the migration of peoples and their cultures, politics, ideas, and other systems from or within Africa to other nations or regions.

Slavery's Metropolis

Unfree Labor in New Orleans during the Age of Revolutions

RASHAUNA JOHNSON

Dartmouth College

CAMBRIDGE
UNIVERSITY PRESS

CAMBRIDGE
UNIVERSITY PRESS

University Printing House, Cambridge CB2 8BS, United Kingdom

One Liberty Plaza, 20th Floor, New York, NY 10006, USA

477 Williamstown Road, Port Melbourne, VIC 3207, Australia

314-321, 3rd Floor, Plot 3, Splendor Forum, Jasola District Centre, New Delhi-110025, India

79 Anson Road, #06-04/06, Singapore 079906

Cambridge University Press is part of the University of Cambridge.

It furthers the University's mission by disseminating knowledge in the pursuit of education, learning and research at the highest international levels of excellence.

www.cambridge.org
Information on this title: www.cambridge.org/9781107591165

© Rashauna Johnson 2016

First published 2016
First paperback edition 2017

A catalogue record for this publication is available from the British Library

Library of Congress Cataloging in Publication data
Johnson, Rashauna, author.
Slavery's metropolis : unfree labor in New Orleans during the age of revolutions / Rashauna Johnson.
New York, NY : Cambridge University Press, 2016. | Series: Cambridge studies on the african diaspora
LCCN 2016026285 | ISBN 9781107133716 (hardback)
LCSH: Slaves – Louisiana – New Orleans – History. | Slavery – Louisiana – New Orleans – History. | Slavery – United States – History. | New Orleans (La.) – History. | United States – History – 1783–1865.
LCC F379.N59 N44429 2016 | DDC 976.3/35–dc23
LC record available at https://lccn.loc.gov/2016026285

ISBN 978-1-107-13371-6 Hardback
ISBN 978-1-107-59116-5 Paperback

For my mother,
Clo Dunn Johnson
(1957–2015)

Contents

Figures

Maps

Preface

"Drowned in the blood of its citizens"

In August 2005, New Orleans officials decided that a mandatory evacuation order applied to people, not prisoners. As the Orleans Parish Prison filled with floodwaters, armed deputies escorted incarcerated citizens from locked jail cells to an interstate highway that, days before, conveyed relatively more privileged residents to safer places. In time I recognized what I call their "confined cosmopolitanism" – bound prisoners detained on a highway that connects Florida to California – but that insight came later. At the time my concerns were more prosaic: Are there my loved ones among the floating corpses? Which cousins are in jail right now? What did eight feet of water do to my home? Will class end early so I can piece together my shattered world from this bench in Washington Square Park?

New Orleans is my home place. I love that city, and I am proud to call it home. I missed Hurricane Katrina by about a week, as I had moved back to New York to prepare for the start of my second year of graduate coursework. As others worried the city would not come back, I worried it would. The poverty and inequality that others "discovered" during Katrina has defined black life in New Orleans and places like it for a very long time. By the mid-1960s, New Orleans "was one of the most impoverished, most unequal, most violent, and least educated places in the United States." Three-fourths of the city's black residents lived below the poverty line, while nearly half of the city's income went to the top 20 percent of the population. Public health and education were abysmal, and the murder rate was double the national average. The 1970s saw shifts thanks to the work of local organizers and War on Poverty programs, but in the 1980s the retrenchment of public will and funding under the Reagan administration and the bust of two major industries – oil and the port – left the local economy dependent on tourism and the service economy. White flight to the suburbs deprived the city of its tax base, and substance abuse, street violence, and mass incarceration ripped families apart. For most poor and black residents, things were far from easy in "The City that Care Forgot."[1]

As in the paradigmatic post-industrial US cities – Detroit, Chicago, Newark – urban communities in New Orleans have been devastated by wealth inequality, the War on Drugs, the prison industrial complex, and substance abuse. The illicit economy offers what legal capitalism does not, so men and women become trapped in cycles of violence, incarceration, poverty, and recidivism. As of 2012, Louisiana imprisoned 1619 inmates per 100,000 residents, a rate higher than that of any other state in the United States and "nearly five times Iran's, 13 times China's and 20 times Germany's." Louisiana's for-profit prisons enrich local law enforcement officials even as its two major cities – New Orleans and Baton Rouge – lead national murder statistics every year. And imprisonment disproportionately limits black men's lives: "About 5,000 black men from New Orleans are doing state prison time, compared with 400 white men from the city."[2] The murder rates are equally grim. In 2012, the city registered 193 murders in a population just shy of 363,000 residents.[3] Each death is a devastation, one that leaves traumatized partners, parents, children, and communities to shoulder a desperate grief.

Hurricane Katrina and the levee failures exposed the poverty that neoliberalism holds in store for many more in the years to come. But it also exposed the grit that persons of color and poor people across the

---

[1] Kent B. Germany, "The Politics of Poverty and History: Racial Inequality and the Long Prelude to Katrina," *Journal of American History* 94, no. 3 (December 2007): 743–751, 744. See also Kent B. Germany, *New Orleans After the Promises: Poverty, Citizenship, and the Search for the Great Society* (Athens: University of Georgia Press, 2007).

[2] Cindy Chang, "Louisiana is the World's Prison Capital," *Times-Picayune* (New Orleans, LA), May 13, 2012. On the rise of mass incarceration, see Dan Berger, *Captive Nation: Black Prison Organizing in the Civil Rights Era* (Chapel Hill: University of North Carolina Press, 2014); Michelle Alexander, *The New Jim Crow: Mass Incarceration in the Age of Colorblindness* (New York: New Press, 2010); Bryan Wagner, *Disturbing the Peace: Black Culture and the Police Power After Slavery* (Cambridge, MA: Harvard University Press, 2009).

[3] Report, "Louisiana: Offenses Known to Law Enforcement by City, 2012," Crime in the United States, 2012, Table 8, U.S. Federal Bureau of Investigations (FBI), available at www.fbi.gov/about-us/cjis/ucr/crime-in-the-u.s/2012/crime-in-the-u.s.-2012/tables/8tabl edatadecpdf/table-8-state-cuts/table_8_offenses_known_to_law_enforcement_by_louisia na_by_city_2012.xls (accessed March 21, 2014).

Global South have long marshaled to survive. Even the guns of private security forces and the market pressures of predatory lending and gentrification did not stop the city's dispossessed citizens from claiming their right to return. The Free Agents Brass Band spoke for me and many others when they declared, "I'm so glad we're back home/I'm so glad we're back home/We made it through that water/That muddy, muddy, water." And in January 2007, the late antiviolence activist and my beloved pastor Rev. John C. Raphael, Jr. proclaimed before protestors of many races and faiths gathered on the steps of City Hall that "A city that could not be drowned in the waters of a storm will not be drowned in the blood of its citizens."[4]

During the Age of Revolution, which witnessed the establishment of racialized citizenship, the emergence of capitalism, and the expansion of chattel slavery, people of African descent harnessed the power of streets and streams to survive a deadly epoch. Generations later, people of all backgrounds are working to transform bloody streets into places of justice and peace. In the present, as in the past, the place of black people in New Orleans remains contested. Their stories remind us that this nation's prosperity rested on the bedrock of exploitation and violence, but they also remind us that pretensions to unbounded power have been – and must be – checked by the determination of the defiant.

---

[4] Stacey Plaisance, "New Orleans Residents March on City Hall," *Washington Post*, January 11, 2007. Though Raphael was the son of New Orleans' first black police officer post-desegregation, was himself a police officer, and was a member of a family of police officers, "antiviolence" for him was not synonymous with "anti-criminal."

Acknowledgments

This book exists, which is testament to, among other things, the generosity and encouragement of many. First, I owe so much to my teachers and advisors. As an undergraduate at Howard University, Greg Carr and Edna Greene Medford mentored me and encouraged me to pursue graduate study. I also enjoyed the warm and generous support of Crystal Evans, Dr. Forrestine Barnes, and the Ronald E. McNair Program. The authors of the first two books that I read toward my undergraduate honors thesis – Michael Gomez and Walter Johnson – became members of my dissertation committee at New York University. There is no way for me to sufficiently thank Dr. Gomez, my dissertation advisor and now series editor. Dr. Gomez trusted me with the freedom to pursue my vision while offering timely feedback and encouragement along the way. And all of the members of that committee – Ada Ferrer, Walter Johnson, Barbara Krauthamer, and Michele Mitchell – have been supportive throughout this process.

I owe a great deal of gratitude to many scholars whose feedback shaped this book. I thank those who participated in the manuscript review at the John Sloan Dickey Center for International Understanding at Dartmouth College: Jennifer Morgan, Adam Rothman, Aimee Bahng, Bob Bonner, Leslie Butler, Reena Goldthree, Udi Greenberg, Sharlene Mollett, and George Trumbull IV. I also thank Chris Hardy Wohlforth for coordinating the seminar. Rosanne Adderley, Daina Ramey Berry, Raymond Gavins, Lara Putnam, Rebecca Scott, and Nayan Shah have all been supportive, and I thank them for their kindness and encouragement. In my time at Dartmouth I have enjoyed the camaraderie of many mentors, colleagues, and friends. I thank the members of the Department of History and the Programs in African and African American Studies (AAAS) and Women, Gender, and Sexuality Studies (WGSS) at Dartmouth. Bob Bonner has given feedback on an infinite number of drafts. Reena Goldthree and Aihmee Bahng helped me to carve out time to write and to reflect. Claudia Anguillano Lisa Baldez, Donnie Brooks, Adrienne Clay, Jay Davis, Laura Edmondson, Udi Greenberg, Jim Igoe, Deborah King, Bruch Lehman, Eng-Beng Lim, Stefan Link, Vincent Mack, Jennifer Miller, Paul Musselwhite, Annelise Orleck, Fran Oscadal, Tanalís Padilla, Gail Patten, Russell Rickford, Naaborko Sackeyfio-Lenoch, Leslie Schnyder, Soyoung Suh, Antonio Tillis, Zeynep Turkyilmaz, Derrick White, and many others have also been so kind and supportive. For his work on the maps, I thank Jonathan Chipman of Dartmouth's Geography Department and Citrin Family GIS/Applied Spatial Analysis Lab. I thank Charles "C.J." Katz for assistance with images and permissions. I thank independent researchers John McNish Weiss and Patrick Davis for their valuable insights. Finally, I thank the anonymous readers at Cambridge for their incisive comments.

I could not have written this book without many knowledgeable and patient archivists. Siva Blake at the Williams Research Center guided me through its collections. I also thank the archivists at the Archdiocese of New Orleans Office of Archives, the Louisiana State Archives, the Notarial Archives of New Orleans, Special Collections at Hill Memorial Library at Louisiana State University, the City Archives and Special Collections of the New Orleans Public Library, the New York Historical Society, the Manuscripts and Archives Division of the New York Public Library, the UK National Archives at Kew, the Louisiana Research Collection at Tulane University, and the West Indiana and Special Collections at the University of the West Indies at St. Augustine in Trinidad and Tobago.

For the funding that made this project possible, I am grateful to the Walter and Constance Burke Research Initiation Awards for Junior Faculty and the Junior Faculty Fellowship at Dartmouth; Jim Basker, Sidney Lapidus, and the Gilder-Lehrman Institute of American History; the Andrew W. Mellon Predoctoral Fellowship in the Humanistic Studies; and the Henry M. MacCracken Fellowship at New York University.

I owe such a debt to Debbie Gershenowitz, who has been a responsive and supportive editor. I also thank David Morris and Amanda George at Cambridge University Press as well as Velmurugan Inbasigamoni for shepherding this project to completion.

Somehow I have assembled the world's most amazing and supportive friends. Taciana Hardmon has generously provided encouragement, feedback, and a listening ear, and Khadija Adams, Charlyn Anderson, Peter Davis, Ashley Spears, Ashley Steele, and Tiffany Watson have all been kind to me for many years. My dear friends from my grad school cohort – Abena Asare, Anne Eller, Kendra Field, Kiron Johnson, Priya Lal, and Franny Sullivan – have made the past decade as fun as it has been intellectually stimulating. Justin Steil offered critical feedback and consistent encouragement, and Brandon Hogan challenged many of my assumptions in our notoriously lengthy and generative conversations.

The love, encouragement, and support of my family have sustained me during a period of major transitions. I thank my brother, Ventress Johnson III, and his children Breanna, Kirklen, and Ventress R. Johnson. I also thank my godmother, Ruth McKession, and cousins, Veronica Henry and Chantell Douglass, as well as Kathie Clark, Debbie Lindsey, Jacqueline Smith, Pamela White, and the members of the New Hope Baptist Church in New Orleans. My mother, Clo Johnson, and grandmother, Ruth Dunn, did not get to see this book in print, but their love, labor, sacrifices, and support made each word possible.

Abbreviations

AANO	Archdiocese of New Orleans Office of Archives, New Orleans, LA
AHR	*American Historical Review*
GRO	Gloucestershire Record Office, Gloucester Archives, Gloucestershire, UK
HNOC	Williams Research Center, Historic New Orleans Collection, New Orleans, LA
LSA	Louisiana State Archives, Baton Rouge, LA
LSU	Special Collections, Hill Memorial Library, Louisiana State University, Baton Rouge, LA
NANO	Notarial Archives, New Orleans, LA
NOC	New Orleans Collection at New-York Historical Society, New York, NY
NOPL	Louisiana Division, City Archives & Special Collections, New Orleans Public Library, New Orleans, LA
NYHS	New-York Historical Society, New York, NY
NYPL	Manuscripts and Archives Division, New York Public Library, New York, NY
THC	The Heartman Collection, 1794–1897, Xavier University, New Orleans, LA.
TNA	The National Archives, Kew, UK
TU	Special Collections, Tulane University, New Orleans, LA
UWI	West Indiana & Special Collections, University of the West Indies at St. Augustine, Trinidad and Tobago

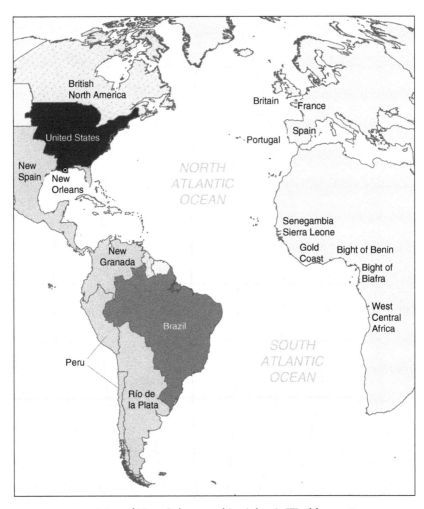

MAP 1 Map of New Orleans and its Atlantic World, ca. 1803.

Introduction

Slave Spaces

Stories about places are makeshift things.

Michel de Certeau[1]

Of all the places I've been in the world, New Orleans is the only place I've ever been where, if you listen, sidewalks will speak to you.

John T. Scott[2]

Charlotte's first Atlantic crossing did not require a passport. Her 1805 Middle Passage from Africa to New Orleans was legal. However, by her second transoceanic journey fifteen years later, the Atlantic currents had shifted. New Orleans, a colonial hamlet, had transformed into a booming American metropolis. Its population exploded from about 8,000 in 1803 to 27,000 in 1820, which made it the fifth largest city in the United States. International slave importation had been illegal since 1807, and Charlotte herself had changed: The prepubescent girl who left Africa had become the property of the prominent Forstall family and a mother in New Orleans. Like Charlotte, the Blancqs of New Orleans also descended from an Atlantic lineage, but unlike the enslaved woman these elite sojourners could visit their relatives in Bordeaux. In preparation for their 1820 journey, Pierre Blancq leased Charlotte, who would leave her daughter Corine behind in New

---

[1] Michel de Certeau, *The Practice of Everyday Life*, trans. Steven F. Rendall (Berkeley: University of California Press, 1984), 107.

[2] John T. Scott, *American Experience: New Orleans*, DVD, directed by Steven Ives (Boston: WGBH Educational Foundation, 2007). Scott (1940–2007), a celebrated visual artist, was a black New Orleanian who, among other accolades, received the Macarthur Genius grant.

Orleans to nurse the three Blancq children. Since such border crossings jeopardized property claims and subjected importers to prosecution, the mayor issued a passport for Charlotte. That paper – the mayor, slave owner, and slave lessee all hoped – would ensure that Charlotte could travel to France and then re-enter New Orleans as she had left it – a slave.[3]

Charlotte's story and others like it suggest that daily experiences of slavery in New Orleans and its environs at the turn of the nineteenth century were international, interconnected, and itinerant – a sharp contrast to the contained, isolated, and stationary bondage long associated with the plantation south. Unlike in the northeastern states of the early republic, where emancipation schemes diminished slave populations, New Orleans became a major American metropolis as its slave population exploded. From 1803, the year of the Louisiana Purchase, until 1830, slaves made up one-third of the urban population. The city became a hub of slavery, diversity, and circulation at the same time that the proper management of people became a measure of civilization and modernity. How did Charlotte and her fellow slaves help to produce the cosmopolitan places of New Orleans, the polyglot port city at the intersection of US imperial expansion and the Atlantic market economy? How did elites seek to establish order among the slaves and rabble in a compact urban core? How was the place of slaves in the city and its terrestrial and maritime conduits informed by the transitions between mercantilism and liberalism, small-scale farming and agro-capitalism, Old World imperialism, and New World republicanism? In short, what do we make of a slave woman with a passport?

Slavery's Metropolis uses slave circulations through New Orleans between 1791 and 1825 to map the social and cultural history of enslaved men and women and the rapidly shifting city, nation, and world in which they lived. In contrast to the prevailing idea that black Atlantic journeys and intimate interracial assemblies were exceptional to or subversive of chattel slavery, this book argues that in New Orleans not only did such

---

[3] I explore Charlotte's story in depth in Chapter 2. See footnotes there for full references.
    On changes in jurisdiction and their implications for slave status, see Rebecca Scott, "Paper Thin: Freedom and Re-Enslavement in the Diaspora of the Haitian Revolution," *Law and History Review* 29, no. 4 (2011): 1061–1087; Edlie L. Wong, *Neither Fugitive nor Free: Atlantic Slavery, Freedom Suits, and the Legal Culture of Travel* (New York: New York University Press, 2009).

journeys and assemblies exist despite that system of domination, but they were essential to it. A monolithic slaveocracy did not conspire to quarantine bondspersons; rather, slaveholders and local and imperial officials disputed over how to regulate and exploit slave mobility to build the city's infrastructure and industries. Bondspersons used this compulsory mobility to enact their own ideas about their proper place in a burgeoning slave society. So that diverse port situated at the intersection of Atlantic circularity and early American imperial expansion offers a rich vantage point for exploring the history of those multidirectional movements and the race-based containment strategies masters and leaders developed to regulate them. Though the master–slave relationship was a property-based arrangement, over time leaders and masters used law and custom to transform a black phenotype into a proxy for slave status. This book charts the uneven contests over the place of enslaved people in a port city to contribute fresh insights into the geographies of slavery and freedom for men and women, the history of racism, and the malleability of modern power.

This book uses everyday life across lines of empire, color, race, and status to offers a novel analysis of a transformational epoch in world history. In a little over three decades, the United States went from a collection of British colonies to a sovereign and imperialistic "nation among nations." The Haitian Revolution became a model for black freedom and an omen for the slaveholding Americas. The Louisiana Purchase doubled the nation's territory, accelerated the dispossession of indigenous nations, and hastened Anglo-American settlement in the continental interior. The transatlantic slave trade gave way to a domestic one that met the skyrocketing demand for slaves during the ascendance of King Cotton, strengthened US national sovereignty, and advanced the global industrial economy. The US victory over Britain in the War of 1812 and Napoleon's defeat at Waterloo ushered in a new era in the history of free trade, globalization, and colonialism. And this period stoked a white supremacist ideology that holds power even in the present. Slavery was central to each development, which put enslaved people in a position to advance, interrupt, shape, and talk back to such geopolitical shifts.

Slavery's Metropolis contributes analytical and historical perspectives to three intertwined fields: African diaspora and black Atlantic studies, cultural studies of American empire, and Louisiana history. First, the book proposes a novel analytical framework, "confined cosmopolitanism," that extends recent scholarship on the geographies of slavery and freedom in the

United States and the black Atlantic. Ex-slave, abolitionist, and orator Frederick Douglass declared, "people in general will say they like colored men as well as any other, *but in their proper place!*"[4] While Douglass likely referred to status, social and geographic positions are intertwined. Space is not a blank slate or an inert setting over which time acts. Rather, over time people produce places through lived experience even as those places shape people's daily lives. As such, contests over place-making offer unique insight into historical processes.[5] For example, auction blocks, whether the centerpiece of an elaborate pen or a slipshod arrangement of wood or stone no more massive than a milk crate, were a trader's showroom and a buyer's prospecting place. For those who mounted it, the auction block was a shattering space. Strangers gathered at that one physical place for a transaction that deepened their social and economic distance from one another.[6]

Slavery studies is heavily indebted to historian Stephanie Camp, whose groundbreaking *Closer to Freedom: Enslaved Women and Everyday*

[4] Frederick Douglass, "The Church and Prejudice" (speech given to the Plymouth County Anti-Slavery Society in Plymouth, County, Massachusetts on November 4, 1841), in *Frederick Douglass: Selected Speeches and Writings*, eds. Philip S. Foner and Yuval Taylor (Chicago: Lawrence Hill Books, 1999), 3–4, 4, emphasis original.

[5] As geographers and environmental historians have long insisted, people and places act on each other in contingent and competing ways. For example, New Orleans owes its existence as much to the rhythmic silt deposits carried by the Mississippi River as to the decision by early French urban planners to situate the city atop a "natural" levee. Geographers have long debated the relationship between space and place. For some, space is the "empty" terrain on which places are built. For others, place connotes the varied and distinctive landscapes associated with the pre-modern past while space refers to the homogenous or uniform landscapes of modernity and the future. In this book, I am interested in the ways that people "produced" places consistent with their competing visions of present and future society. I will generally use "space" to refer to conceptual or analytical schemas, whether those belonging to the historical actors or to me, and I will use "place" to refer to the concrete, material structures and sites that these actors produced and inhabited. On the shifting meanings of space and place in geography, see John A. Agnew, "Space and Place," in *The Handbook of Geographical Knowledge*, eds. John A. Agnew and David N. Livingstone (London: Sage Publications, 2011), 316–330. Important works on space and place in New Orleans history include Lawrence N. Powell, *The Accidental City: Improvising New Orleans* (Cambridge, MA: Harvard University Press, 2012); Shannon Lee Dawdy, *Building the Devil's Empire: French Colonial New Orleans* (Chicago: University of Chicago Press, 2008); Ari Kelman, *A River and Its City: The Nature of Landscape in New Orleans* (Berkeley: University of California Press, 2003).

[6] Katherine McKittrick, *Demonic Grounds: Black Women and the Cartographies of Struggle* (Minneapolis: University of Minnesota Press, 2006); Walter Johnson, *Soul by Soul: Life inside the Antebellum Slave Market* (Cambridge, MA: Harvard University Press, 1999).

Resistance in the Plantation South analyzes the ways that masters and slaves competed over physical space. Rural slave masters, Camp argues, sought to contain slave movement within a "geography of containment," such as fields, housing quarters, and any other space subject to the master's will. Through fences and slave patrols, pass systems and surveillance, they enacted power by containing their slaves. In response, enslaved men and women created a "rival geography" or the "alternative ways of knowing and using plantation and southern space that conflicted with planters' ideals and demands." The rival geography consisted of appropriated plantation space, and the areas to which truant and escaped slaves fled. These competing geographies, she argues, were one terrain in the ongoing struggles between masters and slaves that lasted through emancipation.[7]

While Camp focuses on rural plantations, her insights into the relationship between space and power apply to more capacious and dynamic geographies of slavery and resistance. Though most enslaved people lived, labored, and died on rural plantations, which were the primary sites of staple production, they were not the only contested space of Atlantic slavery. Rural plantations belonged to global geographies of capital and power that connected the African continental interior to the Atlantic, American plantations and mines to European capitals. Trade routes, wars, and displacement in the African interior supplied captives for the coastal trade. Elmina, Gorée, and other slave castles housed human cargo, sometimes for over a year until they passed through doors of no return. After kidnappers stole Olaudah Equiano (c. 1745–1797) from his home he spent years as a captive in West Africa before he embarked upon the Middle Passage and later became a famed sailor and abolitionist. Millions lived and died on the salty Atlantic waters. Those who survived then mounted auction blocks to be scattered across the plantations, ships, mines, and households of the Americas. And after they arrived in port cities like New Orleans and their rural environs, bondspersons maintained "simultaneity" with the Atlantic World through heterogeneous assemblages and urban and rural migrations. Slaves were "citizens of the world."[8]

---

[7] Stephanie M. H. Camp, *Closer to Freedom: Enslaved Women and Everyday Resistance in the Plantation South* (Chapel Hill: The University of North Carolina Press, 2004), 6–7.

[8] On the Middle Passage and the remaking of Atlantic communities, see Stephanie E. Smallwood, *Saltwater Slavery: A Middle Passage from Africa to American Diaspora*

Transnational lives demand transnational histories. The analytical framework "confined cosmopolitanism," I argue, illuminates the global "geographies of containment" that masters hoped would bring land and sea, urban cores, and rural hinterlands into a single geography of Atlantic slavery, and the global "geographies of resistance" that enslaved men and women used to challenge it. It applies the conceptual frameworks pioneered by theorists of the black Atlantic to the populations often addressed by social historians of African diasporic slavery. This phrase "confined cosmopolitanism" may seem paradoxical, since everyday usage of "cosmopolitanism" calls to mind wealthy, educated, or otherwise privileged individuals, many of them male, who comfortably hop from place and place. I hope to subvert this assumption. In New Orleans, enslaved men and women had likely circulated through up to four regions – Africa, continental North America, the Caribbean, and Europe – and belonged, however unequally, to diverse communities of strangers.[9] As recent scholarship shows, slaves manipulated space on and beyond plantations to build complex communities, escape, and revolt.[10] But what about slave movement that was not the result of slaves' attempts to find freedom, but instead the result of masters' efforts to build their own wealth and power? Rather than mark plantations as containment spaces and everything beyond as latent freedom spaces,

(Cambridge, MA: Harvard University Press, 2007); Michael A. Gomez, *Exchanging Our Country Marks: The Transformation of African Identities in the Colonial and Antebellum South* (Chapel Hill: The University of North Carolina Press, 1998); John Thornton, *Africa and Africans in the Making of the Atlantic World, 1400–1800*, second edition (Cambridge: Cambridge University Press, 1998 [1992]).

[9] Nayan Shah, *Stranger Intimacy: Contesting Race, Sexuality, and the Law in the North American West* (Berkeley: University of California Press, 2011).

[10] Recent spatial histories of slavery and freedom include Vincent Brown, "Slave Revolt in Jamaica, 1760–1761: A Cartographic Narrative," http://revolt.axismaps.com, accessed January 10, 2014; Thadious Davis, *Southscapes: Geographies of Race, Region, and Literature* (Chapel Hill: The University of North Carolina Press, 2011); Anthony E. Kaye, *Joining Places: Slave Neighborhoods in the Old South* (Chapel Hill: The University of North Carolina Press, 2007); Katherine McKittrick, *Demonic Grounds: Black Women and the Cartographies of Struggle* (Minneapolis: University of Minnesota Press, 2006). On maritime marronage, see Jorge L. Chinea, "Diasporic Marronage: Some Colonial and Intercolonial Repercussions of Overland and Waterborne Slave Flight, with Special Reference to the Caribbean Archipelago," *Revista Brasileira do Caribe* 10, no. 19 (July–December 2009): 259–284; Linda M. Rupert, "Marronage, Manumission and Maritime Trade in the Early Modern Caribbean," *Slavery & Abolition* 30, no. 3 (2009): 361–382.

I am instead interested in how, under particular conditions, the entire world could become slave space.[11]

An Atlantic perspective on containment geographies contributes to the history of women and gender by disrupting the association between mobility and masculinity and by emphasizing the contingent aspects of slave women's circulations. Historians generally argue that male slaves were more likely to be "hired out," or leased, while, with few exceptions such as midwives and healers, female laborers occupied domestic and plantation spaces.[12] "Over the course of their lives," one historian writes, "bondwomen would leave their home plantations, with permission, extremely rarely."[13] But in the port city of New Orleans, the geographies of slavery for men and women spanned the plantation south and the Atlantic World. Enslaved women also circulated as nurses, chain gang laborers, and peddlers, which allowed them to gain "geographic literacy" or knowledge of the physical and social terrains of the neighborhoods, regions, nations, and empires that converged in New Orleans.[14] At the same time, such

---

[11] Pioneering works on the black Atlantic include Paul Gilroy, *The Black Atlantic: Modernity and Double Consciousness* (Cambridge, MA: Harvard University Press, 1993); Brent Edwards, *The Practice of Diaspora: Literature, Translation, and the Rise of Black Internationalism* (Cambridge, MA: Harvard University Press, 2003); J. Lorand Matory, *Black Atlantic Religion: Tradition, Transnationalism, and Matriarchy in the Afro-Brazilian Candomblé* (Princeton: Princeton University Press, 2005). Important works on slavery and the African diaspora include James Sweet, *Recreating Africa: Culture, Kinship, and Religion in the African-Portuguese World, 1441–1770* (Chapel Hill: The University of North Carolina Press, 2003); Gomez, *Exchanging Our Country Marks*; Gwendolyn Midlo Hall, *Africans in Colonial Louisiana: The Development of Afro-Creole Culture in the Eighteenth Century* (Baton Rouge: Louisiana State University Press, 1992); Thornton, *Africa and Africans in the Making of the Atlantic World, 1400–1800*. Several recent works investigate migrations and the practice of diaspora across slavery and freedom. They include Adam Rothman, *Beyond Freedom's Reach: A Kidnapping in the Twilight of Slavery* (Cambridge, MA: Harvard University Press, 2015); Greg Grandin, *The Empire of Necessity: Slavery, Freedom, and Deception in the New World* (New York: Metropolitan Books, 2014); and James H. Sweet, *Domingos Álvares, African Healing, and the Intellectual History of the Atlantic World* (Chapel Hill: The University of North Carolina Press, 2011).

[12] On midwives and ritual healers, see Sharla M. Fett, *Working Cures: Healing, Health, and Power on Southern Slave Plantations* (Chapel Hill: The University of North Carolina Press, 2002).

[13] Camp, *Closer to Freedom*, 28.

[14] Walter Johnson, *River of Dark Dreams: Slavery and Empire in the Cotton Kingdom* (Cambridge, MA: Harvard University Press, 2013), 161; Camp, *Closer to Freedom*, chapter 2. On geographic literacy, see Phillip Troutman, "Grapevine in the Slave Market," in *The Chattel Principle: Internal Slave Trades in the Americas*, ed. Walter Johnson (New Haven: Yale University Press, 2004), 203–233.

circulations rendered them vulnerable to verbal and physical abuse in that notoriously violent port city.[15]

Beyond that, this focus on slavery in an Atlantic port city allows us to bring the conventions of land and sea into a single analytical frame. Scholars of the early modern Atlantic World are interested in the ways pirates, sailors, merchants, missionaries, and other such "citizens of the world" carved out unconventional lives and, at times, radical politics on the high seas. This association between the Atlantic World and freedom proves especially strong for the black "Atlantic Creoles," a term historian Ira Berlin coined to describe the early generation who traveled freely in ways that would later become difficult. As one historian writes, these "Atlantic Creoles" were "extraordinarily mobile, both geographically and socially ... These were not people who felt constrained by place or defined by slavery. Nor was race their primary identification; that imposition came later." These daring individuals "repeatedly risked danger, found an opening, seized the moment, and freed themselves." This relationship between Atlantic migration and freedom has proven a durable one, and many recent works show the ingenious lengths to which people of African descent traveled to escape bondage.[16]

Yet in its insistence that mobility was integral, not exceptional, to slave life and labor, *Slavery's Metropolis* democratizes and deromanticizes cosmopolitanism and thereby decouples the strong association between mobility and freedom in Atlantic World studies. To be sure, transnational migration afforded some bondspersons an escape from or alternative to the hierarchies of slavery and nation. From the moment of their arrival in the Americas, people of African descent crossed national borders to join

---

[15] On slave women peddlers in Charleston, see Jennifer L. Morgan, *Laboring Women: Reproduction and Gender in New World Slavery* (Philadelphia: University of Pennsylvania Press, 2004), 178–183.

[16] Jane Landers, *Atlantic Creoles in the Age of Revolutions* (Cambridge, MA: Harvard University Press, 2010), 13. According to Ira Berlin, many Atlantic Creoles were predominately male African and African diasporic merchants, *gens de mer*, free blacks, and black landowners who enjoyed broad life possibilities before the lines between slave and free, black and white became more fixed in the seventeenth, eighteenth, and nineteenth centuries. Jane Landers extends Berlin's Atlantic Creole framework to the Spanish Gulf Coast and circum-Mexican Gulf. Ira Berlin, *Generations of Captivity: A History of African-American Slaves* (Cambridge, MA: Belknap Press of Harvard University Press, 2003); Rebecca J. Scott and Jean M. Hébrard, *Freedom Papers: An Atlantic Odyssey in the Age of Emancipation* (Cambridge, MA: Harvard University Press, 2012).

indigenous communities and to form maroon nations. The continued resonance of the Underground Railroad and the North Star as powerful symbols of the African-American experience is a testament to the enduring association between migration and black freedom. But for the vast majority of Africans in the early modern black Atlantic, migration brought them closer to bondage. The stories of slaves in motion across, between, and within physical, social, and imperial borders remind us of the possibilities and, more often, limits of migration and other such spatial fixes to structural hierarchies in the Global South.[17]

In addition to its exploration of slavery's Atlantic geographies this book also investigates the contingent local and imperial efforts to create a rational race regime in a city legendary for disorder. Both Napoleon Bonaparte and Thomas Jefferson saw in Louisiana the solution to the challenges that confronted their respective imperial ambitions. After the Seven Years War (1756–1763), republican revolutions upended thirteen British Northern American colonies, France, and the French Caribbean. At the same time, the Age of Revolution was the age of African slave importation. According to some estimates, the enslaved population in Spanish Louisiana nearly quadrupled from 5,600 in 1766 to 20,673 in 1788.[18] Napoleon Bonaparte envisioned for Louisiana a plantation economy to support his efforts to avenge France's defeat in the Seven Years

---

[17] Philosophers and intellectual historians have long debated the connections between cosmopolitan or universal moralities and particular interests. Even before philosopher Immanuel Kant elaborated on the concept in his influential 1795 essay *Perpetual Peace*, the word "cosmopolitanism" has situated the universal realm as an antidote to the narrow prejudices and hierarchies of home. Cosmopolitanism as a moral project, however, is beyond my scope. Immanuel Kant, *Perpetual Peace: A Philosophical Essay*, trans. M. Campbell Smith (London: Swan Sonnenschein & Co. Lim, 1903). Recent works that interrogate cosmopolitanisms in the black Atlantic include Emmanuel C. Eze, *Achieving Our Humanity: The Idea of the Postracial Future* (New York: Routledge, 2001), chapter 3; Ifeoma C. K. Nwankwo, "'Charged with Sympathy for Haiti': Harnessing the Power of Blackness and Cosmopolitanism in the Wake of the Haitian Revolution," in *The Libertine Colony: Creolization in the Early French Caribbean*, ed. Doris Garraway (Durham: Duke University Press, 2005), 91–112; Pnina Webster, "Vernacular Cosmopolitanism," *Theory, Culture & Society* 23, nos. 2–3 (May 2006): 496–498; K. Anthony Appiah, *Cosmopolitanism: Ethics in a World of Strangers* (New York: W. W. Norton & Co., 2006); Clifford Geertz, "What Is a Country If It Is Not a Nation?" *Brown Journal of World Affairs* 4 (1997): 235–247. On deromanticizing black history, see Clarence Walker, *Deromanticizing Black History: Critical Essays and Reappraisals* (Knoxville: University of Tennessee Press, 1991).

[18] Hall, *Africans in Colonial Louisiana*, 278, 284–285.

War and the Haitian Revolution. He planned to re-enslave the rebellious blacks in Saint-Domingue, return them to cash-cropping agriculture or deport them to Louisiana, and sustain the tiny Caribbean island with staples imported from Louisiana. When anticolonial and antislavery forces in Saint-Domingue defended their revolution, Napoleon sold Louisiana to his archenemy Great Britain's other Atlantic rival: Thomas Jefferson's United States.[19]

To Jefferson, New Orleans was central to US geopolitical interests. In his *Notes on the State of Virginia*, published in 1785, he rightly predicted the Mississippi River would become "one of the principal channels of future commerce for the country west of the Allegheny." It would convey goods from the continental interior out to European markets. In addition, Louisiana promised a peaceable solution to the divisive slavery question that threatened national unity from the start. Jefferson and others thought slavery would decline. By the 1770s, only South Carolina and Georgia had expanding plantation economies, and by 1804 seven of the original states had either abolished slavery outright or instituted gradual emancipation schemes. Jefferson hoped reproduction and geography would lead to a similar result in Louisiana. As Anglo-American settlers migrated west, he calculated, they would take the nation's slaves with them. The "diffusion" of the slave population over space and the presumed superior rates of white reproduction over time would lead to the gradual and, for masters in the Old South, profitable disappearance of blacks and, by extension, slavery in the early republic.[20]

---

[19] Laurent Dubois, "The Haitian Revolution and the Sale of Louisiana," *Southern Quarterly* 44, no. 3 (2007): 18–41. On Saint-Domingue, see Laurent Dubois, *Avengers of the New World: The Story of the Haitian Revolution* (Cambridge, MA: Belknap Press of Harvard University Press, 2004).

[20] Thomas Jefferson, *Notes on the State of Virginia*, ed. Frank Shuffelton (New York: Penguin Books, 1999 [orig. published 1785]), 9. On slavery and Jefferson's vision for American empire in the era of the Louisiana Purchase, see Edward E. Baptist, *The Half Has Never Been Told: Slavery and the Making of American Capitalism* (New York: Basic Books, 2014), 30–35; Adam Rothman, *Slave Country: American Expansion and the Origins of the Deep South* (Cambridge, MA: Harvard University Press, 2005); Walter Johnson, "The Racial Origins of American Sovereignty," *Raritan* 31, no. 3 (Winter 2012): 50–59; Roger G. Kennedy, *Mr. Jefferson's Lost Cause: Land, Farmers, Slavery, and the Louisiana Purchase* (New York: Oxford University Press, 2003). On whiteness in the early republic, see Alexander Saxton, *The Rise and Fall of the White Republic: Class Politics and Mass Culture in Nineteenth-Century America* (London: Verso, 1990).

As Jefferson predicted, strangers from all walks of life indeed converged on the hovels of New Orleans. "The low orders of every colour, white, yellow, and black, mix indiscriminately at these receptacles," one observer wrote of the city's tippling houses. "Such a motley crew, and incongruous scene!"[21] At the 1803 Louisiana Purchase, the city's population stood at 8,000, and though it trailed that of more established American cities – New York, Philadelphia, Baltimore, Boston, Charleston – New Orleans, many thought, was the place of the future. Its geographic location at the crossroads of the Mississippi River and the Atlantic Ocean coupled with its political transfer from the Spanish and French to the notoriously enterprising Americans promised commercial success. "The city every day acquired new population," one traveler wrote. "The population of the city," he estimated, "must be about ten or twelve thousand souls." Those souls included "Frenchmen most of all, but also Spaniards, Anglo-Americans, several Bohemian families, Negroes, and mulattoes, some free, but most of them slaves." By 1810, not even a full decade after the Louisiana Purchase, the city's population had more than doubled to over 17,000 people, which made it the seventh largest American city. Together, if unequally, these citizens of the world transformed a swampy colonial borderland into a crossroads of capital and empire, human streams and freedom dreams.[22]

American inventor Eli Whitney's cotton gin did turn Louisiana into a graveyard for individual black people, but it did not become a graveyard for slavery. Whitney's invention, which mechanized the removal of seeds from short-staple cotton, transformed the political economy of the Deep South. As the Industrial Revolution transformed cloth production by increasing the capacity of textile mills in England and the northern United States, southern planters used technological innovations to optimize crop growth. The gin allowed for the more efficient production of short-staple cotton, which could be grown in a larger territory than its long-staple counterpart. Bellicose expansionism transformed Indian

---

[21] Pierre-Louis Berquin-Duvallon and John Davis, *Travels in Louisiana and the Floridas, in the Year, 1802, Giving a Correct Picture of Those Countries* (New York: I. Riley & Co., 1806), 53–54. On the radical politics of the "motley crew" across the Atlantic World, see Peter Linebaugh and Marcus Rediker, *The Many-Headed Hydra: Sailors, Slaves, Commoners, and the Hidden History of the Revolutionary Atlantic* (Boston: Beacon Press, 2000).

[22] C. C. Robin, *Voyage to Louisiana, 1803–1805*, trans. and ed. Stuart O. Landry, Jr. (New Orleans, LA: Pelican Publishing Co., 1966 [1807]), 36, 32; Richard Campanella, *Bienville's Dilemma: A Historical Geography of New Orleans* (Lafayette: University of Louisiana-Lafayette Press, 2008), 26, 28.

lands into American cotton plantations, trades in human flesh supplied cotton pickers, and methodical torture increased their productivity. By 1820, about 69,000 slaves lived in the state of Louisiana, and they labored until death in the Deep South's cotton fields. Two decades after the founding of the first republic, slavery was not a vanishing relic of a colonial past; it was ascendant. And New Orleans was poised to become its capital.[23]

Slaves in motion became central to the New Orleans economy even as the proper management of people in space became a marker of modernity. The contests over the place of slaves in the port city reflected and heightened the tensions of republican state-building during an era of emergent agro-capitalism. As art historian Dell Upton argues, the American city was a physical place, political symbol, and commercial hub. As republican leaders reorganized cities, they hoped transformations in the built environment would transform wayward slum dwellers into good citizens and productive workers. The rise of the culture of capitalism hastened the stigmatization of poverty and idleness. Reformers laid roads and built buildings, criminalized vagrancy, and regulated gatherings. Asylums, prisons, hospitals, and other therapeutic institutions exemplified and enforced Enlightenment values – order, cleanliness, uniformity, and classification. And gridded streets, uniform street names, and other developments in infrastructure allowed information, commodities, and laborers to circulate.[24]

Capitalism did not reshape the American landscape uniformly. In the North, the transition from mercantilism to a free market hastened the decline of slavery and the rise of a caste society. Northern industrialists erased slavery – and blacks – from memory and from the streets

---

[23] Historians debate whether Whitney invented the gin, but he patented it – and that technology transformed the Lower Mississippi River Valley. On empire, capitalism, and slavery in Louisiana and the Atlantic World, see Sven Beckert, *Empire of Cotton: A Global History* (New York: Knopf, 2014); Baptist, *The Half Has Never Been Told*; Johnson, *River of Dark Dreams*; Rothman, *Slave Country*.

[24] Gordon S. Wood, *Empire of Liberty: A History of the Early Republic, 1789–1815* (Oxford: Oxford University Press, 2009); Seth Rockman, *Scraping By: Wage Labor, Slavery, and Survival in Early Baltimore* (Baltimore, MD: The Johns Hopkins University Press, 2009); Dell Upton, *Another City: Urban Life and Urban Spaces in the New American Republic* (New Haven: Yale University Press, 2008); Clare A. Lyons, *Sex among the Rabble: An Intimate History of Gender and Power in the Age of Revolution, Philadelphia, 1730–1830* (Chapel Hill: The University of North Carolina Press, 2006). On capitalist space, see David Harvey, *Spaces of Capital: Towards a Critical Geography* (New York: Routledge, 2001).

through curbs on African-American citizenship rights, mob violence, colonization schemes, and disproportionate incarceration.[25] In the US South, by contrast, the emergent sugar and cotton economies depended on slave labor. Regional elites refused to eliminate black slaves, so the demands of racial slavery refracted their debates about urban space and the place of workers in it. The slave population increased even as the region attracted Anglo-American settlers and immigrants from the Caribbean and Europe. Those influxes compounded fears about the physical place of laborers, both slave and free, and their relationship to each other. To become a modern American capital, to go to the future, New Orleans had to put slaves in their places.[26]

During the territorial period (1804–1812), the racialization and regulation of black people became key to Louisiana's preparation for inclusion in a modern, imperialistic nation-state. Urban space became a key site on which leaders sought to impose an ideological geography onto the diverse and fractured territory through hierarchies of race, class, gender, sexuality, and ability. The modernizing imperial state used what theorist Michel Foucault calls "biopower," or strategies to classify and regulate bodies – their migrations, assemblages, domesticities, sexual relations, reproduction, punishment, and execution – to turn white supremacist ideologies into everyday practice. In this conception, chains, fences, and property lines did not necessarily delineate the geographies of containment, since masters and leaders needed slaves to be able to move. Instead, those in power did so through policy, legislation, social customs, and architecture. This transformation was neither linear nor harmonious. Generally, masters privileged profit, imperial officials valued social order, and small entrepreneurs favored regulated slave latitude. When those values came into conflict, as they often did, varying sectors of the propertied, powerful classes lobbied for their version of blackness in the city.[27]

[25] James T. Campbell, *Middle Passages: African American Journeys to Africa, 1787–2005* (New York: Penguin Press, 2006); Allan Yarema, *The American Colonization Society: An Avenue to Freedom?* (Lanham, MD: University Press of America, 2006); Joanne Pope Melish, *Disowning Slavery: Gradual Emancipation and "Race" in New England, 1780–1860* (Ithaca, NY: Cornell University Press, 1998).

[26] Berquin-Duvallon and Davis, *Travels in Louisiana*, 53–54. On "terrorist assemblages," see Jasbir K. Puar, *Terrorist Assemblages: Homonationalism in Queer Times* (Durham: Duke University Press, 2007).

[27] Michel Foucault, *The History of Sexuality, Volume 1: An Introduction*, trans. Robert Hurley (New York: Vintage Books, 1990); Ann Laura Stoler, "Tense and

Even as leaders and masters fought over the place of slaves in New Orleans, enslaved men and women had their own ideas about where to place themselves on the urban frontier. To be sure, chattel slavery was an institution sustained by violence. Bondspersons confronted asymmetrical power relations at every turn.[28] Nonetheless, enslaved persons appropriated the places assigned them toward their own ends, a point that broadens the received gendered geographies of slave resistance. Because New Orleans was an important port city, it offered a diffuse set of pathways for escape – and recapture. If the politics of place could oppress, slaves reasoned, movement could also become an avenue to freedom. The connectedness that made the city's location so desirable to merchants and imperial officials – its land passageways, river outlets, and Atlantic access – gave runaways an array of escape options. The fugitives redefined themselves in local "geographies of resistance," or fled to other parts of the Atlantic World. But truancy and escape carried costs. Even when they escaped the purview of one master or even one empire, they remained trapped on a trans-imperial terrain shaped by racism. They remained vulnerable to capture, kidnapping, rape, and even death. But many still set out toward freedom, and their individual journeys subverted the imperial cartographies of the Atlantic World.[29]

This book's third contribution rests in its examination of racism, sexism, classism, and sexual exploitation in enslaved daily life to challenge the persistent myth of New Orleans exceptionalism in history and memory. New Orleans presents a paradox: a capital of slavery was a capital of free blacks. Due to lenient manumission policies during the Spanish period and the influx of the Saint-Dominguan diaspora, New Orleans became home to one of the largest free black populations in the United States. Some formed political, cultural, and literary institutions, owned land and slaves (whether to "free" relatives or as masters in a more conventional sense), and fought in the nation's wars. Influential and exciting recent scholarship on Louisiana and the black Atlantic focuses on those who secured freedom through migration and contestation. And

Tender Ties: The Politics of Comparison in North American History and (Post) Colonial Studies," *The Journal of American History* 88, no. 3 (December 2001): 829–865; John Fiske, "Surveilling the City: Whiteness, the Black Man and Democratic Totalitarianism," *Theory, Culture & Society* 15, no. 2 (May 1998): 67–88.

[28] Saidiya V. Hartman, *Scenes of Subjection: Terror, Slavery, and Self-Making in Nineteenth-Century America* (New York: Oxford University Press, 1997).

[29] "Geographies of resistance" is taken from Camp, *Closer to Freedom*, 6–7.

the shifting classifications of free persons of color from a tripartite race regime in the colonial era to the binary regime instituted after the Louisiana Purchase became a barometer of race-making in colonial and early American Louisiana.[30]

Yet such attention to free and freed blacks risks privileging freedom stories when slave labor became the engine of a global industrial economy and New Orleans a capital of the slave trade and slavery.[31] New Orleans was (and remains) a unique city, but it was not an exception to the Atlantic plantation complex; it was fast becoming a hyperreal space of capitalism and slavery. From a comparative perspective, New Orleans was arguably suspended between the Caribbean and Latin America on the one hand and the US South on the other. Its colonial history of French and Spanish rule and the conventions that stemmed from it – including a sizable free black population – remained salient after the Louisiana Purchase. But the city underwent significant changes upon entry into the United States that shortened the distance between that port city and its neighbors on the Eastern Seaboard. A transnational African diasporic perspective allows us

---

[30] Works that highlight the experiences of free blacks include Emily Clark, *The Strange History of the American Quadroon: Free Women of Color in the Revolutionary Atlantic* (Chapel Hill: The University of North Carolina Press, 2013); Scott and Hébrard, *Freedom Papers*; Shirley Elizabeth Thompson, *Exiles at Home: The Struggle to Become American in Creole New Orleans* (Cambridge, MA: Harvard University Press, 2009); Jennifer M. Spear, *Race, Sex, and Social Order in Early New Orleans* (Baltimore, MD: The Johns Hopkins University Press, 2009); Sybil Kein, *Creole: The History and Legacy of Louisiana's Free People of Color* (Baton Rouge: Louisiana State University Press, 2000); Virginia Meacham Gould, *Chained to the Rock of Adversity: To Be Free, Black and Female in the Old South* (Athens, GA: University of Georgia Press, 1998); Caryn Cossé Bell, *Revolution, Romanticism, and the Afro-Creole Protest Tradition in Louisiana, 1718–1868* (Baton Rouge: Louisiana State University Press, 1997); Kimberly S. Hanger, *Bounded Lives, Bounded Places: Free Black Society in Colonial New Orleans, 1769–1803* (Durham: Duke University Press, 1997).

[31] Important works that explore the history of enslaved Louisiana include Baptist, *The Half Has Never Been Told*; Johnson, *River of Dark Dreams*; Jean-Pierre Le Glaunec, "'Un Nègre nommè [sic] Lubin ne connaissant pas Sa Nation': The Small World of Louisiana Slavery," in *Louisiana: Crossroads of the Atlantic World*, ed. Cécile Vidal (Philadelphia: University of Pennsylvania Press, 2014); Jean-Pierre Le Glaunec, "Slave Migrations and Slave Control in Spanish and Early American New Orleans," in *Empires of the Imagination: The Transatlantic Histories of the Louisiana Purchase*, eds. Peter J. Kastor and François Weil (Charlottesville: University of Virginia Press, 2009), 204; Rothman, *Slave Country*; Judith K. Schafer, *Becoming Free, Remaining Free: Manumission and Enslavement in New Orleans, 1846–1862* (Baton Rouge: Louisiana State University Press, 2003); Johnson, *Soul by Soul*; Joseph R. Roach, *Cities of the Dead: Circum-Atlantic Performance* (New York: Columbia University Press, 1996), 1–31; Judith K. Schafer, *Slavery, the Civil Law, and the Supreme Court of Louisiana* (Baton Rouge: Louisiana State University Press, 1994); Hall, *Africans in Colonial Louisiana*.

to appreciate how New Orleans was a crossroads of the expanding US empire and the Atlantic World.[32]

In no case is this approach more valuable than in understanding the practice of intersecting hierarchies of race, gender, class, and sexuality in everyday life. The persons introduced in this work belonged to diverse categories and classifications that had contextual meanings in the intimate and international spaces they inhabited, and the close attention to the contextual meanings of race in individual lives is one of this work's most critical contributions.[33] Rather than considering free blacks, people of so-called mixed race, or interracial sex as evidence of comparatively lenient race regime, this book instead examines the contingent lived experiences of racism across all levels of a complicated society.[34] Historian Doris Garraway makes this point about colonial Saint-Domingue, where one of the most brutal slave systems in the Americas gave rise to a politically active, economically independent, and largely mixed-race free black class. "Rather than viewing the coincidence of racially exclusionary law and

---

[32] "Scholars' efforts to understand the black world beyond the boundaries of nation-states have profoundly affected the way we write the history of the modern world." Tiffany Ruby Patterson and Robin D. G. Kelley, "Unfinished Migrations: Reflections on the African Diaspora and the Making of the Modern World," *African Studies Review* 43, no. 1 (April 2000): 11–45, 13. See Cécile Vidal, ed., *Louisiana: Crossroads of the Atlantic World* (Philadelphia: University of Pennsylvania Press, 2014); Alexander X. Byrd, *Captives and Voyagers: Black Migrants Across the Eighteenth-Century British Atlantic World* (Baton Rouge: Louisiana State University Press, 2008); Laurent Dubois, A *Colony of Citizens: Revolution and Slave Emancipation in the French Caribbean, 1787–1804* (Chapel Hill: The University of North Carolina Press, 2004); Linebaugh and Rediker, *The Many-Headed Hydra*; W. Jeffrey Bolster, *Black Jacks: African American Seamen in the Age of Sail* (Cambridge, MA: Harvard University Press, 1997); Julius S. Scott, "The Common Wind: Currents of Afro-American Communication in the Era of the Haitian Revolution" (Ph.D. diss., Duke University, 1986).

[33] Barbara Fields, "Ideology and Race in American History," in *Region, Race and Reconstruction: Essays in Honor of C. Vann Woodward*, eds. J. Morgan Kousser and James M. McPherson (New York: Oxford University Press, 1982), 143–177; Barbara Fields, "Slavery, Race, and Ideology in the United States of America," *New Left Review* 181 (1990): 95–118; Thomas C. Holt, "Marking: Race, Race-Making, and the Writing of History," *The AHR* 100 (February 1995): 1–20.

[34] Frank Tannenbaum, *Slave and Citizen: The Negro in the Americas* (New York: A. A. Knopf, 1946); Peter Wade, *Blackness and Race Mixture: The Dynamics of Racial Identity in Colombia* (Baltimore, MD: The Johns Hopkins University Press, 1993); Aline Helg, *Our Rightful Share: The Afro-Cuban Struggle for Equality, 1886–1912* (Chapel Hill: The University of North Carolina Press, 1995); Ada Ferrer, *Insurgent Cuba: Race, Nation, and Revolution, 1868–1898* (Chapel Hill: The University of North Carolina Press, 1999); Nancy Appelbaum, Anne Macpherson, and Karin Alejandra Rosemblatt, *Introduction to Race and Nation in Modern Latin America* (Chapel Hill: The University of North Carolina Press, 2003).

interracial libertinage as a contradiction," she writes, "I consider these phenomena to be mutually constitutive of the system of white supremacy and racial domination that shaped French slave societies." This insight is also instructive for New Orleans, where in the early nineteenth-century slaves and free blacks both contended with the hardening lines of white supremacy.[35]

It is easy to romanticize nineteenth-century New Orleans as a foil for its twentieth-century version, when *Plessy* v. *Ferguson* (1896), the US Supreme Court case, enshrined Jim Crow nationwide. The polyglot colonial capital seems an almost perfect antithesis of the fixed lines of twentieth-century Jim Crow segregation. But such a perspective fails to take into account the ways white supremacy and diversity can work in tandem with one another. Melting pot, gumbo, and jazz metaphors notwithstanding, chattel slavery allowed New Orleans to become a modern city. This book explores how that happened.[36]

In his influential essay "Walking the City," anthropologist Michel de Certeau calls for increased attention to "the stories and legends that haunt urban space like superfluous or additional inhabitants."[37] For the stories of enslaved New Orleans, however, this effort is easier said than done. The first challenge is that local elites transformed the city's inconvenient history into enchanted myths for tourists' consumption. The commoditization of slave culture is as ubiquitous as slaves are invisible.[38] In New Orleans as in the nation, as Toni Morrison theorizes in *Playing in the Dark: Whiteness and the Literary Imagination*, "a nonwhite, Africanlike (or Africanist) presence or persona was constructed," and she explores the

---

[35] Doris Garraway, *The Libertine Colony: Creolization in the Early French Caribbean* (Durham: Duke University Press, 2005), 30.

[36] As recent works show, multinational communities also thrived at the heart of Jim Crow in New Orleans at the dawn of the twentieth century. See Vivek Bald, *Bengali Harlem and the Lost Histories of South Asian America* (Cambridge, MA: Harvard University Press, 2013), chapters 1–2; Emily Landau, *Spectacular Wickedness: Sex, Race, and Memory in Storyville, New Orleans* (Baton Rouge: Louisiana State University Press, 2013); Alecia P. Long, *The Great Southern Babylon: Sex, Race, and Respectability in New Orleans, 1865–1920* (Baton Rouge: Louisiana State University Press, 2004), chapter 2; Peirce F. Lewis, *New Orleans: The Making of an Urban Landscape* (Sante Fe, NM: Center for American Places in Association with the University of Virginia Press, 2003).

[37] De Certeau, *The Practice of Everyday Life*, 106. See also Roach, *Cities of the Dead*, Introduction and chapter 1.

[38] On culture and tourism in New Orleans, see Kevin Fox Gotham, *Authentic New Orleans: Tourism, Culture, and Race in the Big Easy* (New York: New York University Press, 2007); J. Mark Souther, *New Orleans on Parade: Tourism and the Transformation of the Crescent City* (Baton Rouge: Louisiana State University Press, 2006).

"imaginative uses this fabricated presence served." One thing that made people white was the ability to "play in" or enjoy imagined blackness.[39] In New Orleans, "voodoo," which began as a subversive spiritual practice that empowered Africans to survive and challenge slavery and colonialism, now modifies the names of lattés, ghost tours, sports franchises, radio stations, and rock festivals. Yet such visibility can be as violent as erasure, as with Congo Square, one of the few sites in the United States where slaves could drum, dance, and trade on Sundays well into the antebellum period. At the risk of seeming flippant, only in New Orleans could the paradigmatic site of slavery be a party. Again, this tendency is a problem of framing: Bondspersons partied there, but those gatherings took place within the daily traumas of enslavement. What did enslaved people do, see, think, fear, and dream beyond Congo Square? And how might their shifting places in space and society be read as barometers of the sweeping changes of a revolutionary age?

If histories of individual slaves are difficult, then a history of slave transience might seem methodologically impossible. Laws and customs prohibited literacy among most New World slaves, and even the literate lacked the resources to preserve documents. Few archives hold their words. As historian Nell Irvin Painter asks in her biography of abolitionist and women's rights activist Sojourner Truth, "What sources can generate a history of the kind of person Truth was – black, female, poor, nineteenth-century? Do people like Truth *have* a history?" As Painter concludes, "People like Truth do have a history, of course. But a Truth biographer, like the biographer of any poor person, any person of color, or a woman of any stratum, cannot stick to convention, for conventional sources mostly are lacking." Such histories are possible, but they require a creative approach to the archives.[40]

As Painter and others insist, bondspersons were real-time actors in their societies, and their histories should show as much. For important reasons, scholars have sought to identify the core elements that defined the status of enslavement across time and space, an approach that allows for comparisons across different periods and places. But when scholars across disciplines distill the experiences of millions into a single, transhistorical

---

[39] Toni Morrison, *Playing in the Dark: Whiteness and the Literary Imagination* (Cambridge, MA: Harvard University Press, 1992), 6. See also Clyde Taylor, *The Mask of Art: Breaking the Aesthetic Contract – Film and Literature* (Bloomington: Indiana University Press, 1998).

[40] Nell Irvin Painter, *Sojourner Truth: A Life, a Symbol* (New York: W. W. Norton & Co., 1996), 289–291, 289, emphasis original.

essence of slavery, we lose the texture of their daily lives in relation to one another and to their societies. We exclude them as subjects of and actors in history, which has the effect of inscribing otherness onto them.[41] Similarly, though enslaved men and women in scholarly literature are often aggregated into categories, such as sex, nationality, or skill set, this work instead uses "mini-biographies" to situate them within their rapidly shifting milieus and lived to gain fresh insight into the macro-level processes that shaped their lives.[42]

For historians, such accounts require documents, but archives are themselves products of the histories we use their contents to examine. As Michel-Rolph Trouillot argues, "silences" in the archives are neither haphazard nor apolitical. Power shapes source creation, preservation, evaluation, and narration. Conversely, the presence of documents raises challenges, since their materiality amid so many archival voids raise the temptation to confer disproportionate significance on them. Some documents, as musicians James Brown and Bobby Byrd might say, are "talking loud and saying nothing." But rather than focus on what the archives do not hold, I investigate the sources that remain. I engage in informed speculation, and I consider the multiple possibilities embedded in each scene. Together, these documents and perspectives allow for fresh insight into the history of slavery in New Orleans and the larger Atlantic World.[43]

To construct this history, I relied on primary sources held in over a dozen archives and penned in English, French, and Spanish. Early New Orleans was home to an unusually literate population that read mono-lingual and bilingual newspapers published in French, Spanish, and English. I have read select Gulf Coast newspapers for editorials and letters to the editor to discern political contests between the master classes. More importantly, I have also relied on runaway slave

---

[41] As Vincent Brown argues, some scholars expanded historical sociologist Orlando Patterson's distilled concept of "social death," or "the permanent, violent domination of natally alienated and generally dishonored persons," into a transhistorical definition of slavery. As a consequence, everyday slave experiences go unexamined. Vincent Brown, "Social Death and Political Life in the Study of Slavery," *The AHR* 114, no. 5 (December 2009): 1231–1249. On the politics of coevality, see Johannes Fabian, *Time and the Other: How Anthropology Makes Its Objects* (New York: Columbia University Press, 1983).

[42] Lara Putnam, "To Study the Fragments/Whole: Microhistory and the Atlantic World," *Journal of Social History* 39, no. 3 (Spring 2006): 615–630.

[43] Michel-Rolph Trouillot, *Silencing the Past: Power and the Production of History* (Boston: Beacon, 1995), chapter 1.

advertisements and slave sale announcements for insight into the ways enslaved persons inhabited and shaped the interlocked spatial, commercial, and discursive worlds of early New Orleans. Even the briefest advertisements recount slaves' names, genders, nationalities, physical features, past migrations, and, for runaways, presumed destinations. The facticity of these individual advertisements matters, but of equal value is the collective understandings of slave trajectories that these ads established. These ads divulge what masters thought individual slaves had done, and in so doing they created knowledge about what slaves do.[44]

To track the ways that states saw slaves in space and society, I have drawn on executive, judicial, legislative, and commercial sources. I have used Governor William C. C. Claiborne's published correspondence, the New York Historical Society's extensive New Orleans Collection, and Xavier University's Heartman Collection for the receipts and ledgers of state-building in an occupied territory. The state met the market in every act of sale, succession, and other such transaction, so notarial records offer invaluable insight into the biographies and valuations of enslaved people as well as the social and economic transactions that eased their sales. Finally, to explore British geographies of Louisiana in the context of the War of 1812, I have relied on documents from the colonial, admiralty, and treasury offices housed at the UK National Archives at Kew and at the Gloucestershire Records Office. These documents reveal the ways adversarial states regarded slaves in Louisiana in war and peace.

As officials constructed empires, patriarchs and priests consolidated the domestic and spiritual spheres that were the building blocks of society. In family papers, housed at the Historic New Orleans Collection's Williams Research Center and at Tulane Special Collections, I read personal correspondence, acts of sale, invoices, receipts, diaries, wills, and other personal writings. In a single archival folder, correspondence that overflows with the sentimental language of paternalism and maternalism

---

[44] On runaway advertisements, see David Waldstreicher, "Reading the Runaways: Self-Fashioning, Print Culture, and Confidence in Slavery in the Eighteenth-Century Mid-Atlantic," *The William and Mary Quarterly* 56, no. 2 (April 1999): 243–272. On print culture in the Atlantic, see Benedict Anderson, *Imagined Communities: Reflections on the Origin and Spread of Nationalism*, Rev. and extended edition (London; New York: Verso, 1991). On the hispanophone press in New Orleans, see Kirsten Silva Gruesz, *Ambassadors of Culture: The Transamerican Origins of Latino Writing* (Princeton: Princeton University Press, 2002).

toward slaves sits atop a will in which masters affixed monetary values to those same slaves. Such sources capture like few others the bizarre banalities of chattel slavery. The Catholic Church also tracked the lines of family, class, and race in a society filled with people whose bodies subverted neat categories. Sacramental records offer accounts of births, marriages, and deaths, which I used to follow individual people and families, particularly those who immigrated to Louisiana from Saint-Domingue.

The rare sources that give a glimpse into the words and perspectives of enslaved persons themselves are the Holy Grail of slavery studies. I draw on Louisiana Works Progress oral interviews conducted in the 1930s and very early 1940s. Like all sources, these interviews present challenges. They were conducted nearly seven decades after emancipation during the Great Depression in the Jim Crow South. Predominately white interviewers used what today would be considered questionable survey design methods, such as leading questions, that compromised the level of transparency these elderly black informants offered. These and other limitations have prompted some scholars to set aside these testimonies. But trauma travels the generations. A discursive analysis of these interviews from the early twentieth century proves useful even if only to bear witness that the geographies of slavery seared the memories of survivors well into the twentieth century. Published slave narratives also communicates perceptions of slavery from the survivors who lived to tell.[45]

This work is rooted in archival sources, but it also draws on other ways of knowing, including critical theory and literature. Novels rest alongside theorists of power, literary scholars, and historians of diverse times and spaces. The rewards of such intellectual promiscuity far outweigh the risks of casting aside the contributions of such diverse thinkers. Together, this rich literature allows me to improvise the inner lives of the men and women who traveled across the physical and social borders of early American society. This approach has proved especially fruitful in black women's history where, all too often, traditional sources that recount individual thoughts and experiences have been made to not exist.[46]

---

[45] John W. Blassingame, "Using the Testimony of Ex-Slaves: Approaches and Problems," *The Journal of Southern History* 41 (November 1975): 473–492.

[46] Nell Irvin Painter, "Three Southern Women and Freud," in *Southern History across the Color Line* (Chapel Hill: The University of North Carolina Press, 2002), 93–111.

The structure of this book mimics the incongruities of the society it examines. First, New Orleans was a polyglot society, so I do not standardize names into one language. Instead, I follow the sources to trace when, for example, the bondwoman named Maria Redas, before a Spanish notary, became Marie Rose when her French master reported her to local authorities after the Louisiana Purchase. Second, this book is not a linear, "change over time" story, nor does it follow one narrative arc. Some chapters are synchronic, while others trace changes over time. I focus as much on fleeting encounters as I do longitudinal sequences, so many of the people who appear on these pages step into focus and disappear just as quickly. There are methodological and conceptual reasons for this approach. Though I do so when possible, it is difficult to trace these actors beyond a single scene, and the juxtaposition of synchronic encounters is as illuminating as diachronic narratives. The approach adopted here revels in the messiness and contingencies of this diverse society. Finally, this work offers no essential truths about "the" slave experience. In fact, it does the opposite by presenting a pastiche at odds with itself. Some evidence charts race-making, others its unmaking. Rather than refining the typologies of slavery, this book presents biographies and kaleidoscopic snapshots that reveal the contingencies and complexities of slavery and modernity.

This book consists of five chapters, each of which explores a specific circuit or site of New Orleans slavery. It is bookended by two chapters that are transnational in scope, while the middle chapters explore the local, regional, national, and Atlantic circulations of enslaved people through New Orleans. Chapter 1 uses migrations from Saint-Domingue into Louisiana during the era of the Haitian Revolution to examine the resilience of racist hierarchies amid trans-imperial journeys in an era of republican revolution. Chapter 2 illuminates the sanctioned and illicit circulations of enslaved men and, significantly, women that connected the markets and communities of urban and rural Louisiana. This chapter gives particular attention to enslaved female peddlers because their labor complicates notions that enslaved women were rendered uniquely immobile during slavery. They were commodities and they transported commodities across the Deep South. Such circulations allowed them to maintain diverse and far-flung communities.

Play was serious business in early New Orleans. Chapter 3 analyzes the ways intimate yet public places such as brothels, taverns, boarding houses, sports, and Congo Square became microcosms of national and global contests over gender, race, sexuality, and class. Chapter 4 examines the shifting race and space practices inside the New Orleans jail and on its chain gangs. It shows how the nascent prison industrial complex in the slave south helped to create categories of race, status, gender, class, and sexuality as well as the multiracial politics that inmates used to challenge it. Finally, Chapter 5 charts the complicated imperial freedom that a handful of black sojourners from Louisiana realized in Trinidad after the War of 1812. It uses their journey from Louisiana to the British Caribbean to illuminate the competing imperial visions of black modernity – chattel slaves and somewhat free laborers – to meditate on the possibilities and limits of freedom in the Global South.

Revolutionary Spaces

RANAWAY from Lafourche on the 2d. of October instant, a negro man named Figaro creole from St. Domingo, 30 years of age, 5 feet 1 inches French measure, of very black skin, speaking good French and bad English, bending his body when in march, looking false ... He makes him pass as a free negro and is bearer of a forged title of liberty.

Louisiana Courier, October 24, 1810

I ain't 'shamed of my pa.

Marie Brown, ca. 1940

In his three decades, Pierre lived in as many Atlantic port cities. Described as mulatto, he was born sometime around 1781 in Cap Français, a cosmopolitan capital in northern Saint-Domingue. Home to about 7,000 people, Le Cap was, according to Moreau de Saint-Méry, "the largest urban center in the French colony, the principal seat of its wealth and its luxury; the place of greatest commerce." It was also where Pierre learned to drum. The exact date is unclear, but after the start of the Haitian Revolution in 1791 a pubescent Pierre migrated from Le Cap to Charleston, South Carolina. That port city was home to some 16,000 people, which made it the fourth largest in the United States, and it was the national capital of slave importation. Pierre might have been classed as free from birth or freed in Le Cap with French emancipation in 1794. But in Charleston, he was held as a slave and labored as a barber. There a man named Claude Guillaud purchased Pierre and branded his initials, "C.G.," into the teenager's chest. In 1796, Pierre defied the wound inscribed into his flesh by relocating his body. Fifteen-year-old Pierre ran away.[1]

---

[1] "Runaway Negro," *Courrier de la Louisiane*, July 23, 1810; August 1, 1810. Susan M. Socolow, "Economic Roles of the Free Women of Color of Cap Français," in

In 1810, nearly fifteen years later, both men converged on the crowded streets of yet another cosmopolitan Atlantic port city, this time New Orleans. Pierre, now a man of about thirty years, allegedly ran a barbershop under the scatological alias "La Pisse" (or else "La Puce") and was assumed to have lived in the diverse Faubourg Marigny (a neighborhood described in depth in Chapter 3). Guillaud placed a runaway advertisement in the local paper. He "was seen last Sunday," Guillaud's ad proclaimed. Pierre reportedly carried "a Tambarine unstrung in his hand and a pair of razors, from which it is presumed he plays on it" and "a great quantity of clothes." On the Sunday streets of New Orleans, Pierre transformed the tools of his trade into instruments of African diasporic culture and community. For a decade and a half, Pierre's friends harbored him from the individuating power of Guillaud's property claims, but not entirely. "He has been a runaway 16 years," Guillaud declared in a second advertisement. "He will no doubt endeavor to pass for a free man," Gillaud wrote, using the future tense to deny the recent past. Pierre, a "Creole of Le Cap," circulated through three Atlantic port cities and lived as a free man for sixteen years, but two runaway slave advertisements collapsed the distance between him and the New Orleans auction block.

Like Pierre, many others saw New Orleans as a space of refuge. In an age of republican and antislavery revolutions, Spanish Louisiana became a point of confluence for at least two diasporas, one Anglo-American and the other Saint-Dominguan. During and after the Seven Years War (1754–1763), European monarchs consolidated power even as their subordinates – both on the continent and in the colonies – challenged traditional hierarchies. Enlightenment thinkers, the working classes of Europe, Euro-American colonists, and enslaved Africans contested royal rule. In Jamaica, the center of British sugar production, an estimated 1,500 enslaved men and women launched Tacky's Revolt of 1760, the largest antislavery insurrection in the Americas to that point. In 1776 Scottish thinker Adam Smith published *The Wealth of Nations*, promoting the "invisible hand" of the free market over state-centered mercantilist economies. That same year, colonists in British North America revolted against the Crown to secure political independence

More than Chattel: Black Women and Slavery in the Americas, eds. David Barry Gaspar and Darlene Clark Hine (Bloomington: Indiana University Press, 1996), 279–297, 281. On black barbers, see Douglas W. Bristol, *Knights of the Razor: Black Barbers in Slavery and Freedom* (Baltimore, MD: The Johns Hopkins University Press, 2009).

and economic power. Then in 1789 radical republicans stormed the
Bastille and began the French Revolution. The common winds of republican revolution manifested in French Saint-Domingue, the premier sugar-
producing Caribbean colony, where local elites hoped that the French
Revolution would bring them increased autonomy and prosperity.
In 1791 their efforts were overshadowed by demands for liberty from
the colony's insurgent bondspersons. Their revolt prompted slavery's
abolition in Saint-Domingue in 1793 and across the French Empire the
following year. In principle, the French Republic's Declaration of Rights
of Man and Citizen (1789) applied to every citizen in France and its
colonies, which transformed former slaves, free persons of color, and
French colonists alike into citizens of the French republic. When
Napoleon came to power in 1799, he sought to depose Toussaint
L'Ouverture and to subjugate the freedpersons of Saint-Domingue.
Colonists defended their antislavery revolution, declared independence
from France, and in 1804 founded Haiti, the first black republic.
The Haitian Revolution and its aftermath propelled tens of thousands of
the colony's residents to Louisiana and across the Atlantic World.[2]

The advantageous placement of slaves in New Orleans was essential to
the efforts of elite members of two revolutionary diasporas – one Saint-
Dominguan and the other American – to recreate themselves and, their
fortunes during the region's transition from colony to state. American
settlers, liberated from their already limited respect for colonial-era
Anglo-Indian treaties, flooded the continental interior in pursuit of life,
liberty, and property. Elite colonists displaced from Saint-Domingue
hoped to escape the radical republicanism associated with the French
and Haitian Revolutions and to recreate the planter's lifestyle. How did
the elite strangers in New Orleans transcend cultural differences to unite
around a shared commitment to proslavery republicanism? Who were the
"Creoles of St. Domingue" who came to populate New Orleans' auction
blocks and slave advertisements? How did these migrants from the French
Caribbean survive and contest the bondage many of them entered or re-
entered upon crossing the emergent US national border? And how did the
afterlives of this migration reveal the promises and limits of collective
uprisings against global structures of modern power?

---

[2] On Tacky's Revolt, see Brown, "Slave Revolt in Jamaica, 1760–1761." Vincent Brown,
The Reaper's Garden: Death and Power in the World of Atlantic Slavery (Cambridge,
MA: Harvard University Press, 2008), 144–156. On the Haitian Revolution, see Dubois,
Avengers.

This chapter uses the trans-local migrations of individuals from a former capital of slavery, Saint-Domingue, to an emergent one, Louisiana, in the era of the Haitian Revolution to emphasize the sheer unpredictability and utter vulnerability of black life in the Americas. The first section details the efforts of some members of the Saint-Dominguan diaspora to reconstitute themselves through the importation of fellow migrants as slaves into Louisiana. The debate over the admittance of migrants of visible African ancestry as slaves became a proxy for larger debates between French Creole and Anglo-American planters and US imperial officials over the place of slaves and slavery in the nation's future. Sections two and three analyze how so-called Creoles of Saint-Domingue inhabited and transformed the geographies of slavery in New Orleans. For those for whom crossing the US border meant a passage into bondage, New Orleans became the new terrain of an old struggle between masters and slaves. The migrants held as slaves performed faithfulness, revolted, and did everything in between to survive and resist their enslavement. The final part of the chapter uses the testimonies of slavery survivors to illuminate the figurative place of Saint-Domingue and its intertwined legacies of slavery and freedom in the Jim Crow South. This chapter traces freedom stories, but it also illuminates how racist hierarchies could be made resilient not in spite of the trans-imperial journeys of a revolutionary age, but because of them.

Where the Haitian Revolution's claim to black citizenship once represented an "unthinkable" event to be "disavowed," scholars now recognize it as a foundational event in the history of republican, anti-imperialist, and antislavery movements.[3] Persons of African descent and their allies found – and continue to find – inspiration in Haiti, "the glory of the blacks and terror of tyrants."[4] Those formerly enslaved persons revolutionized a revolutionary ideology in a way that inspires quests for liberty and equality well into the present. The Haitian Revolution also inspired antislavery revolts across the Americas. For example, former residents of

---

[3] On the erasure of the Haitian Revolution, see Trouillot, *Silencing the Past*; Sybille Fisher, *Modernity Disavowed: Haiti and the Cultures of Slavery in the Age of Revolution* (Durham: Duke University Press, 2004). On the Haitian Revolution in Atlantic history, see David Patrick Geggus, *The Impact of the Haitian Revolution in the Atlantic World* (Columbia: University of South Carolina, 2001); Alfred N. Hunt, *Haiti's Influence on Antebellum America: Slumbering Volcano in the Caribbean* (Baton Rouge: Louisiana State University Press, 1988).

[4] David Walker, *Appeal in Four Articles; Together with a Preamble, to the Coloured Citizens of the World, but in Particular, and Very Expressly to Those of the United States of America* (Boston, MA: David Walker, 1829), 24.

Saint-Domingue held as slaves in Louisiana took part in a series of revolts between 1793 and 1811.

What is less appreciated is that thousands of phenotypically black members of the Saint-Dominguan diaspora found in Louisiana not a revolutionary freedom, but a revolutionary slavery. Through a series of contingent events, by choice and by coercion, these migrants' presence in Louisiana effectively augmented the ascendant slaveocracy in Lower Louisiana.[5] For the most vulnerable of them, those of visible African descent, their ingenuity, their claims, and even their papers did not preclude their enslavement. This insight does not diminish individual efforts to escape desperate situations or the Haitian Revolution as a foundational black freedom struggle. It does present a sobering view of how elites met their demand for property and cheap labor by manipulating race and status at imperial borders, and how intertwined republican and market revolutions reverberated across the lowest frequencies of society across the Global South.

"FUGITIVE DEBRIS" IN "THE SHADOW OF GRANDEUR"

Beginning in August 1791, insurgent slaves in Saint-Domingue displaced colonial elites from their households and high society. As early as March 1792, one such refugee wrote from Kingston to an acquaintance in Louisiana about the "revolution which we rejected from the start ... because the rabble, with their blind ingratitude and injustice, would make us their victims." In Philadelphia, another member of the planter diaspora fantasized that he and others would return to Abricots, Jérémie, reunite with their loyal slaves, and enjoy "tambourines and bamboulas" (*Nous aurons tambours et bamboulas*).[6] The consumption of slave culture as spectacle was

---

[5] Recent works that interrogate the liberatory associations with the Haitian Revolution include Ada Ferrer, *Freedom's Mirror: Cuba and Haiti in the Age of Revolution* (New York: Cambridge University Press, 2014); Sara E. Johnson, *The Fear of French Negroes: Transcolonial Collaboration in the Revolutionary Americas* (Berkeley: University of California Press, 2012); Scott and Hébrard, *Freedom Papers*; Scott, "Paper Thin," 1061–1087.

[6] Montault to Livaudais, Kingston, March 2, 1792, in *Favrot Family Papers*, ed. Guillermo Náñez Falcón (New Orleans: Tulane University Howard Tilton Memorial Library, 1988), 2: 113; De Bordes to Pierre-Antoine Lambert, July 22, 1805, Lambert Family Papers, TU, my translation; J. M. Bart to Hugues de La Vergne, Paris, February 25, 1812, De La Vergne Family Papers, TU, my translation. "Bamboula," which likely stems from a Ki-Kongo term for memory, "referred to a drum, a dance, dancers, and a rhythm in some cases" that diasporic Africans practiced in New Orleans and across the Caribbean. Africans "in numerous parts of the West Indies including Trinidad, St. Lucia, Guadeloupe,

part of the mastering experience, so former elites mourned the loss of those African rhythms and the bound hands that played them. They also missed the money. "You know that I have been stripped of a large independent fortune in St. Domingo," a former planter wrote from Napoleon's beautified Paris in 1812. From Kingston to Philadelphia, Paris to New Orleans, the fraternity of former planters gazed on the shards of their shattered lives: "For my part, I was designed by my Father to keep a high station in Society, but the shadow of grandeur is all that remains now for me."[7]

For one French observer, the presence of the colony's white expatriates in New Orleans and other parts of the Atlantic World was evidence of their ineptitude as masters. While in authority, he argued, they "divided themselves into rich and poor whites ... non-resident whites versus residents who are coffee growers versus residents who are sugar growers." Had they united, he continued, they would have maintained control of their colony and slaves. Instead, as elite colonists produced white supremacy to better produce sugar and coffee, its attendant hierarchies stoked resentment in three of the four tiers of colonial society. The *grands blancs*, or wealthy white planters and colonial officials, enjoyed concentrated wealth and power. *Petits blancs* labored as merchants, traders, and clerks. *Gens de couleur libres*, or free people of color, owned nearly one-third of the colony's land and about one-fourth of its slaves. In the eighteenth century, as many as 685,000 enslaved Africans entered Saint-Domingue, with some 37,000 arriving each year between 1783 and 1792. Elites enjoyed concentrated wealth and power while the masses lived in misery.[8]

The attack on the *ancien régime* accelerated after a *Vodun* ritual at the Bois-Caïman in August 1791. Boukman Dutty, a spiritual and military leader, reportedly exhorted the island's slaves to "[t]hrow away the image of the god of the whites who thirsts for our tears and listen to the voice of liberty which speaks in the hearts of all of us." In 1794, as former slaves on the island fought their former rulers, radical republicans in France further

---

St. Domingue (Haiti), Puerto Rico, and the Virgin Islands" practiced it then and into the present. Freddi Williams Evans, *Congo Square: African Roots in New Orleans* (Lafayette: University of Louisiana at Lafayette Press, 2011), 102.

[7] J. M. Bart, Paris, to Hugues de La Vergne, February 25, 1812, De La Vergne Family Papers, Manuscript Collection 146, Manuscripts Department, TU. It is unclear whether this predestination came from his earthly father or his heavenly one.

[8] Robin, *Voyage*, 251. Dubois, *Avengers of the New World*, 39. See also Ashli White, *Encountering Revolution: Haiti and the Making of the Early Republic* (Baltimore, MD: The Johns Hopkins University Press, 2010). On the legal system in colonial Saint-Domingue, see Malick W. Ghachem, *The Old Regime and the Haitian Revolution* (Cambridge: Cambridge University Press, 2012).

undermined the power of colonial planters when they abolished slavery across the empire. In the years that followed, the former colony declared its independence from France, and the coachman-turned-emperor Toussaint Louverture engaged in state building, foreign relations, and controversial labor management initiatives. Haiti became a beacon of black freedom as merchants and planters in Brazil, Cuba, and the Lower Mississippi River Valley deepened their investments in chattel slavery.[9]

In an inversion of the Middle Passage, the Haitian Revolution dispersed former elites to uncertain futures across the Atlantic World. Their exodus began in 1791 but accelerated after the 1793 burning of Cap Français. One man named Sabouraud was in Le Cap when insurgents set it aflame. He later recalled that he escaped "the unfortunate revolution in St. Domingue" thanks to a free black man (*Le Negre* [*sic*] *Libre*) who recognized him as a "good white" (*bon blanc*) and facilitated his escape. Sabouraud fled toward Haut du Cap River, where he and his brother boarded a vessel bound for New England. They disembarked at Baltimore, but, like many other Frenchmen, they hesitated to settle in the young republic. That port city was home to a significant Francophone population, but increasing hostilities between the United States and the French Republic made the United States an unwelcoming destination. Britain and France remained locked in a Second Hundred Years War. US interest in neutral trade with both combatants prompted the Quasi-War with France (1798–1800) and restrictive Alien and Sedition and Naturalization Acts designed to curb French espionage. Little wonder that after a visit to Baltimore one French planter from Martinique concluded: "It took me no more than three months to become completely disgusted with [the United States] and to decide never to live there. France is the only country where I ardently wish to live." Sabouraud agreed: Six months after his arrival in Baltimore he and 300 other Frenchmen sailed to Bordeaux.[10]

---

[9] Ada Ferrer, "Haiti, Free Soil, and Antislavery in the Revolutionary Atlantic," *AHR* 117, no. 1 (February 2012): 40–66; Carolyn E. Fick, *The Making of Haiti: The Saint Domingue Revolution from Below* (Knoxville: University of Tennessee Press, 1990), 93. See also John K. Thornton, "'I am the Subject of the King of Congo': African Political Ideology and the Haitian Revolution," *Journal of World History* 4 (1993): 181–214. On the first French abolition, see Dubois, *A Colony of Citizens*.

[10] "la Malheureuse Revolution De St Domaingue [*sic*]" Sabouraud's letter, 13 Germinal An 10 [1799] my translation, MSS 339, HNOC; Pierre Dessalles to [Pierre Nicholas de Sainte-Catherine] Bence, Martinique, August 6, 1811, in *Sugar and Slavery, Family and Race: The Letters and Diary of Pierre Dessalles, Planter in Martinique, 1808–1856*, ed. and trans. Elborg Foster and Robert Foster (Baltimore, MD: The Johns Hopkins University Press, 1996), 39. Dessalles, a French planter, wrote these lines to his

Between 1791 and 1803 the people whom French observer C. C. Robin called "the fugitive debris of this superb colony" left Saint-Domingue to settle in New Orleans, where they invigorated the local Francophone population. "As New Orleans had been also under French rule," one migrant explained, some "Creole refugees finally settled [in New Orleans] after landing elsewhere in the United States."[11] Their attraction to New Orleans was intuitive enough. As one of the few planned cities in the Americas, New Orleans sprang from the imaginations of French merchants and architects.

After decades of French rule, the cultural Francophilia persisted in part as a political reaction against the subsequent Spanish administration. At the time of the Louisiana Purchase of 1803, the French influence in New Orleans remained palpable. The migrants from Saint-Domingue doubled the urban population, bolstered the politically and demographically embattled Francophone population, and increased the free black population by 90 percent. "I have discovered with regret," US Territorial Governor William C. C. Claiborne lamented in the first days of his administration, "that a strong partiality for the French Government still exists among many of the inhabitants of this City."[12]

When Napoleon's failed efforts to re-enslave Saint-Domingue prompted him to sell the entire Louisiana Territory to the United States, immigration from the French Caribbean became one of Claiborne's first

father-in-law, who, like Sabouraud, was a French émigré to Baltimore. On Baltimore as a microcosm of the early republic, see Rockman, *Scraping By.*

[11] Althea du Puech Parham, working papers for "My Odyssey: Experiences of a Young Refugee from Two Revolutions, by a Creol of Saint Domingue," 85-117-L, HNOC. On this population in New York, see Martha S. Jones, "Time, Space, and Jurisdiction in Atlantic World Slavery: The Volunbrun Household in Gradual Emancipation New York," *Law and History Review* 29, no. 4 (November 2011): 1031–1060.

[12] William C. C. Claiborne (hereafter WC) to James Madison, January 10, 1804, in Dunbar Rowland, ed., *Official Letter Books of W.C.C. Claiborne, 1801–1816* (Jackson, MS: State Department of Archives and History, 1917), I: 329–333.

In the 1720s, engineer Adrien de Pauger drew on an intellectual history that stretched to French military architect Sebastien Le Prestre, Marshal Vauban (1633–1707) to imprint New Orleans into the swampy sediment deposited by a temperamental river. During Louisiana's French period (1699–1763), locals enjoyed the autonomy sometimes granted to the marginal, as the French monarchy focused its administrative efforts on the more profitable Saint-Domingue. During the Spanish period (1763–1803), French Creoles in Louisiana defended their language and culture even as they benefitted economically from the increasing rates of slave importation that Spanish rule facilitated.

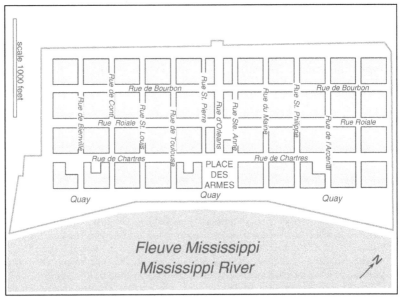

MAP 1.1 *Plan de la Nouvelle Orleans* by Jacques Nicolas Bellin, 1764. (Library of Congress, Geography and Map Division). The complementary map of the old city shows the street names.

administrative challenges.[13] The state creates itself at its borders. There officials, residents, and migrants contend over which people are fit to become part of the body politic (and in what capacity) as well as who should be excluded. In one instance, Claiborne decided that the hundred or so French migrants denied asylum in Jamaica were not "the best description of Settlers for Louisiana."[14] At the border, representatives of the early republic decided who fit "the best description" based on a matrix of labor needs and racist ideologies. In other words, at the border the nation constructs its future one migrant at a time.[15]

The problem was that the majority of the migrants from the French Caribbean appeared to have been of African descent, and Claiborne, like Thomas Jefferson, considered increases in the black population, slave or free, a threat to American sovereignty. "The Searcher of all hearts," Claiborne wrote Jefferson in late 1804, "knows how little I desire to see another of that wretched race set his foot on the Shores of America, & how from my Heart I detest the rapacity that would transport them to us." Whether by "race" Claiborne meant slaves or all black people, his sentiment stemmed not from abolitionism but from white supremacy. Through the end of transatlantic slave importation, the "diffusion" of resident slaves over continental North America, the colonization of free blacks, and superior rates of white reproduction, the nation would rid itself of black people and become a beacon of white republicanism in a cosmopolitan hemisphere.[16]

Louisiana planters, whether French Creole or Anglo-American, wanted a federal border that was closed to antislavery radicals, yet open to

---

[13] Dubois, "The Haitian Revolution and the Sale of Louisiana." On the Haitians' final defeat of Napoleon's forces at Vertières, see Jean-Pierre Le Glaunec, *L'armée Indigène: La Défaite de Napoléon en Haïti* (Montréal: Lux Editeur, 2014).

[14] WC to Madison, February 6, 1804, *Letter Books*, I: 363–365; WC to Madison, January 31, 1804, *Letter Books*, I: 352; WC to Officer, January 20, 1804, *Letter Books*, I: 343; WC to Madison, April 9, 1804, *Letter Books*, II: 88.

[15] Lara Putnam, *Radical Moves: Caribbean Migrants and the Politics of Race in the Jazz Age* (Chapel Hill: University of North Carolina Press, 2013), 11.

[16] Claiborne, New Orleans, to Thomas Jefferson, November 25, 1804, in Claiborne and Jared William Bradley, *Interim Appointment: W.C.C. Claiborne Letter Book, 1804–1805* (Baton Rouge: Louisiana State University Press, 2002), 100–103, 102. See also Jefferson, *Notes on the State of Virginia*, 9. On slavery and Jefferson's vision for American empire in the era of the Louisiana Purchase, see Baptist, *The Half Has Never Been Told*, 30–35; Rothman, *Slave Country*; Johnson, "The Racial Origins of American Sovereignty," 50–59; Kennedy, *Mr. Jefferson's Lost Cause*. On whiteness in the early republic, see Saxton, *The Rise and Fall of the White Republic*.

masters and slaves. "But on this Point the People here were united as one man," Claiborne wrote to Jefferson, "that they must import more Slaves or the Country was ruined forever." By "Country" Claiborne likely referred to the Lower Mississippi River Valley, but he could have just as easily meant the trans-imperial society of Atlantic planters whose material interests diverged from those of the empires to which they belonged. While Claiborne was "desirous to exclude those Slaves who (from Late habits) are accustomed to blood and devastation, and whose counsel & communication with our present Black population may be pregnant with much future Mischief," planters looked to speculators who supplied slaves from Africa and the Caribbean. Those slave dealers supplied a booming market, and demand for slave importation was one thing that could unite the factious planters of Louisiana.[17]

If the smaller migrations highlighted the difference in priorities between the governor and the planters, then the prospective place of about 10,000 migrants from Cuba between 1809 and 1810 caused a federal crisis. From the beginning of the Haitian Revolution and most notably after the defeat of French Major General Charles Victor-Emmanuel-Leclerc's expedition in 1803, tens of thousands of Saint-Dominguans fled to Baracoa and Santiago de Cuba. By 1808 they numbered about 25,000, and they had a significant impact on the economy and culture of Cuba's Oriente Province. They introduced cutting-edge techniques for coffee production; expanded citrus, indigo, cotton, and other staple production; and modernized the sugar industry. Though Spanish officials saw benefits in the capital and skills the migrants brought, others suspected the migrants of republicanism, piracy, and other undesirable traits. But in this age of empire, Napoleon's quest for control of the Iberian Peninsula transformed Cuba from a haven into yet another point of departure for French colonists. In 1807, Napoleon allied with Spain to invade Portugal.

---

[17] Claiborne to Jefferson, November 25, 1804 ("country"); Claiborne to Lt. Col. Freeman, Commg. U.S. Troops, New Orleans, July 17, 1804, *Letter Books*, II: 254–255 ("mischief"). Many Louisiana planters experienced this rift between empire and colony during the Spanish era. In 1796 Spanish administrators banned the importation of foreign slaves due to the events in Saint-Domingue, but at planters' insistence the Cabildo reopened the international slave trade in 1800 with the explicit exclusion of slaves imported from Saint-Domingue. After the Louisiana Purchase, Louisiana briefly became subject to the US ban on slave importation of 1803, and this became a point of disagreement between empire and planters.

After a successful campaign, Napoleon turned on his ally and invaded Spain. The fighting in Europe prompted policy shifts in Havana. Governor Salvador de Muro y Salazar, El Marquis de Someruelos "resolved for ... greater tranquility, to send away ... all those who [were] not indissolubly united to [Spain], and detached from France by their known adherence to the royal family of Bourbon." The Spanish military expelled the refugees, and over 9,000 of them migrated to Louisiana.[18]

Elite migrants from Saint-Domingue by way of Cuba sought to ensure that the polychromatic shadows of Caribbean slavery extended to New Orleans, but by that point Louisiana had become subject to the 1807 federal law that made it illegal for slaves to cross the border into the republic and its territories. After a maritime voyage that one passenger described as "two months [of] struggling against the horrors of hunger, thirst and despair ... [a] distressing situation," this law jeopardized elite migrants' ability to import the over 3,000 persons they claimed to own.[19] If the migrants were slaves, then they could not be allowed entry into New Orleans. If they were free, then those who claimed to own them would lose the material and social privileges of mastery. More than that, they would be added to Louisiana's already sizable free black population.[20]

Edward Livingston recognized in this border conflict an opportunity to use a proslavery federal action to win support from the powerful, if colonized, planters of Louisiana. Livingston, a freemason, former congressman, and US attorney, came from a prominent family in New York (his brother Robert helped to negotiate the Louisiana Purchase), but

---

[18] Marquis of Someruelos, Havana, March 12, 1809, reprinted in *Louisiana Gazette*, April 11, 1809; Scott and Hébrard, *Freedom Papers*, chapter 3; Thomas Fiehrer, "From La Tortue to La Louisiane: An Unfathomed Legacy," in Carl A. Brasseaux, Glenn R. Conrad, and David Cheramie, eds., *The Road to Louisiana: The Saint-Domingue Refugees, 1792–1809* (Lafayette: Center for Louisiana Studies, University of Southwestern Louisiana, 1992), 1–30, 23.

[19] Gallien Preval, Letter to the editor, *Courrier*, reprinted in *Louisiana Gazette*, July 14, 1809.

[20] Jeremy Adelman, *Sovereignty and Revolution in the Iberian Atlantic* (Princeton: Princeton University Press, 2006); Ashli White, "The Limits of Fear: The Saint Dominguan Challenge to Slave Trade Abolition in the United States," *Early American Studies* 2, no. 2 (Fall 2004): 362–397; W. E. B. Du Bois, *The Suppression of the African Slave-Trade to the United States of America, 1638–1870* (New York: Longmans, Green and Co., 1896), 81. For an analogous situation involving Chinese laborers who migrated from Cuba to Louisiana in the post-emancipation period, see Moon-Ho Jung, "Outlawing 'Coolies': Race, Nation, and Empire in the Age of Emancipation," *American Quarterly* 57, no. 3 (September 2005): 677–701.

dubious business dealings sent him to Louisiana for a fresh start.[21] He lobbied associates across the country in support of the "wretched victims of revolutionary insurrection," and he insisted that his archrival Governor Claiborne furnish the "essential relief which in cases like this becomes a national concern." Livingston argued that refugees could prosper in the new land only if allowed ownership of the Africans they claimed as slaves:

The only property by which any of them can hope to import consists of a few slaves who either followed them from affection in their first flight or who have been acquired since by the success of their labor – these slaves are by the existing laws of the United States [illegible] and their owners to an heavy fine – It is to call your attention and that of the committee to the necessity of some general provision for the relief of men who have so many claims on our Constitution that I have taken the charity of addressing you.[22]

Though Louisiana statehood was still a few years off and these migrants had barely traded the high seas for land, Livingston was already making arguments about their constitutional rights to human property.

Those and other arguments swayed local and federal officials, and they enacted policies that defined membership in the migrant elite and endowed them with capital in the form of human property. In May 1809, the New

---

[21] Livingston, one champion of the Louisiana Civil Code of 1825, was also an active freemason, which became another point of connection between the migrant and native elites. In an 1809 address to fellow freemasons, Livingston stated: "Faith, hope, and charity form the triple mystic base, on which our constitutions rest; and the greatest of them, says the inspired poet, is charity." Many prominent Saint Dominguans, including Médéric-Louis Moreau de Saint-Méry, Etienne Polverel, and Vincent Ogé, were freemasons. Radical freemasonry, with its rejection of race, class, and religious hierarchies, predominated in French lodges during the 1790s and early 1800s, which allowed people of African descent, Muslims, Jews, and women entrance into lodges. Many free people of color from Saint-Domingue, including Polverel, joined the Masonic lodges when they pursued educations in France. Saint-Dominguan émigrés undoubtedly joined or started lodges upon arrival in the United States. On Livingston's speech, see *Louisiana Gazette*, May 16, 1809. These words were taken from his address to the Louisiana Lodge on the festival of St. John. In that speech, he resigned as Master of the Lodge. See also Susan Buck-Morss, "Hegel and Haiti," *Critical Inquiry* 26 (Summer 2000): 821–865; DuBois, *Avengers*, 142.

[22] Edward Livingston to James H. Causten, Washington, June 14, 1809, MSS 68, Folder 1, HNOC. Causten (1788–1874), was part of the prominent Baltimore merchant family headed by Isaac Causten. They traded staples such as flour, coffee, and tobacco across the Atlantic, including South America, Europe, and the Caribbean. James Causten's legal career began when he represented US citizens in their claims against Congress, which assumed the spoliation claims against the French in the aftermath of the Quasi-War. Carlton Fletcher, "James H. Causten," Glover Park History: Historical Sketches of Glover Park, Upper Georgetown, & Georgetown Heights, http://gloverparkhistory.com /estates-and-farms/weston/james-h-causten/, accessed February 17, 2014.

Orleans City Council formed "a committee of benevolence, for the purpose of relieving the refugees from the Island of Cuba."[23] Also in 1809 the US Congress passed an exemption that allowed the importation of the select group as slaves. The migrants whom officials recognized to be free – those who either appeared to be white, which was proof enough of freedom, or people of African descent who had documentation of free status – colluded with the state to classify about one-third of the immigrants as slaves: 962 men, 1,330 women, and 934 children. Race became its own passport, one that allowed those who appeared to be white to pass into the country as free people and that subjected all people of color to heightened scrutiny. Whatever their legal status before they crossed the US border, for thousands of persons of African descent who came from Saint-Domingue by way of Jamaica, Cuba, and other points in the circum-Gulf of Mexico, Louisiana became not an "asylum from affliction," but a sanctuary for slavery.[24]

Though as a caste they had just deprived thousands of persons of their freedom, the elites of Saint-Domingue displaced to counter-revolutionary New Orleans clung to their sense of victimization. They ostracized fellow white colonists who had supported the revolution, and they remained as adamant as ever in their antiblack racism. "The colonists of San Domingo who survived the massacre of their loved ones, saw their wealth pillaged, and now drag out their days in indigence are hardly constrained to listen to the counsels of moderation," one observer wrote. "Embittered by these misfortunes, it would seem that their vengeance can only be satisfied by the torture of the blacks."[25]

---

[23] Charles Trudeau, President of City Council, "Records of the City Council, Providing for the Forming of a Committee of Benevolence, for the Purpose of Relieving the Refugees from the Island of Cuba," *Louisiana Gazette*, June 6, 1809. Members of the committee included Governor Claiborne, Mayor Mather, and Judge Moreau Lislet.

[24] Edward Livingston to James H. Causten, Washington, June 14, 1809. These figures are given in the *Louisiana Courier* from March of an unknown year. Preval, letter to the editor, *Courier*, reprinted in *Louisiana Gazette*, July 14, 1809; Scott, "Paper Thin"; Nathalie Dessens, *From Saint-Domingue to New Orleans: Migration and Influences* (Gainesville: University of Florida Press, 2007); Paul F. Lachance, "The 1809 Immigration of Saint-Domingue Refugees to New Orleans: Reception, Integration, and Impact," *Louisiana History* 29, no. 2 (Spring 1988): 109–141.

[25] Robin, *Voyage*, 261. In 1804, exile DeBordes warned fellow refugee Lambert: "There will arrive in Annapolis, Maryland, a French Ambassador. His name is Mr. Charlot, and I strongly believe that he was a general of Brigands in St. Domingue." In another instance, in 1810 a group of exiled planters motivated by "the recollection of their past sufferings" went before the Superior Court of the Territory of Orleans to have Pierre Dormenon, a refugee from Jacmel, disbarred. They alleged that he had fought alongside Étienne

"FORGED TITLE OF LIBERTY"

On October 2, 1810, a "negro man named Figaro creole from St. Domingo"
ran away from his purported owner in Lafourche, Louisiana. According to
the runaway advertisement, Figaro based his right to freedom on the ascendant ideology of the era: "He makes him pass as a free negro." In this
ambiguous phrasing, "pass" could have been either verb or noun. On the
one hand, "makes him pass" might have referred to a radical action, Figaro's
ability to perform freedom. When persons classed as slaves "passed," or
pretended to be whites or free blacks to escape bondage, they highlighted the
malleability of those social categories even though those designations held
extraordinary power in everyday life. The phrase also alludes to the passes or
permits that masters used to authorize slave movement. Perhaps Figaro
literally made himself a written pass, since the advertisement specified that
Figaro was the "bearer of a forged title of liberty." Figaro might have secured
his freedom at birth in Saint-Domingue, with the French emancipation of
1794, or through manumission in Cuba. Figaro would have carried that
paper from sea to land and from freedom to slavery, but in 1810 Louisiana
he became a runaway slave. For Figaro and thousands of other phenotypically black migrants from the Caribbean into Louisiana, the border crossing
illuminated the ephemerality of the 1794 French emancipation in the face of
the insatiable labor demands of industrial sugar and cotton production. In an
age of republican revolution, one word in a runaway slave advertisement
turned a freedom paper into a forgery.[26]

Enslavement at the border was a common experience for phenotypically black migrants from the French Caribbean into Louisiana, where

Polverel and Léger-Félicité Sonthonax, the two French Revolutionary Civil Commissioners
of Saint-Domingue who abolished slavery on the island in 1793. Mr. Guiet and other "men
of veracity" swore that Dormenon "headed, aided and assisted the negroes of St. Domingo,
in their horrible massacres, and other outrages against the whites, in and about the year
1793." Dormenon was allegedly an "intimate friend of De Lisle, Brissot, Faubert and Gai."
He paid for his politics with his profession – the court in Louisiana initially disbarred him
nearly two decades after the offending act. He later became a judge and planter in Pointe
Coupée Parish. DeBordes/Joubert (?), to Lambert, Philadelphia, September 27, 1804,
Lambert Family Papers, MC 244, Folder 1, TU; *Dormenon's Case*, 1 Mart. (o.s.) 129,
1810 WL 841 (La.Terr.Super.Orleans); Nathalie Dessens, *Creole City: A Chronicle of
Early New Orleans* (Gainesville: University Press of Florida, 2015), 178. On white refugees
in New Orleans, see Thomas N. Ingersoll, *Mammon and Manon in Early New Orleans:
The First Slave Society in the Deep South, 1718–1819* (Knoxville: University of Tennessee
Press, 1999), 257; Lachance, "1809 Immigration of Saint-Domingue Refugees to New
Orleans," 127. On the animus that white refugees had for Polverel and Sonthonax, see
White, *Encountering Revolution*, chapter 3.

[26] St. Marc, "Runaway Negro," *Louisiana Courier*, October 24, 1810.

dark skin increasingly carried the presumption of slave status. Because of French emancipation in 1794, it is virtually certain that many of the people who appeared to be black were free at the time they migrated to Louisiana. But for those who, like Figaro, had "very black skin," liberty was not a right. Livingston, the migrant elite, and others cited two interlaced justifications for the ownership of their fellow sojourners: a paternalistic notion of "affection," or the volitional servitude that – masters convinced themselves – enslaved people performed, and "acquisition," or a claim based on the sanctity of private property across borders. Consequently, black migrants from the French Caribbean became a critical demographic in the city's growing slave population. Those who became slaves at the border, one historian writes, "accounted for a full quarter of the growth of the Orleans Territory's slave population, from 22,701 to over 34,000, between 1806 and 1810"; that is, "for 16 percent of the 3,000 people sold as slaves in New Orleans between 1809 and 1811." By 1810, black migrants from Saint-Domingue "represented almost a third of the 1810 slave population of New Orleans and its precincts (10,824) and 10 percent of the slaves of Orleans Territory (34,660)." Whatever their status before, these migrants sailed into Louisiana's slave places.[27]

The auction block was among the first places that these migrants entered, and through naked force it transformed them from free persons into Louisiana slaves. For the migrants who sold their fellow sojourners, the slave market laid bare the material interests beneath their paternalistic discourses. "Among the fugitives from San Domingo who came to Louisiana there were some whose slaves had followed them out of attachment for their masters," one observer wrote. "The reward of these too faithful servants was to be inhumanly sold."[28] The Chancerels provide one example of the short distance between these loyal slaves and the auction block. During the course of the revolution (the date is unclear), Pierre Marie Chancerel, a Major General in the French army, and his household left his plantation in the Cul de Sac-Leogane region of

---

[27] Baptist, *The Half Has Never Been Told*, 56; Fiehrer, "An Unfathomed Legacy," 25; Lachance, "1809 Immigration of Saint-Domingue Refugees to New Orleans," 117. As Rebecca Scott argues, these migrants were likely once freed and then re-enslaved. On the other hand, I hesitate to label these migrants as "wrongfully enslaved," which risks suggesting that others were "rightfully enslaved." As Adam Rothman writes, "nobody is a natural-born slave." The force of law, custom, and lash turned people into the property of others. Scott, "Paper Thin"; Rothman, *Beyond Freedom's Reach*, 17.
[28] Robin, *Voyage*.

Saint-Domingue for Santiago de Cuba. There, in April 1805, Chancerel granted to his wife, Marie Ursule Marin Chancerel, authority to sell two of the people held as slaves who had accompanied the couple on that initial exodus: "un nègre" named Pierre-Charles and the "nègresse" Evoline. After mistress and slaves migrated to New Orleans, she sold Pierre-Charles in 1810, and Evoline three years later, to a free woman of color. Chancerel signed both acts of sale herself.

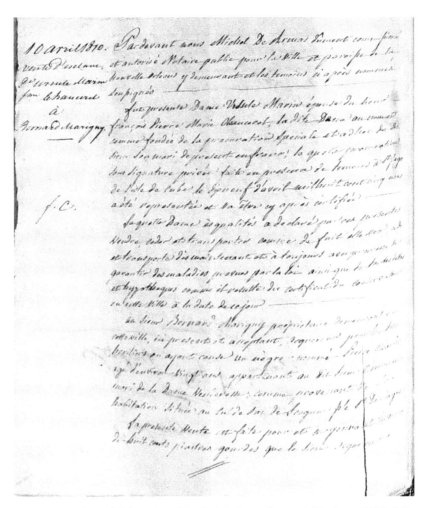

FIGURE 1.1 Act of Sale, Marie-Ursule Marin to Bernard Marigny, Michel De Armas, Notary, June 10, 1810, Office of the Clerk of Civil District Court, Notarial Archives Division, New Orleans. Courtesy Dale N. Atkins, Clerk of Civil District Court. In this document, Marin sold Pierre-Charles to Bernard Marigny.

About a decade later, in testimony taken after a different one of Chancerel's bondspersons ran away, a witness swore that the fugitive had faithfully exhibited his "good character, and tried fidelity and attachment to his mistress, who he constantly followed everywhere," most notably during her escape from the embattled island. When it became convenient for Chancerel, the slaves' journey from Saint-Domingue to Louisiana became evidence of fidelity. But years before, the "fidelity and attachment" that Pierre-Charles and Evoline showed by migrating did not protect them from the New Orleans auction block.[29]

Pierre-Charles and Evoline were not alone; local newspapers and estate sales overflowed with advertisements and transactions for unfree laborers who had migrated from Saint-Domingue to New Orleans. In 1807, one seller marketed "A HANDSOME MULATRESS, born in St. Domingo, seventeen years old, an excellent seamstress, a pretty good washerwoman, and an excellent chambermaid." A different ad listed "A Negress, creole of St. Domingo, about 25 years old, with her daughter 13 years old ... several other young Negresses, creoles of the same place."[30] In an 1810 auction, the firm Patton & Mossy advertised "a handsome young Mulatto, active and industrious, creole of St. Domingo, about 5 or 6 years in the States and this country 20 years old."[31] Estate sales document the despair of those migrants from Saint-Domingue to New Orleans for whom one master's death meant a life of continued bondage in Louisiana. Marie Mercier widow Daulase's estate consisted of three enslaved "creoles of St. Domingue": Catherine, described as a forty-five-year-old quadroon; Manda, a fifty-year-old negro woman; and twenty-six-year-old Dieu Donné. All three (even the latter bondsperson, whose name meant "God-given") met the auction block in 1810. A master's death sent them to the New Orleans slave market.[32] These migrants ended up on the auction blocks of New Orleans, not despite, but because of their circum-Caribbean circulations.

---

[29] Act of Sale, Dame Ursule Marin to Bernard Marigny, Michel De Armas, Notary, June 10, 1810, New Orleans, volume 3, page 84, NANO; Act of Sale, Ursule Marin to Minette Chiffré [free woman of color], Michel De Armas, Notary, New Orleans, June 10, 1810, volume 7A, page 982, NANO; Deposition, Marie-Ursule Marin widow Chancerel to Gallier Préval, Justice of the Peace for the Second Section of New Orleans, New Orleans, June 18, 1821; Deposition, Charles Joseph Robert Peyrac to Préval, New Orleans, June 18, 1821, both in Slave Evaluation Report, MSS199, HNOC.

[30] Louis Lecesne, "A Vendre," *Telegraphe, General Advertiser*, October 13, 1807; *Telegraphe*, October 17, 1807, my translation, both MF5700, LSU.

[31] *Courrier*, September 28, 1810.

[32] *Courrier*, August 6, 1810.

But who would buy them? Concerns about the latent insurrectionist potential of Saint-Dominguan slaves notwithstanding, Louisiana's planters knowingly purchased these men, women, and children. As the above listings demonstrate, some sellers, who had every incentive to minimize unseemly qualities, listed slaves' provenance in Saint-Domingue in advertisements. To be sure, some sellers likely divulged such a background upfront to avoid redhibitory actions from buyers.[33] In Louisiana, purchasers had the right to contest sales by claiming that a seller knowingly concealed a defect in the property. In this case, that defect would have been Saint-Dominguan origins. In addition, there are likely other compelling reasons that these sellers advertised the "Creoles of St. Domingue" as such. First, planters' high demand for labor meant they would buy just about anyone. Second, as experienced domestics, peddlers, and sugar makers, for example, these laborers possessed valuable skills. Third, if we take seriously the power of the loyalty myth, then those faithful slaves who supposedly left Saint-Domingue under the authority of their masters embodied the colonial past that was a source of nostalgia for displaced Saint-Dominguan planters and inspiration to Louisiana ones. Notably, these men and women were generally listed as "Creoles," a term that meant any number of things depending on context. In this particular usage, it might have connoted a domesticated or loyal black in contrast to the unseasoned, African-born rebels left behind in Saint-Domingue.[34]

A close examination of one act of sale illuminates the ways that elite migrants and Louisiana planters together reconstructed the plantation workforces of colonial Saint-Domingue in the early republic. In March 1812, Claude François Jean Bellanger sold to Joseph Fouque sixteen people of African descent classed as slaves. Bellanger claimed to have the standing to do so because they "all belong[ed] to the seller having been born in his plantation in St. Domingue & brought by him ('ammenés

---

[33] In one instance, the firm Dutillet & Peyrellade faced legal actions because they sold a "Negro wench" from Baltimore to a purchaser "who was guaranteed a good servant, washer, and seamstress, and who far from having these qualities has entirely different ones." Ducourneau, "Notice," *Courier*, November 20, 1811.

On redhibition laws (or warranty laws) in Louisiana that governed and shaped slave sales, see Johnson, *Soul by Soul*, 12–13, 130–131.

[34] "Caliban is a 'noble savage' if properly domesticated or extirpated," Fiehrer writes. "But Caliban becomes a menacing brute once the relations of power are challenged, as in Saint-Domingue." Fiehrer, "An Unfathomable Legacy," 29. Ashli White sees in this demand for Saint-Dominguan slaves an act of Anglo-American chauvinism. US slave owners assumed they could exercise better authority over Saint-Dominguan slaves than their French masters did in the colony. White, *Encountering Revolution*, 151–154.

par lui') to this city." This point is telling because in the years that preceded the revolution the colony's slave population was overwhelmingly African-born, so the seller's claim that they were all born on his plantation is doubtful. Second, the age of the youngest migrant seems to undermine his already suspect claim. The act of sale lists "Farine, *griffone* aged about 19 years with her three-month old child." It is unlikely that Farine had given birth on a Saint-Dominguan plantation in January 1812. In the act of sale, Bellanger nonetheless cemented the association between their births on his plantation in Saint-Domingue and their journey to Louisiana.[35]

In that one purchase, Fouque secured a miniature version of a Saint-Dominguan plantation's workforce. Bondspersons included men, women, and children, and Bellanger classified them into such racial categories as *mulatresse* and *griffone, negresse* and *negritte*. Many possessed skills, including Moïse, listed as a carpenter, and Lise, described as a washer and seamstress. And their status followed them. In early 1813, when Fouque became insolvent and died only a month or so thereafter, his estate sale included two slaves purchased from Bellanger: Aime, a thirty-year-old quadroon man, and Georgette, a twenty-five-year-old black woman. Both were listed as "creoles L'Artibonite," the region in western Saint-Domingue that includes Gonaïves and Saint-Marc. These two migrants would again be sold in New Orleans as slaves from Saint-Domingue.[36]

"LOOKING FALSE"

In addition to his purportedly forged "title of liberty," Figaro also used his body, possessions, and skills to challenge the slave status assigned to him. This thirty-year-old man reportedly spoke "good French and bad English," which allowed him to communicate with a broad segment of the local population. He carried only the clothes on his back, "a

---

[35] Act of Sale, Claude François Jean Bellanger to Joseph Fouque, Pierre Pedesclaux, Notary, New Orleans, March 3, 1812, volume 64, Folder 7, page 130, NANO.

[36] On *Joseph Fouque v. His Creditors*, see Thomas Kennedy, Clerk of Court, "City Court – Parish of Orleans, January 20, 1813," *Courier*, February 1, 1813. On Fouque's over one hundred other slaves between 1808 and 1813 and the February 8, 1813 estate sale that included Georgette and Aime, see Gwendolyn Midlo Hall, *Databases for the Study of Afro-Louisiana History and Genealogy, 1699–1860* (Baton Rouge: Louisiana State University Press, 2000). Curiously, Fouque died shortly after the public became aware of his financial difficulties.

pantaloons and a shirt of check with [an] old hat," but his modest clothes covered a deceptive body. According to the runaway advertisement, Figaro had a habit of "bending his body when in march, looking false." Perhaps he slouched to escape detection, since erect posture might draw undue attention. More than that, since liberty was primarily the province of white people, any black person who claimed it "looked false." In a society in which blackness carried a presumption of enslavement, migrants of African descent from Saint-Domingue employed diverse strategies to make their bodies "look false," or to place them outside of the accepted confines of blackness.[37]

Because freedom "looked false" on black bodies, migrants of African descent who hoped to preserve their free status needed the sworn statements of credible witnesses before local officials to support their claims.[38] In an 1808 affidavit before Mayor James Mather, a presumably white woman named Michele Amfoux (or Amphoux) swore that Marie Justine, called Sangosse, was a "free quadroon, 29 years old, daughter of Marie Jeanne Breton, resident of la Ville du Cap" until 1799. Amfoux further stated that Marie Justine "was generally recognized as free from birth" and lived in enjoyment of those rights. Though classified as a quadroon, Marie Justine nonetheless needed the testimony of a woman recognized to be white to authenticate her freedom claim. In August 1816, five men made a similar claim before a notary on behalf of the incarcerated Saint Louis Vallon, also known as Voltiques. They swore that he had been free from birth ("libre de naissance") in Port au Prince and that he had lived in New Orleans as a free man for three and a half years. Again, since he appeared to be "negre" [sic], these men's testimonies were critical to Vallon's effort to claim free status in the new territory.[39]

Even slaveholding Saint-Dominguans of African descent struggled to secure recognition and financial independence in New Orleans. In *Tonnelier v. Maurin's Executor*, a case brought before the Superior Court of Louisiana in 1812, the plaintiff, a free woman of color, claimed

---

[37] St Marc, "Runaway Negro," *Courier*, October 24, 1810. On the body and performativity of social categories, see Judith Butler, *Bodies that Matter* (London: Routledge, 1993).

[38] For a discussion of the importance of freedom papers for these migrants as well as a family history of one such migration, see Scott and Hébrard, *Freedom Papers*.

[39] Affidavit, Michele Amfoux before Mayor James Mather, New Orleans, May 7, 1808, Free Persons of Color and Slave Documents, 91–42-L, HNOC; Deposition, Joseph Blactraud (or Blactot), Marcellin Gillot, Fontagne Leger, Sirille Mollet, and Jules Plantin, h. c. l. [homme de couleur libre, or free man of color] before Gallien Préval, New Orleans, August 10, 1816, NYHS NOC, Box 8, Folder 12.

to have lived as the deceased Maurin's "menagère" (which could have meant housewife, partner, or domestic servant) in Hispaniola, Santiago de Cuba, and New Orleans. "She had with her in his family, several grown daughters of hers," the court's awkward prose divulged. During their partnership, Tonnelier testified, she allowed Maurin to profit from her bondspersons' wages, earnings that Maurin likely reinvested. Louisiana's authorities did not recognize their relationship, so Tonnelier and her daughters lacked the legal protections given to widows and so-called legitimate children. After his death Maurin's legal heirs claimed his estate. Tonnelier sought financial redress, which the court denied. As this case shows, contingent events over consecutive border crossings left even slaveholding free blacks, especially women, from Saint-Domingue vulnerable in New Orleans.[40]

So why did people of African descent move to New Orleans? Some persons once held as slaves in Saint-Domingue left an antislavery revolution for Cuba and then Louisiana, both territories where slavery was expanding, and perhaps for good reason. First, some masters could simply force their slaves into the Saint-Dominguan diaspora. Even the flames of revolution did not instantaneously eradicate the physical, psychological, and sexual coercions of slavery. Second, due to French emancipation in 1794 many people of African descent in Saint-Domingue did not consider themselves to be "mobile slaves," but instead considered themselves to be free persons who, like countless others, sought a better life abroad. Some might have hoped to become slave owners. Third, it is hard to know what each migrant knew about their destinations at their points of departure. Due to the extensive martial and trade networks that linked people and places across the circum-Mexican Gulf, it is quite likely that the migrants maintained "simultaneity" with Cuba, Louisiana, and other territories prior to their departures from Saint-Domingue, but this is not certain. And finally, with the order of expulsion from Cuba in 1809, they had to go somewhere. And their journey to New Orleans reveals much about the relationship between race, slavery, and nation.[41]

The uncertainties of revolution, when coupled with masters' desperate promises of patronage and manumission, made trans-imperial migration

---

[40] *Tonnelier v. Maurin's Ex'r*, 2 Mart. (o.s.) 206, 1812 WL 767 (La. Super. 1812). See also Hortense Spillers, "Mama's Baby, Papa's Maybe: An American Grammar Book," *Diacritics* 17 (Summer 1987): 65–81.

[41] On simultaneity in the Atlantic World, see Anderson, *Imagined Communities: Reflections on the Origin and Spread of Nationalism*, Rev. and extended ed. (London; New York: Verso, 1991).

a viable option for some persons of African descent. Indeed, strategic faithfulness might have been the reason that some of them migrated to Louisiana in the first place. No matter how self-serving their masters' narratives, faithfulness cannot be discounted as one tactic that those formerly held as slaves in Saint-Domingue used to reconstitute their lives in diaspora. Slaveholders manipulated their human property's virtues, such as loyalty, and emotions, such as fear and love, to better exert control. And though certainly disadvantaged by systematic domination, bondspersons nonetheless used their agency in contingent and counterintuitive ways. For example, masters heavily rewarded those who informed on conspiracies. Informants secured for themselves extra quantities of food, cash payments, and even manumission. After the 1811 Deslondes Revolt in Louisiana, for example, the descendants of one murdered planter sought to free Bazile "in consideration of his good conduct and zeal with which he has extinguished the fire which the brigands had set to the principal house of the plantation."[42] Finally, resistance and collaboration are not necessarily antithetical. Trusted slaves, such as coachmen and drivers, used their positions to better facilitate individual escapes and collective revolts. In 1810, for example, Scaramouche's master issued the enslaved man a pass ("un billet") so the bondman could pursue an escaped slave. Scaramouche used the opportunity to become a runaway himself.[43]

Some women of African descent who may have been free or freed in the French Caribbean and then re-enslaved at the Louisiana border were subsequently manumitted in Louisiana, though it is impossible to know whether they migrated in the capacity of slaves in hopes of subsequent manumission or were unexpectedly enslaved at the border and later freed again. Agathe, described in a petition for manumission as "a negro wench creole of Saint Domingue, about fifty years old," was born sometime

---

[42] Petition du héritier Meuillon demandant l'affanchisement du plusier slaves, St. Charles Parish, Louisiana, March 20, 1811, in Albert Thrasher, *"On to New Orleans!": Louisiana's Heroic 1811 Slave Revolt* (New Orleans: Cypress Press, 1996), 224. I discuss the Deslondes Revolt in depth below.

[43] Jumoville, "Parti Marron," *Courrier*, July 30, 1810; de Certeau, *The Practice of Everyday Life*, 37. See also Stephanie Li, *Something Akin to Freedom: The Choice of Bondage in Narratives by African American Women* (Albany: State University of New York Press, 2010); Walter Johnson, "On Agency," *Journal of Social History* 37, no. 1 (2003): 113–124; Hartman, *Scenes of Subjection*; James C. Scott, *Weapons of the Weak: Everyday Forms of Peasant Resistance* (New Haven, CT: Yale University Press, 1985).

The trope of the faithful black-turned-armed revolutionary has a long history in popular culture, from Sam Greenlee's novel, *The Spoke Who Sat by the Door*, to the 2015 music video for rapper J. Cole's song "G.O.M.D."

around 1770. She lived in that colony for two to four decades before her 1810 arrival in New Orleans. There she became classified either for the first or second time as a slave. Agathe, now in her forties, labored in bondage in that port city for another seven years before her owner filed a petition for her manumission. She gained her freedom in New Orleans in 1817 at the age of fifty. Prudence may have made a similar calculation but to a different result. Described as a faithful bondsperson, Prudence also reportedly fled with her owner from Saint-Domingue during the revolution. Her owner manumitted her in his will, but his heirs successfully sued to preserve their inherited wealth in her. Some masters may have simply preferred to manumit bondspersons of a certain age rather than remain responsible for them in their later years, but it is also possible that these women remained faithful to their masters during the journey from Saint-Domingue to New Orleans with the promise of patronage and an eventual freedom.[44]

As Prudence's case shows, sometimes even a master's intention to manumit did not necessarily confer a meaningful freedom on his bondsperson. Marie Lanesse's passages across borders and statuses illuminate the lengths to which freed persons and their allies went to preserve their freedom. Raymond Labatut served as militia captain of Cap Français and acquired La Tortue (or Tortuga) – the small, tortoise-shaped island north of Saint Domingue – in 1795. He subsequently established three coffee plantations: Basse-Terre, Cayenne, and Palmiste.[45] Sometime around February 1803, Pierre-Clement Laussat, en route to Louisiana to serve as Napoleon's appointed Colonial Prefect, claimed to have observed the revolutionaries' attack on La Tortue: "During the entire forty-eight hours of our layover, [the insurgents] pillaged, slaughtered, and devastated the small isle of La Tortue and massacred its proprietor Labatut, a descendent of the family of the original land holders."[46] Raymond

[44] Robert De St. Leger, petition to Louisiana Parish Court (Orleans Parish), Petitions for the emancipation of slaves, 1814–1843, New Orleans Public Library, microfiche VCP320; *Prudence v. Bermodi*, No. 1888, 1 La. 234 (1830). See also Schafer, *Slavery, the Civil Law, and the Supreme Court of Louisiana*, 186–199.

[45] Jean-Louis Clavier, "Toussaint Louverture d'après le Mémoire abrégé des événements de l'Île de Saint-Domingue depuis l'année 1789 jusqu'à celle de 1807," in *Toussaint Louverture Et L'indépendance D'haïti : Témoignages Pour Un Bicentenaire*, Hommes Et Sociétés, ed. Jacques Cauna (Paris: Karthala: Société française d'histoire d'outre-mer, 2004), 77–81.

[46] Pierre-Clément de Laussat, *Memoirs of My Life to My Son during the Years 1803 and after, Which I Spent in Public Service in Louisiana as Commissioner of the French Government for the Retrocession to France of That Colony and for Its Transfer to the United States* (Baton Rouge: Published for the Historic New Orleans Collection by the Louisiana State University Press, 1978), 9.

Labatut's wife, Marie-Thérèse Gansefort Labatut, was killed in 1803. Labatut, his brother Benjamin, and his "Negro wench" Marie Lanesse fled.[47] Raymond Labatut died later that year in Newport, Rhode Island, and was survived by one of his three sons, Pierre-Isidore, who settled in Charleston, South Carolina.[48]

The times and spaces of her journeys are unclear, but Lanesse later arrived in New Orleans, where she immediately confronted the threat of enslavement. Aimée Copman, a free woman of color ("mestiza libre") and property owner from Saint-Domingue by way of Santiago de Cuba, purchased Lanesse and arranged to sell her. Perhaps Copman, an unmarried mother, needed the money from Lanesse's sale to support herself and her newborn daughter in this new territory.[49] Whatever Copman's motives, an anonymous former resident of La Tortue took the unusual step of publishing a notice on July 4, 1810, that warned that the initial sale of Lanesse to Copman was invalid, which would render any subsequent sales illegitimate. The author claimed that Lanesse's master, the deceased Labatut, had long "manifested a desire at different times, to make that negro wench, Lanesse, free" in recompense for "the services which she rendered to him."[50] The author defined those "services" as Marie's "following him faithfully in his precipitate retreat in the recesses of the forests, when the revolted negroes invaded the island." It is also possible that this phrase euphemistically refers to an unspoken if common sexual

[47] An Ancient Inhabitant of La Tortue, "To the Public," *Louisiana Courier*, July 4, 1810. Here "ancient" is likely an Anglicization of the French "ancien," or "former."

[48] Jacques de Cauna, "93–24 LABATUT (St-Domingue et Martinique, 18°)," *Généalogie et Histoire de la Caraïbe* Bulletin 63 (Septembre 1994): 1149–1150. The editors of Laussat's published memoirs note that Jean-Baptist Labatut was massacred in La Tortue. This La Tortue resident should not be confused with the Jean-Baptiste Labatut who moved to New Orleans in 1781, held public office, and fought alongside Andrew Jackson during the War of 1812.

[49] Marie Estelle Copman, the "natural" daughter of Aimée Copman, was born on August 28, 1809, and baptized November 2, 1809, at the St Louis Church in New Orleans. In the baptismal certificate, the priest, Claude Thomas, listed Aimée Copman as "habitante et proprietaire en Ville du Cap." Marie Estelle's father's name was omitted, which is why she was listed as a "natural," that is, not a "legitimate," child. Slave and Free People of Color Baptismal Records, Sacramental Records of the Roman Catholic Church of the Archdiocese of New Orleans, Book 23, page 22, available at http://archives.arch-no.org/sfpc.php. On the racial politics of baptisms, see Spear, *Race, Sex, and Social Order*; Verena Stolcke, *Marriage, Class and Colour in Nineteenth-Century Cuba: A Study of Racial Attitudes and Sexual Values in a Slave Society* (London; New York: Cambridge University Press, 1974).

[50] *Louisiana Courier*, July 4, 1810.

relationship between male master and female slave. Marie's story opens several possibilities. Perhaps Labatut forced Lanesse to relocate to New Orleans. Perhaps he (or someone else) intentionally defrauded Copman by "selling" Lanesse to her only to anonymously sabotage the transaction at a later stage. But perhaps Lanesse engaged in the reproductive and sexual labor demanded of her in hopes of securing favor and manumission.[51]

Marie Lanesse's fate is not certain, but circumstantial evidence suggests that she remained free in New Orleans. The Saint Louis Church's burial records show that a Marie Magdelaine Labatut, "femme de couleur libre, natif du Port au Prince dans l'isle de St. Domingue," was buried on March 17, 1824. Church officials estimated her age to have been about sixty years old. Her birthplace coupled with the absence of listed family members suggests she likely had no connection to the white Labatuts of New Orleans, whose progenitors migrated directly from France to Louisiana. Marie Magdelaine Labatut might have been Marie Lanesse, who, once freed, took the surname of her late owner and perhaps partner. And while Marie Lanesse would have perhaps been in her mid-forties at the time, not sixty as the decedent was thought to have been, it is possible that she looked older. After enslavement in Saint-Domingue, flight from an unthinkable revolution, a fight against re-enslavement, and life as a freed black woman on the urban frontier, her weathered face bore the etchings of an epic story.[52]

Other migrants from Saint-Domingue escaped the auction block in New Orleans by running away, a process that tore apart some relationships while creating and reuniting others. While it is difficult to document, it is certainly likely that, given the interconnectedness that the elite diaspora fostered through correspondence and travel, the people they held as slaves had knowledge of each other's whereabouts across the United States. It is further conceivable that they would again migrate, whether legally or illegally, to rejoin their friends and families. Indeed, former bondspersons often enacted their freedom by reconstituting the bonds that the slave market severed. François, described as a twenty-five-year-old *grif* (a term for mixed black and Indian ancestry) with a "red face," purportedly migrated from Saint-Domingue to Louisiana in 1803 and ran

---

[51] For a discussion of the relationship between gender, sexual labor, and manumission, see Sue Peabody, "*Négresse, Mulâtresse, Citoyenne*: Gender and Emancipation in the French Caribbean, 1650–1848," in *Gender and Slave Emancipation in the Atlantic World*, eds. Pamela Scully and Diana Paton (Durham: Duke University Press, 2005), 56–78.

[52] "Labatut, Marie Magdelaine," St. Louis Cathedral Funerals Slaves/Free People of Color, volume 7, part II, record 2401, March 17, 1824, AANO.

away in 1810. Honoré, a twenty-two-year-old baker and cook, ran away the following year. By 1813, persons who had previously migrated from Saint-Domingue to New York and Philadelphia started to arrive in New Orleans, whether pushed to get away from owners in the northeast or pulled by a desire to reconnect with the Saint-Dominguans in New Orleans. Emille, a twenty-year-old mulatto, reportedly belonged to an owner in New York. Acts of sale sent him first to Tennessee and then Alabama. He escaped his owners there and journeyed to New Orleans before local authorities apprehended him. Perhaps the vagaries of the domestic slave trade would have sent him to New Orleans anyway. But it is compelling to consider that a combination of factors, both within and beyond Emille's control, sent him from one major point of entry for the Saint-Dominguan diaspora, New York, to another, New Orleans.[53]

Women who had ties to Saint-Domingue and Cuba also ran away, sometimes to escape the gendered oppression they experienced under slavery. Finette, a twenty-five-year-old woman, traveled from Cuba to New Orleans in 1809, where upon arrival Marguerite Dangluse claimed ownership of her. After Dangluse's death, a testamentary sold Finette to Manuel Perez *fils* (an appellation that indicates the son was named after his father). The sale occurred on December 8, 1811, and Finette ran away from Perez's plantation almost exactly seven months later. In the runaway advertisement, Perez described her as "a negro wench ... of the Congo nation, and came from Cuba to this place about two years ago ... 6 or 7 months gone with child ... She has no country marks whatsoever on her face." This woman was born in West Central Africa, survived the Middle Passage to either Saint-Domingue or Cuba, and then undertook a subsequent journey to New Orleans, where one owner's death sent her into the possession of another. Her travails had not ended. Perhaps she was already pregnant at the act of sale, but the timing of her pregnancy suggests that the testamentary, Perez, or someone else raped Finnete as soon as he took possession of her. No wonder she ran.[54]

---

[53] Chaniau, *aîné*, "*Esclave en Maronnage*," *Courrier*, July 11, 1810 (Francois); J. Laymuse & Grounche, "Thirty Dollars Reward," *Courrier*, September 11, 1811 (Honoré); B. Puche, "Runaway Slave in Jail," *Courrier*, March 26, 1813 (Emille).

[54] Act of Sale, Jean Francois Pigal to Manuel Perrez, Jr., Michel De Armas, Notary, New Orleans, December 8, 1810, volume 4B, page 431, NANO; Manuel Perez, *Louisiana Courier*, July 29, 1811. On rape and slavery, see Edward E. Baptist, "'Cuffy,' 'Fancy Maids,' and 'One-Eyed Men': Rape, Commodification, and the Domestic Slave Trade in the United States," *AHR* 106 (December 2001): 1619–1650; Melton McLaurin, *Celia: A Slave* (Athens, GA: University of Georgia Press, 1991).

    Other enslaved women from Saint-Domingue also absconded in the New Orleans metropolitan area. They included "Pauline, 22 or 23 years, creole of the Windward

In addition to fidelity and escape, some bondspersons escalated their everyday resistance into antislavery revolt, and in the process they drew in part on ideas from the revolutionary isle to stage the largest antislavery revolt in US history. In a letter to her father, Harriet Peters Deslondes offered a restrained description of what she called "the attempt at a revolt which took place, amongst the negroes." The events left her so shaken that her "reason almost fled," but "the combination, not being very extensive, it being the negroes but of a few plantations collected, the Insurrection was immediately quelled."[55] That was certainly one way to describe it. On January 8, 1811, the mulatto bondman Charles of the Deslondes plantation and an estimated 500 co-conspirators set out from the German Coast, an area about thirty-six miles upriver, toward New Orleans. They burned plantations and killed two white residents in their wake. Two days later, US troops stationed nearby intercepted the revolutionaries, and, with the assistance of militiamen and other volunteers, massacred the rebels. Sixty-six enslaved persons died, and another seventeen went unaccounted. Following court trials in New Orleans, twenty-one accused rebels were sentenced to death and subsequently shot. "The unfortunate insurrection which took place here Jan'y last," Harriet Peters Deslondes wrote, reduced their household income, "some of our Negroes were accomplices of course killed, [and] at the same time they plundered my trunk containing 500 dollars, & much of our wearing apparel." Some rebels, inspired as they were by Haiti, lost far more than cash and clothes. They met the same fate as some Saint-Dominguan rebels: their corpses were decapitated, their severed heads placed on stakes along the Mississippi River to deter any other slaves who would use force to resist enslavement.[56]

Islands, speaking creole French and a little English." A "young Negro Girl born in St. Domingo, named Anne and Rose" ran away from Miss Nouchet in September 1813. And on December 29, 1815, Ursule, a thirty-two-year-old woman from Saint-Domingue, ran away from Jayme Jordan, and she took her eight-year-old daughter and three-year-old son with her. "It is presumed that she was enticed away by some person," her owner reasoned. J. Joly, *Courier*, August 7, 1811 (Pauline); Nouchet, "Runaway Slave," *Courier*, September 20, 1813 (Anne and Rose); Jayme Jorda, "Ten Dollars Reward," *Courier*, January 3, 1816 (Ursule).

[55] Harriet Peters to John Peters, New York, February 16 [1811], Peters Family Letters, MssCol 4578, NYPL.

[56] *Louisiana Gazette*, January 10, 1811; Harriet [Peters] Delonde to John Peters, May 14, 1811, NYPL. See also Robert L. Paquette, "Revolutionary St. Domingue in the Making of Territorial Louisiana," in *A Turbulent Time: The French Revolution in the Greater Caribbean*, eds. David Barry Gaspar and David Patrick Geggus (Bloomington: Indiana University Press, 1997), 204–225; Junius P. Rodriguez, "'Always En Garde': The Effects

In the aftermath of this armed revolt, officials again resorted to a combination of brute force and incentives to keep rebellious slaves in place. The 1811 revolt in Louisiana and the 1812 Aponte Conspiracy in nearby Cuba inspired Louisianans to strengthen colonial laws that governed slaves. Louisiana's first *Code Noir* of 1724 was derived almost wholesale from Louis XIV's 1685 version. Spanish officials replaced some parts of the *Code Noir* and implemented some progressive elements, such as the right to self-purchase. In 1806, three years after the Louisiana Purchase, Louisiana's legislature passed the Black Codes, which were quite strict in comparison to the previous *Code Noir*. The Black Code already granted freedom to any slave who informed on a conspiracy, and a June 1813 ordinance added to it a monetary reward for such information. That law called for a $500 payment to free persons and freedom to slaves who successfully informed on an arson plot.[57]

"WE WERE FREE PEOPLE"

"My grandmother was Sylphid Sacriste and she was from Santo Domingo. She came over to Louisiana during the Revolution," Anita Fonvergne explained to the Louisiana Works Progress interviewer around 1940. "When the Revolution broke out, she was separated from her mother and never saw her again."[58] Fonvergne, who spoke French and English, was a New Orleans resident. At nearly eighty years old, she lived in the Jim Crow South during the Great Depression. Her transnational and

---

of Slave Insurrection upon the Louisiana Mentality," *Louisiana History* 33 (1992): 399–416; Thomas Marshall Thompson, "National Newspaper and Legislative Reactions to Louisiana's Deslonde Slave Revolt of 1811," *Louisiana History* 33 (1992): 5–29.

[57] "Ordinance Allowing a Reward to Any Persons Denouncing One or More Incendiaries," *L'Ami des Lois*, July 1, 1813. On the Aponte Rebellion in Cuba, see Matt D. Childs, *The 1812 Aponte Rebellion in Cuba and the Struggle against Atlantic Slavery* (Chapel Hill: The University of North Carolina Press, 2006). On ongoing revolts in the British Caribbean, see Michael Craton, *Testing the Chains: Resistance to Slavery in the British West Indies* (Ithaca, NY: Cornell University Press, 1982). The Black Code was amended over the nineteenth century, but remained in place through the Civil War. Spear, *Race, Sex, and Social Order*, chapter 7.

[58] Interview, Anita Fonvergne in Ronnie W. Clayton and Louisiana Writers' Project, *Mother Wit: The Ex-Slave Narratives of the Louisiana Writers' Project* (New York: P. Lang, 1990), 73–82. The date of the interview is unrecorded, but likely occurred in 1940 or 1941. Clayton, the editor of the published volume, assumes Fonvergne spoke of the American Revolution, but the context makes clear that she meant the Haitian Revolution.

interracial family history, however, confounded the binary racism of Jim Crow. She claimed Spanish maternal ancestry and Swiss and French lineage on her father's side, and US census takers found it impossible to consistently assign Fonvergne's race. They listed her as mulatto in 1880, white in 1900, then mulatto again in 1910.[59] "We don't class ourselves as negroes and we don't class ourselves as white," Fonvergne insisted, "but with our connections and what we know, there is no house in New Orleans that could close their door on us if we wanted to go in." Whatever the census workers' confusions about race, Fonvergne was quite clear about status: "None of my family were ever slaves[;] we were free people."[60]

Marie Brown also recounted a family history that stretched from Hispaniola to Louisiana, one that crossed both sides of the slave-free divide, and she was proud of it. "My mother's grandma lived durin' the revolution in San Domingo. My mother's mother, she come [sic] from San Domingo, but she was born in [Martinique] and was a f.w.c. [free woman of color]." As with the shipmates of the Middle Passage, Brown recalled the people who journeyed to Louisiana alongside her relatives: "My grandma came from San Domingo with the Duplantiers, and Miss Jule Duplantier was her godmother." Like Fonvergne, Brown also emphasized the importance of family and status in the recreation of migrant communities. But where Fonvergne highlighted her distance from slavery, Brown claimed the slave status that was her patrimony: "Grandma didn't want [Brown's mother] to have Pa because he was a slave, but they just had they [sic] way anyhow. He made money and lived high." She acknowledged the status distinctions that cleaved free blacks from ex-slaves during slavery and emancipation, and she celebrated the ways her parents transcended them.[61]

The afterlives of colonialism and slavery in Saint-Domingue did not vanish in nineteenth-century New Orleans; they partitioned Brown's kinship networks even in 1940. The hierarchies of color, gender, and sexuality that gave rise to a caste of fair-skinned, elite blacks in Saint-Domingue and Louisiana continued to structure affections. "I got a sister

[59] "1880 United States Federal Census," "1900 United States Federal Census," and "1910 United States Federal Census," Database, *Ancestry.com*, http://ancestry.com, accessed October 27, 2008, entry for Anita Fonvergne [b.] 1861, New Orleans.

[60] Clayton and Louisiana Writers' Project, *Mother Wit*, 74–75.

[61] Interview, Marie Brown by Zoe Posey, New Orleans, May 29, 1940, Clayton and Louisiana Writers' Project, *Mother Wit*, 33–36. The editor lists the location as "Montenegro," but given the context "Martinique" is the likelier site.

in Carrollton. She's like white, and her family pass for white folks."
The lines of race in the Jim Crow South separated Marie from her sister's
family. So did values: "She thinks I ain't good 'nough for her, but I say she
ain't good 'nough for me for she's only white man's leavin's. I ain't
'shamed of my pa." Even as she judged her sister's choice to "pass" as
white and to engage in asymmetrical sexual relationships with white men,
Brown inverted the language of white supremacy. She was not ashamed of
her father's enslavement. Rather she found shameful those descended
from the people who had enslaved him and those people of African
descent who "passed" to associate with them. This subversion of the
white supremacy in Jim Crow New Orleans might be considered
Brown's personal inheritance of the Haitian Revolution.[62]

In the Age of Revolutions, migrants from across the Atlantic World
converged on Louisiana, and the ones who left an antislavery revolution
became among those most involved in that institution's expansion in
Louisiana, whether as slaveholders or as slaves. As a result, thousands
of black migrants from Saint-Domingue landed in the slave spaces of
republican empire. And all of the migrants from Saint-Domingue fled
one slavery-centered revolution for another: the former, an antislavery
revolution, was so radical that its aims – liberty and equality for all –
remain unrealized, and the latter, a sugar and cotton revolution, was so
thoroughly dependent on black slave labor that a Second Middle Passage
developed to supply it. The place of slaves in New Orleans would never be
the same.

---

[62] Carrollton, now one of the city's neighborhoods, was politically independent before it
was annexed in 1874. Campanella, *Bienville's Dilemma*, 28–29.
    On the economic, political, and social incentives for passing in this period, see Cheryl
I. Harris, "Whiteness as Property," *Harvard Law Review* 106, no. 8 (1993): 1707–1791;
Allyson Hobbs, *A Chosen Exile: A History of Racial Passing in American Life*
(Cambridge, MA: Harvard University Press, 2014).

2

Market Spaces

One of our carriers, a negro man named James, ranaway [*sic*] yesterday from the office, and is lurking about the suburbs. We therefore request those of our subscribers who are served by him to be so good as to send to the office for their paper of this day, requesting also, should any of you see the said negro, to stop & confine him.

Louisiana Courier, September 4, 1811

The enslaved man James held the whole world in his hands. As a carrier for the bilingual *Louisiana Courier*, with each footstep he connected Francophone and Anglophone readers and listeners in New Orleans to the Atlantic public sphere. Those pages informed planters and merchants about sugar and cotton markets, notified citizens about diplomatic events, and kept stylish urbanites somewhat current with continental fashions. James probably could neither read nor write, but newspapers connected him to a cosmopolitan world. His labor required him to circulate across the city, which likely allowed him to build the social networks and gather the reconnaissance that facilitated his escape. But if newspapers enlightened free persons, periodicals also disseminated runaway advertisements, announcements of slave sales, and other knowledge essential to the everyday functioning of chattel slavery. The *Courier* even published a runaway advertisement for James himself, and they deputized the paper's entire readership to "confine" this deliveryman within a slave's place.[1]

---

[1] *Louisiana Courier*, September 4, 1811. On runaway advertisements, see Waldstreicher, "Reading the Runaways," 243–272.

On "geographic literacy" among slaves, see Troutman, "Grapevine in the Slave Market," 203–233. On the role of newspapers in maintaining simultaneity across the Atlantic World, see Anderson, *Imagined Communities*.

The circulation of slaves was essential to the early market economy, a dynamic especially observable in port cities like New Orleans. International and domestic slave trades forcibly transported laborers to New World mines, plantations, households, and other workplaces. The transatlantic slave trade funneled some eleven to fourteen million captives from the coasts of Africa to communities across the Americas, and domestic slave trades tore apart and brought together diverse peoples from disparate places, assemblages then tasked with the hard work of crop production, community formation, and personal survival.[2] Such motion continued in port cities like New Orleans, where local leaders, masters, merchants, and slaves themselves contended over the best uses of enslaved people's mobility toward the construction of the metropolitan area's commercial infrastructure. There, slaves were commodities in the flesh trade, laborers who produced addictive staple crops, consumers who purchased local and imported goods, vendors who peddled products to multilingual customers, and modes of transport for buyers and sellers. These economic geographies extended across New Orleans, into its rural environs, and out into the larger maritime world. Commodity flows across those interlaced spheres offer a unique perspective on the spatial and social histories of slavery in New Orleans and the world.[3]

This chapter examines the market spaces of early New Orleans to reveal the underappreciated geographies of slave circulation, congregation, and escape that connected New Orleans to its region and world. As it shows, economic space sometimes reinforced the political boundaries of city limits and national borders, but at other times commodity flows subverted such man-made lines and organized slave communities

---

[2] Smallwood, *Saltwater Slavery*; Gomez, *Exchanging Our Country Marks*. On domestic slave trades, see Johnson, *Soul by Soul*; Johnson, ed., *The Chattel Principle*.

[3] On the circulation and ownership of goods and complex communities, see Sophie White, *Wild Frenchmen and Frenchified Indians: Material Culture and Race in Colonial Louisiana* (Philadelphia: University of Pennsylvania Press, 2012); Sophie White, "'Wearing Three or Four Handkerchiefs around His Collar, and Elsewhere about Him': Slaves' Constructions of Masculinity and Ethnicity in French Colonial New Orleans," in *Dialogues of Dispersal*, eds. Sandra Gunning, Tera Hunter, and Michele Mitchell (Malden, MA: Blackwell Publishing, 2004), 132–153; Dylan C. Penningroth, *The Claims of Kinfolk: African American Property and Community in the Nineteenth-Century South* (Chapel Hill: The University of North Carolina Press, 2003); Roderick A. McDonald, *The Economy and Material Culture of Slaves: Goods and Chattels on the Sugar Plantations of Jamaica and Louisiana* (Baton Rouge: Louisiana State University Press, 1993); Arjun Appadurai, *The Social Life of Things: Commodities in Cultural Perspective* (Cambridge: Cambridge University Press, 1986).

in latitudinous ways. The chapter begins with the laboring itinerancy of enslaved deliverymen, sailors, cart men, and, notably, female nurses. Their journeys afforded them knowledge of the physical and social terrain of New Orleans, its rural environs, and the Atlantic World. The next section focuses on the female enslaved peddlers and free male boatmen who likely worked in tandem to integrate masters and slaves alike into a global web of commodities. The routes that eased the circulation of raw goods, such as sugar and cotton, as well as consumer goods from clothes to produce facilitated the escape of human property, which is the subject of the third section. Though entry into the rival geography was one tactic of political and economic resistance, it came with costs. The chapter concludes with an extended consideration of a murder trial in St. John the Baptist Parish, Louisiana. In that vignette, an enslaved woman crossed from one plantation to another to confront a fellow bondswoman over the destruction of personal property, in this case a dress. Together these accounts show that when people circulated goods they also formed complex communities across the metropolitan area.

The Age of Revolution witnessed contested political transitions from monarchism to republicanism, but it was defined just as much by the economic transition from mercantilism to free trade and industrial, slave labor. As New Orleans elites renovated the colonial cityscape to facilitate the exchange of commodities, the place of slaves in the city became a proxy in larger contests over blacks in a capitalist economy. To manage the economic logic of slave circulation alongside the political and ideological imperative of regulating blackness, the master classes contended over laws, customs, hierarchies, and social networks to govern, or "structure the possible field of action of," unchained, circulating slaves.[4] Enslaved men and women labored within capacious and elastic geographies of containment to build New Orleans. The multidirectional geographies of enslaved men and women, both legal and illegal, allowed them to create and sustain multiracial social and commercial networks. In the contests over the many places of blacks in the free market economy, we again witness the contested making of race and power during a period of rapid and lasting transitions.

---

[4] Michel Foucault, afterword to *Michel Foucault, Beyond Structuralism and Hermeneutics*, 2nd edition, eds. Hubert L. Dreyfus, Paul Rabinow, and Michel Foucault (Chicago: The University of Chicago Press, 1983), 219–221.

"YOU MUST HAVE A FEMALE SERVANT WITH YOU"

Port cities like New Orleans offer a unique observatory onto the possibilities and risks of slave labor at sea and on land. Certainly, the revolutionary Atlantic facilitated freedom journeys. In 1772 the *Somerset* decision effectively turned England and Wales into "free soil," until 1790 the Spanish empire granted refuge to certain escaped slaves who converted to Catholicism, and Haiti's 1816 constitution offered full citizenship to men of African descent who remained in residence for one year.[5] As a conduit to free-soil territories, New Orleans offered enslaved persons the prospect of exploiting their geographic situation to improve their social position. But that Atlantic port also became a site for the intensification of slavery's hierarchies. Seafaring, whether as sailors or nurses, left travelers of African descent, male and female, subject to unlawful enslavement, violence, and rape. The port of New Orleans, like all other worksites, offered a contingent range of experiences and possibilities.

By the early 1800s, thousands of black seamen, free and enslaved, labored on Atlantic ships, occupations that often afforded them lucrative skills and furthered radical political visions. The most prominent black seaman was Olaudah Equiano (or Gustavus Vassa), an Igbo man alleged to have been born in present-day Nigeria in the 1740s. After a lengthy Middle Passage from the continental interior to the coast, Africa to the Americas, Equiano became the property of a lieutenant in the Royal Navy. Equiano traveled across the British Atlantic, learned to read and write, and, in 1766, purchased his freedom. He campaigned for slavery's abolition and published his autobiography in 1789.[6] In the 1820s, abolitionist, early black liberation theologian, and tailor David Walker hid copies of his incendiary political tract, his *Appeal . . . To the Colored Citizens of the World*, inside the linings of black sailors' clothing, using their maritime

---

[5] Ferrer, "Haiti, Free Soil, and Antislavery in the Revolutionary Atlantic," 40–66. On *Somerset*, see Wong, *Neither Fugitive nor Free*. On free soil in France, see Sue Peabody, *"There Are No Slaves in France": The Political Culture of Race and Slavery in the Ancien Régime* (New York: Oxford University Press, 1996), 107–119.

[6] Olaudah Equiano, *The Interesting Narrative of the Life of Olaudah Equiano, or Gustavus Vassa, the African*, 2 vols. (London: Printed for and sold by the author, 1789). See also Vincent Carretta, *Equiano, the African: Biography of a Self-Made Man* (Athens: University of Georgia Press, 2005); Leon Fink, *Sweatshops at Sea: Merchant Seamen in the World's First Globalized Industry, from 1812 to the Present* (Chapel Hill: University of North Carolina, 2011), chapter 1; Linebaugh and Rediker, *The Many-Headed Hydra*; Bolster, *Black Jacks*; Scott, "Common Wind."

travel to disseminate his revolutionary message across the Eastern Seaboard and into New Orleans.[7]

Shipboard passages carried their own hazards – "what is one's life at sea but the most miserable thing in the world," a white British sailor confided to his journal – but when sailors of African descent journeyed through the port from sea to land, they walked into risks.[8] Disembarkation at New Orleans and other labor-hungry ports where slavery remained legal carried the risk of enslavement, no matter one's previous status. In 1804, officials at the Bayou St. John checkpoint barred entry to three men "employed as Sailors on Board the Schooner *L'Esperance* and belonging to Pierre Bailey." The controversial Governance Act of 1804 forbade the international importation of Africans for enslavement in Louisiana in an effort to limit black immigration from Saint-Domingue. Officials likely suspected that Bailey hoped to sell these men illegally, but Governor Claiborne authorized their entry into New Orleans. Had border agents successfully convicted Bailey of slave smuggling, the three men would still have been sold in the New Orleans slave market.[9]

Free black sailors pursued in New Orleans opportunities denied them on the high seas, but such efforts carried the risk of imprisonment and enslavement. In January 1809, the sailor Frederick arrived in New Orleans on a vessel commandeered by Captain Torry of Charleston. Frederick fled about six weeks after his arrival. Torry advertised a $50 reward to anyone who recaptured Frederick. "As he is by profession a sailor, he generally keeps on board vessels," Torry wrote.[10] A different instance involved a free black man, named Narcés Bastian. According to testimony, Bastian "signed articles in the Port of London on a voyage to New Providence and from thence to any Port of the United States, and

---

[7] Walker, *Appeal in Four Articles: Together with a Preamble, to the Coloured Citizens of the World, but in Particular, and Very Expressly to Those of the United States of America.* On black sailors in the dissemination of Walker's *Appeal,* see Peter P. Hinks, *To Awaken My Afflicted Brethren: David Walker and the Problem of Antebellum Slave Resistance* (University Park, PA: Pennsylvania State University Press, 1997).

[8] Journal entry, October 30, 1814, Sir John Maxwell Tylden diary, 1814–1815, MssCol 3050, NYPL.

[9] WCCC to The Officer Commanding at Bayou St. Jean, New Orleans, February 29, 1804, *Letter Books,* I: 393. The Governance Act, Peter J. Kastor argues, proved controversial not simply due to ethno-national tensions between whites and free blacks and American imperial officials, but due to concerns about the applicability of citizenship rights under a colonial administration. See Peter J. Kastor, *The Nation's Crucible: The Louisiana Purchase and the Creation of America* (New Haven: Yale University Press, 2004), chapter 3.

[10] *The Telegraphe, General Advertiser,* April 13, 1809.

back to England." He labored as a cook aboard the *Marz Causon* before
deserting in New Orleans. Bastian "was apprehended on a nearby brig
and brought to the Guard House." Perhaps he sought a better employment opportunity on the other ship, or else he simply enjoyed the company of his fellow sailors. Either way, this black sailor traveled from
London to The Bahamas and then to the New Orleans jail.[11]

As in the port of New Orleans, arrival at smaller Louisiana harbors also
introduced local hazards to those international sailors deemed black. José
Barbosa, a sailor from Brazil, worked on a vessel headed from South
America to Pointe Coupée, Louisiana. Once Barbosa exchanged the seas
for the swamps, however, his black phenotype carried a presumption of
slave status. *Adéle Auger* v. *Frederick Beaurocher et al.* (also given as *Adelle
v. Beauregard*), an 1810 case decided by the Superior Court of the Territory
of Orleans, placed the burden of proof of documenting a mixed-race
person's status as a slave on the master and made it incumbent upon
persons deemed "Negro" to document their own freedom. Barbosa, who
presumably appeared to be black, carried no evidence of his freedom.
A judge in Des Allemands (French for "The Germans"), a hamlet southeast
of New Orleans that straddles St. Charles and Lafourche Parishes, sent him
to jail. As his fellow crewmember testified before the New Orleans mayor to
secure the man's release, Barbosa languished in a rural prison cell. Perhaps
Barbosa felt demoralized due to his wrongful incarceration or socially
isolated due to language barriers. It is equally possible that this sailor,
a cultural broker who traveled and met new people as a matter of course,
may have spoken English or French. If so, he likely brought news from the
Atlantic World to the cramped Des Allemands jail.[12]

Sailor John Wild proved particularly adept at using Atlantic ports to
crisscross borders of land and sea, slave and free. Described as a "dark
mulattoe," Wild claimed to have been born free in Charleston, South
Carolina. According to the testimony of men who knew him, Wild maintained that he had been part of the crew on a slaver bound from
Charleston to New Orleans. Upon arrival, the captain sold him alongside
the slaves – an occupational hazard for black sailors but also a likely story

[11] Deposition, David Gibson before Macarty, New Orleans, January 16, 1817 NYHS NOC
8:13.
    On the radical political worlds of sailors and pirates, see Linebaugh and Rediker,
The Many-Headed Hydra; Bolster, *Black Jacks*.
[12] Deposition, Manuel Borgès before Macarty, New Orleans, June 7, 1816 NOC 8:12,
NYHS; *Adelle v. Beauregard*, 1810, 1 Mart. (o.s.) 183, 1810 WL 869 (La.Terr.Super.
Orleans).

for a freedom-seeking bondman. Wild worked as a slave in Louisiana, but his Atlantic journeys did not end there. At some point he stowed away in the forecastle of a US naval ship named, fittingly, the *Thomas Jefferson,* which set sail from Louisiana for England in March 1808. In the geography of naval ships, common sailors were generally quartered "before the mast," or at the upper decks on the front end while officers and other elites lodged on the opposite end. Wild's hiding place in the forecastle suggests that he insinuated himself into and perhaps enjoyed the support of members of the rank and file. Upon arrival at Liverpool, a far larger Atlantic port, the ship's captain discovered Wild and ordered the stowaway detained. When the captain left the ship to seek guidance from the US consulate, Wild and several others deserted. Their collective escape further suggests that Wild conspired with certain crewmembers. Wild's fate is unclear. According to the grapevine, British officials impressed him into the Royal Navy, a practice so common that it hastened a war between the British Empire and its former colony. This one black sailor's odyssey took him from freedom in Charleston to slavery in New Orleans, concealment on a US naval ship to impressment into the Royal Navy. The maritime routes that radiated from New Orleans could bring black sailors just about anywhere.[13]

For enslaved female nurses, as for sailors, regional and Atlantic circulations intensified, not subverted, the hierarchies of the urban and plantation south. Like John Wild, Charlotte (whose story opens this book) also passed through the port of New Orleans more than once. She was born in Africa sometime around 1793, and she remained in her community long enough to undergo the ritual scarification associated with puberty.[14] Somehow, perhaps through war captivity or kidnapping, she came to be held as a slave. Perhaps after overland journeys in a coffle full of loved

---

[13] Deposition, Francis Whitmell before James Brown, November 28, 1808, Brown (James) Papers, MSS 44, Folder 4. See also Rothman, *Slave Country,* 98–99. On the ways that such impressments stoked in the making of US nationalism, see Nicole Eustace, *1812: War and the Passions of Patriotism* (Philadelphia: University of Pennsylvania Press, 2012), chapter 3.

[14] The ritualistic scarification marks pressed into her face suggest that she crossed the Middle Passage after the onset of puberty, so she likely learned some ideas about motherhood in West Africa. Women in the Senegambia, Sierra Leone, and the Gold Coast regions of West Africa, for example, maintained societies dedicated to the transition from girlhood to womanhood, and in them they shared information about sex and reproduction, such as the use of breastfeeding to space pregnancies. Morgan, *Laboring Women,* 66–67. On so-called "secret societies," see Gomez, *Exchanging Our Country Marks,* 94–100.

ones or strangers, she arrived on the coast. Traders might have locked her inside a *barracoon*, or holding cell, in Elmina or some other slave castle before passing through a Door of No Return. Not more than ten years after her birth, she became part of the "cargo" (*cargaison*) of a brig named *the Rivario*. During this first transatlantic journey, perhaps she bonded with "shipmates" or withdrew into an envelope of trauma. She survived that journey to New Orleans, where in 1805 Joseph Faurie, a local merchant, aide-de-camp to Governor Claiborne, and city council member, sold the "negritte" Charlotte to another businessman, Edouard Forstall.[15] At roughly fourteen years old, she gave birth to a daughter named Corine, and their values increased in successive sales between the wealthy Forstalls. In 1815, Edouard Forstall sold the "negress" Charlotte, now twenty-three years old, and her daughter, aged about seven and a half, to his brother Edmond Forstall and his sister-in-law Céleste DeLaville

---

[15] Act of Sale, Joseph Faurie to Edouard Forstall, Pierre Pedesclaux, Notary, New Orleans, September 17, 1805, volume 51, page 775, NANO. Faurie was party to at least twenty-six slave sales in Louisiana between 1801 and 1807. Hall, *Database*. On Faurie, see Bradley, *Interim Appointment*, 326 n. 113; 590.

On African slave coffles and the Middle Passage, see Smallwood, *Saltwater Slavery*; Gomez, *Exchanging Our Country Marks*, chapter 7. On the average length of Middle Passage voyages to the Gulf Coast, see David Eltis and David Richardson, *Atlas of the Transatlantic Slave Trade* (New Haven: Yale University Press, 2010), 167.

Economic historian John G. Clark writes, "Nicholas Forstall, who migrated to Louisiana from Martinique in the 1740s, was a wealthy man and prominent official in the 1760s and 1770s and his heirs maintained their prominence into the pre–Civil War decades." John G. Clark, *New Orleans 1718–1812: An Economic History* (New Orleans, LA: Pelican Publishing Company, 1982), 105.

Edmond Jean Forstall (1794–1874), a son of Nicholas, was born in New Orleans. He rose to local and international prominence as a merchant, banker, and financial agent. By age twenty-four, he was director of the Louisiana State Bank and a friend and agent of British merchant Thomas Baring. He then became managing partner of M. de Lizardi & Co. His daughter married Louisiana Governor A. B. Roman's son, which, his detractors argued, gave him unfair advantages with state-backed bond issues. Forstall also purchased a sugar plantation in St. James Parish, and he was also instrumental in inventor and free man of color Norbert Rillieux's return to New Orleans. Rillieux briefly worked as chief engineer of Forstall's sugar refinery. Forstall suffered financial losses during the Panic of 1837 and the Civil War. Between 1780 and 1820, Forstalls were party to at least eighty-seven slave sales in Louisiana. See Hall, *Database*; Beckert, *Empire of Cotton*, 206, 219–220; Scott P. Marler, *The Merchants' Capital: New Orleans and the Political Economy of the Nineteenth-Century South* (New York: Cambridge University Press, 2013), 32–33; Irene D. Neu, "Edmond Jean Forstall and Louisiana Banking," *Explorations in Economic History* 7 (Summer 1970): 383–398; Irene D. Neu, "My Nineteenth-Century Network: Erastus Corning, Benjamin Ingham, Edmond Forstall," Presidential Address, Indiana University, reprinted in *Business and Economic History* 14 (1985), available at www.h-net.org/~business/bhcweb/publica tions/BEHprint/vo14/p0001-p0016.pdf, accessed January 26, 2010.

Forstall before another sale in January 1818, when Edmond and Céleste sold mother and daughter back to Edouard. In not quite two decades, Charlotte traveled from adolescence in Africa to enslaved motherhood in New Orleans.[16]

Like her first Atlantic journey, Charlotte's second trip, this one from New Orleans to Bordeaux in 1818, expanded both her personal geographies and the reach of slaveholders' power. Pierre Blancq, a French Creole and American citizen, hired Charlotte "to nurse one of his children" during the passage to France. Charlotte would likely labor in support of Blancq's entire family, which included his wife Maria Marta Favre D'Aunoy, daughter of a Spanish colonel, and their three children: Juana Eliza (four years old), Clemente (two years old), and Cipriano (four months old). By that year, international slave importation had been illegal for over a decade. The US Constitution forbade a ban on the international slave trade for twenty years, and in 1807 Congress passed an act that designated such importation an act of piracy punishable by slave confiscation, fines, and incarceration. Forstall obtained a passport from New Orleans Mayor Augustin Macarty to protect his property rights and to protect himself from federal penalties. Issued in April 1818, that document contained a biometric description akin to those offered in deeds of sale. It describes Charlotte as "a negro wench ... aged about twenty-three years ... having several of her country marks under both temples." This journey perhaps set in motion one of the most intimate exploitations of slavery – the enslaved woman's coerced proffering of her breasts to her master's child – even as each nautical mile increased the distance between her and her own daughter.[17]

---

[16] Both the 1815 and 1818 acts of sale included five slaves: "Clarice, quadroon aged about 21 years; Célestine, quadroon aged about 19 years; *Le Nègre* Jean aged about 50–60; Charlotte, *negresse* aged 23 years, & Corine, her daughter, aged about seven and a half years old." Act of Sale, Edouard Jean Forstall to Edmond Forstall and Céleste DeLaville Forstall, Michel De Armas, Notary, New Orleans, July 15, 1815, volume 9, act 256, NANO; Act of Sale, Edmond Forstall to Edouard Forstall, Michel De Armas, Notary, New Orleans, January 22, 1818, volume 14 part 1, Act #22, NANO. Curiously, though the same notary oversaw the 1815 and 1818 transactions and cited the first act of sale in the second, he nonetheless listed each slave as being the same age in 1818 as they were in 1815. Based solely on notarial records, then, the slaves would appear to have not aged in three years. For historians, this transcription error reminds us of the imprecisions even in official property records.

[17] Passport, Augustin Macarty to Edward Forstal [*sic*], New Orleans, April 20, 1818, MSS 44, Folder 11, HNOC; Earl C. Woods and Charles E. Nolan, *Sacramental Records of the Roman Catholic Church of the Archdiocese of New Orleans* (New Orleans (1100 Chartres St., New Orleans 70116–2596): Archdiocese of New Orleans, 1987), XI: 39,

If she completed the journey, Charlotte's mobility likely resulted in cosmopolitan confinement in France. As early as 1716 and again in 1738, the French monarchy established laws to bar the entry of slaves from the colonies. France passed legislation that included free-soil components in 1759 and 1777, but that same year Louis XVI issued the *Police des Noirs*, which barred entry based on phenotype rather than status. That controversial legislation called for slaves who accompanied masters from colonies to be housed in *depôts de noirs*, or prison camps, located in Brest, Nantes, Marseille, Bordeaux, and other key cities. The facilities were largely unsuccessful – naval officials chafed at the bureaucratic labor demands of the policy and masters chafed at having their personal slaves kept in depots rather than in their own possession – but the sentiment persisted. After the French Revolution, the republican government abolished slavery in 1794. At his ascendance, Napoleon prohibited the entry of blacks and mulattoes into France, reinstituted slavery in 1802, and reaffirmed the ban on the entry of persons of African descent. Perhaps Charlotte met other persons of African descent from the French Atlantic, but she likely longed for the daughter abandoned in Louisiana. Ties of biology and affect perhaps pulled her back to New Orleans more strongly than could any passport.[18]

If the geography of Charlotte's job seems unusual, the job itself was not: enslaved nurses and attendants routinely traveled across

XII: 36, XIII: 43. Because their privileged parents could marry, baptismal records list the children as legitimate. See, for example, "Blancq, Clemente," SLCB, volume 8, part 1, page 84, record 501, AANO.

Blancq likely carried his own proof of citizenship issued to him in the months that followed the Louisiana Purchase. In that document, Blancq swore to "be faithful and bear true allegiance to" the United States and to "renounce and abjure all allegiance and fidelity to any & every Foreign Prince, Potentate & State or Sovereignty whatever and particularly to the King of Spain and the French Republic." Deposition, Peter [Pierre] Blancq before William Brown, New Orleans, November 27, 1804, Proofs of Citizenship Used to Apply for Seamen's Protection Certificates for the Port of New Orleans, Louisiana, 1804–1812, NARA microfilm publication M1826, 12 rolls, LSA.

[18] Peabody, *"There Are No Slaves in France,"* chapters 7 and 8. Corine "lost her mother," not to the Middle Passage, but to another Atlantic journey. Saidiya V. Hartman, *Lose Your Mother: A Journey along the Atlantic Slave Route* (New York: Farrar, Straus and Giroux, 2007).

Charlotte's story is reminiscent of the journeys that brought Sally Hemings to Paris with Thomas Jefferson or Phillis Wheatley to England. Such travel involved crossing into different legal jurisdictions, which – depending on context – carried with it the possibility of freedom. Annette Gordon-Reed, *The Hemingses of Monticello: An American Family* (New York: W.W. Norton & Company, 2008), 224–248; Vincent Carretta, *Phillis Wheatley: Biography of a Genius in Bondage* (Athens: University of Georgia Press, 2011).

metropolitan New Orleans and beyond to perform material and symbolic work. They nursed, cleaned, hauled, and consoled even as their blackness performed the symbolic work of making visible the whiteness of their owners. Travel records from two generations of the prominent Mathews family reveal as much. An itemized receipt from General George Mathews' 1790s travels recorded his essentials: port wine, "Jill Whiskey for boy," supper, food and lodging for horses, and, on the last line, provisions for one servant. The race of that servant went unrecorded, but he was likely a black man, and his accommodations cost far less than those of his master, a former governor of Georgia.[19] In 1815, his son, Louisiana Supreme Court Justice George Mathews, and the younger man's second wife Harriet planned her move from St. Francisville to her husband's New Orleans household. "You will have need of a maid in coming down," he wrote to her. Judge Mathews was reluctant to pay the $700 it would cost to buy one, especially since in New Orleans he already had "servants in abundance." "Still," he concluded, "you must have a female servant with you." Harriet Matthews' whiteness alongside her female slave's blackness would ensure both women's proper entry into urban society.[20]

"SELLING DRY GOODS IN THE STREETS"

Enslaved sailors and nurses who traveled internationally endured separation from their communities and unrelenting togetherness with masters. Another set of laborers – enslaved women peddlers – left their masters' immediate purview when they circulated across city streets and rural roads to bring the slaves and citizens of Lower Louisiana into overlapping spheres of consumption and communication. Enslaved women peddlers circulated to earn profits for their masters, and as they did so they cultivated diverse networks, slave and free, urban and rural, that became the sinews of cosmopolitan communities.

In Louisiana and across the Atlantic World, women of African descent established and managed marketplaces that became sites of commerce and

---

[19] Receipt, Samuel Clark to George Mathews, Staunton, VA, July 14, 1797, Mathews-Ventress-Lawrason Family Papers, Mss. 1358, Subgroup 1, Box 4, Folder 2, LSU.
[20] George Mathews, New Orleans, to Harriet Mathews, St. Francisville, Louisiana, December 15, 1815, Mathews-Ventress-Lawrason Family Papers, Mss. 1358, Subgroup 1, Box 1, Folder 1, LSU.
  On the relationship between the white marriage market and the black slave market at a later date, see Johnson, *Soul by Soul*, 92–96.

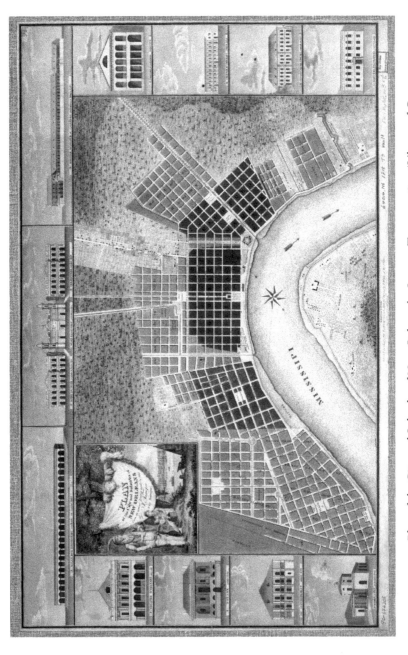

MAP 2.1 *Plan of the City and Suburbs of New Orleans* by Jacques Tanesse, 1815 (Library of Congress, Geography and Map Division).

community. As early as the sixteenth century, observers recorded that Mandinka men and women in the Upper Guinea Coast plied local water-ways for transportation and to circulate food. A German minister who resided in the Gold Coast in the 1660s wrote that, apart from "a few peasants" who brought specific goods to the market, "there are no men who stand in public markets to trade, but only women. It is remarkable to see how the market is filled every day with ... women selling [food]."[21] Across West Africa, Latin America, the Caribbean, and continental North America women of African descent, both slave and free, sold goods at market. "Provisions are in plenty," Trinidad's Governor Ralph Woodford wrote in 1814. "[M]any Negroes are on Sundays better drest [sic] than their owners & make 10 or 20 Dollars by the sale of the superabundance of vegetables from their garden grounds in the market," he claimed.[22] And in colonial Charlestown, South Carolina, enslaved women also dominated local markets, which earned them money – and detractors – in the process.[23]

Enslaved peddlers possessed commercial expertise honed across the Atlantic World, but especially in Saint-Domingue, and such expertise made them coveted workers in Louisiana, where commerce required business acumen, multilingualism, and interpersonal skills. In 1803, an advertiser sought "to lease a Negress who is a good vendor." The poster agreed to "pay 15 piastres a month to an owner who can guarantee her fidelity."[24] An 1804 advertisement listed for sale "a Mulatto Wench, about thirteen years old, a good servant, able to do everything as to what relates to the House, and knows how to sell."[25] In 1807 a newspaper advertised for sale "Several ... young Negresses, creoles of

---

[21] Wilhelm Johann Muller, "Wilhelm Johann Muller's Description of the Fetu Country, 1662–9," in *German Sources for West African History, 1599–1669*, ed. Adam Jones (Weisbaden: Steiner, 1983), 243, quoted in Morgan, *Laboring Women*, 62, 159–161.

[22] Ralph Woodford, Trinidad, to Charles Bathurst, March 25, 1814, Woodford Letters, GRO.

[23] Frederick C. Knight, *Working the Diaspora: The Impact of African Labor on the Anglo-American World, 1650–1850* (New York: New York University Press, 2010); Robert Olwell, "'Loose, Idle and Disorderly': Slave Women in the Eighteenth-Century Charleston Marketplace," in *More Than Chattel: Black Women and Slavery in the Americas*, eds. David Barry Gaspar and Darlene Clark Hine (Bloomington: Indiana University Press, 1996), 97–110; McDonald, *The Economy and Material Culture of Slaves*. On the history and present challenges of so-called African market women, see Gracia Clark, *Onions Are My Husband: Survival and Accumulation by West African Market Women* (Chicago: University of Chicago Press, 1994).

[24] *Moniteur de la Louisiane*, September 17, 1803, my translation.

[25] *The Telegraphe, Commercial Advertiser & New Orleans Price Current*, January 28, 1804.

['St. Domingo']" who labored as "hawkers of goods and home servants."
Given the demographics and diasporas of Saint-Domingue, these women
likely traded goods in West Africa, Jérémie or Cap Français, or Santiago
de Cuba before doing the same work in New Orleans.[26] An 1810 advertisement drew attention to "A Negro Boy, About 12 years old, of the
Mandingo nation, very honest, a good servant, has some knowledge of
selling goods, and was commenced learning to cook."[27] These multipur-
pose laborers performed domestic tasks, but they also peddled in the
streets to earn profits for slaveholding households. In an 1804 dispute
over the ownership of a particular slave, a Spanish official wrote to
Governor Claiborne "it is proved that all the female Slaves paid the
revenue of their daily wages into the hands of Mrs. Villamil." In the
absence of clear titles, this official argued, the peddlers' submission of
their earnings to this woman became a form of possession and, therefore,
proof that she owned them.[28]

The peddlers' circulations brought profits to their masters, but they also
presented economic competition to the less-nimble brick-and-mortar stores,
so disadvantaged merchants complained before the state. In 1804, the retai-
lers' petition before the Orleans Legislative Council complained, "negroes
and negresses [were] permitted to sell articles of merchandize about the
streets and in the neighborhood of this city, to the injury of the petitioners,
and of society at large." They urged the council to "extirpate such abuse."
Though not identical, the similarity of wares gave shopkeepers cause for
concern, especially since peddlers did not pay rent, buy newspaper advertisements, pay employees, or meet other fixed costs. Hugh Monro & Co. on
Toulouse Street and the slave woman Thérèse offer an illustrative contrast.
Shopkeepers like Munro purchased advertisements in local papers that
listed blankets, cloths, cashmeres, sailor and negro jackets, linen, cotton,
handkerchiefs, and other wares. To compare, François Ménière charged
his bondwoman Thérèse with "selling dry goods in the streets." Those
goods included assorted fabrics and other merchandise, such as toile,
cotton cloth, handkerchiefs, stockings, and assorted accessories. Little
wonder, then, that local shopkeepers complained about these women on
the loose. The council responded in the way that bureaucratic governments

---

[26] *Telegraphe, General Advertiser*, October 17, 1807.
         On urbanization in these sites, see Scott and Hébrard, *Freedom Papers.*
[27] L. Bailly Blanchard & Co., *Courrier*, July 20, 1810.
[28] The Marquis of Casa Calvo, New Orleans, to William C. C. Claiborne, New Orleans,
         September 12, 1804, in Bradley, *Interim Appointment*, 154–157, 156.

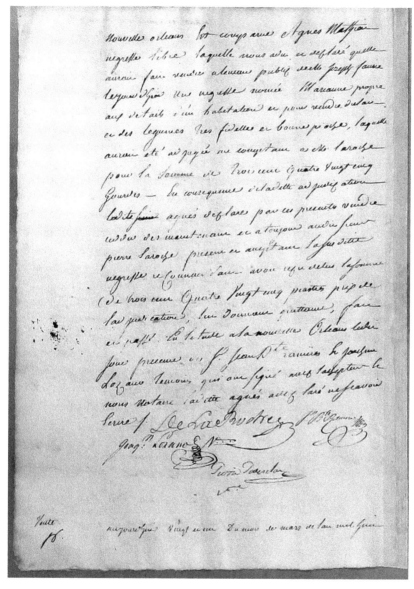

FIGURE 2.1 Act of Sale, Agnes Mathieu to De La Rodres, Pierre Pedesclaux, Notary, March 21, 1806, Office of the Clerk of Civil District Court, Notarial Archives Division, New Orleans. Courtesy Dale N. Atkins, Clerk of Civil District Court.

often do when pressed for action: They appointed a committee of three men to consider the matter.²⁹

Legislators also regarded the peddlers' circulations as threats to the social order, and they responded with a pass system designed to regulate such movement. Section fourteen of the 1806 Black Code empowered "every person or persons" to stop "any slave carrying corn, rice, greens, fowls, or any other provisions whatever, for the purpose of selling the same."³⁰ If the slave could not produce a written pass, the person who stopped her could seize the goods. This law deputized people to determine slave status by sight, presumably by black phenotype, in a city that was home to a significant free black population, and it created incentives for the harassment of all persons of African descent. "In order to keep slaves in good order and due submission," Section 30 of that same code stated, masters were prohibited from allowing slaves to go beyond their jurisdictions, whether the city or districts in the countryside, without a standardized pass that read: "The bearer (negro or mulatto,) named ... has leave to go from ... to ... for ... days, or (hours,) dated the same day of the delivery." Any bondsperson caught without a pass "or without a white person accompanying him," would receive twenty lashes and be returned to his master at a cost of $1.³¹

The Black Code did not end these circulations, so leaders passed more regulations designed to curb the flow of enslaved peddlers who moved between New Orleans and its rural environs. In 1811, a Louisiana law required New Orleans peddlers to secure a license from the mayor or, in

---

²⁹ Report on December 17, 1804 meeting of the Orleans Legislative Council, *Louisiana Gazette*, January 4, 1805; Deposition, Francois Ménière before Girod, New Orleans, February 14, 1813, my translation, NYHS NOC 8:11; Munro, "Seasonable Goods," *Louisiana Courier*, November 6, 1811.

The shopkeepers' identities are unclear, but they might have been diverse. Agnes Mathieu, a free woman of color, was listed in a later city directory as a shopkeeper, but she also owned at least one enslaved peddler. As shown in Figure 2.1, in 1806, she sold *"une negresse"* named Marianne, described as "good for details of a plantation and for selling milk and vegetables, very faithful." New Orleans City Directory, 1811, NOPL; Act of Sale, Agnes Mathieu to De La Rodres, Pierre Pedesclaux, Notary, New Orleans, March 21, 1806, volume 52, page 259, NANO, translation from Hall, *Database*.

³⁰ An Act Prescribing the Rules and Conduct to be Observed with Respect to Negroes and Other Slaves of this Territory, June 7, 1807, in Louis Moreau Lislet, *A General Digest of the Acts of the Legislature of Louisiana* (New Orleans: Benjamin Levy, 1828), 102.

³¹ Ibid., 107. Presumably the issuer would circle the applicable racial category.

The local government also mandated annual inspections of the weights and measures of those who "hawk about or caused to be hawked about dry goods in the streets, and other public places, without having a shop or a fixed store." Nicolas Girod, "Mayoralty of New Orleans," *L'Ami des Lois*, June 10, 1813.

the case of rural peddlers, the parish judges. These peddlers (or, presumably, their masters) would have to pay $500 "as surety for their good behaviour." The heftiness of the sum virtually guaranteed that peddlers would continue to operate without licenses. That same law also prohibited masters from "send[ing] any slaves in the country for the purpose of selling merchandize, and that the said slaves are bound to keep themselves within the limits of the town & suburbs of New Orleans." The inclusion of this provision suggests bondspersons regularly moved between the city and the rural parishes, which allowed them to trade goods and information along the way. Again, this legislation did not curb the peddlers. Two years later officials in St. Charles Parish complained, "daily negro women and mulatto wenches, slaves, come from the city for the purpose of selling salt, meats, tobacco, cakes, &c." These women carried written passes that were easily forged, officials complained, which allowed them to move freely, so to speak, a practice that leaders thought would lead to social disruptions.[32]

Peddling had its privileges. Mobile labor excused these women from the master's immediate gaze and gave them opportunities to socialize with a diverse set of customers, and they gained geographic literacy that allowed them to plan escapes. When the enslaved peddler Thérèse ran away, her master claimed to have had "three strong reasons to believe she [was] living at Mr. Lacroix's, resident of this city" (reasons he did not include in the runaway advertisement). Her relative autonomy as a peddler likely allowed her to foster a relationship with Lacroix, who assisted her escape. Zoe, a "milk retailer" from the Congo, ran away from her owner, and, years later, so did "the negro woman NANCY, accustomed to selling cakes." Daily interactions and circulations may have eased enslaved women's escapes.[33]

Privileges notwithstanding, peddling also exposed laborers to environmental hazards. Disease-transmitting mosquitos terrorized passersby, and the streets were putrid. One visitor complained: "the filth from the houses remains where it was thrown; and, during a great part of the year, [the streets] are a common sewer; a sink of nastiness, dirt, and corruption." Smallpox and yellow fever threatened public health. Like the physical

---

[32] James Mather, "Mayoralty of New Orleans," *Louisiana Courier*, August 23, 1811; F. Bazile, "Notice to the Coasting Traders, Hawkers, and to the Masters Who under Their Sole Permission Send Their Slaves for Selling Goods in the Country," Extract from the Deliberations of the Jury of Police of the Parish St. Charles, in Their Sitting of the 28th of August 1813, *Louisiana Courier*, September 10, 1813.

[33] Deposition, Ménière before Girod, February 14, 1813; Vincent Ramos, "Runaway Slave," *Louisiana Courier*, May 7, 1813; "$15 Reward," *L'Argus*, January 29, 1828.

environment, the social environment was also hazardous. Bondspersons had no recourse to the law – in fact, the law encouraged free residents to harass enslaved peddlers – which left them vulnerable to taunts, robbery, and assault. James McDormant allegedly assaulted an enslaved cart man "who was passing by quietly with a bucket of shoes." McDormant threw a handful of dirt at him "and struck the boy with his fists and took up a stick with the intention of beating the boy with it[,] but the boy luckily got out of his reach." Another witness to that same incident noted that a bystander attempted to intervene but "was also abused most greatly by said James McDormant." Walking while black nearly cost this carter his life.[34]

Bondwomen were also vulnerable to arbitrary assault, and a legal pass from a master offered only limited protection. An anecdote recounted the experience of one enslaved woman in rural Louisiana who peddled to devastating consequences. In "a country seat a few miles from New Orleans," a Saint-Dominguan émigré gave his bondwoman permission to sell goods on a neighboring plantation owned by German Creole. On her first visit to his plantation, the woman sold her wares without incident. On her second visit, the planter "caused the innocent wench to be laid along the ground, to be disrobed of her under garment, and saw the discipline of the whip severely inflicted on her naked body." Such sadistic beatings were not unusual in Lower Louisiana. C. C. Robin, another traveler, also witnessed many such beatings, and decades later Solomon Northup described similar beatings inflicted on the bondwoman Patsey. Authorized circulation did not protect this woman, but instead left her more vulnerable to violence from another planter.[35]

---

[34] Berquin-Duvallon, *Travels in Louisiana*, 19; Deposition, Benjamin Bartlow before Roffignac, New Orleans, May 19, 1821, NYHS NOC 9:2; Deposition, Loran Ginoux before Roffignac, New Orleans, May 19, 1821, NYHS NOC 9:2; Medical Reports: Yellow Fever, David Ker to Macarty, 1817, NYHS NOC 10:5. "Boy" could refer to a bondman of any age.

[35] When the bondwoman's master's son confronted the German Creole, the offending planter allegedly replied: "I have lived thirty years in this colony, and your father only two." The chronicler cited this anecdote as evidence of the xenophobia that Saint-Dominguan émigrés faced in Louisiana, which extended to the summary maltreatment of their slaves by other planters. A traveler claimed to have heard this account and recorded it in his narrative, which suggests the tale communicates a credible truth no matter the factuality of this specific event. Berquin-Duvallon and Davis, *Travels in Louisiana*, 19, 24, 63–64; C. C. Robin and Stuart Landry, *Voyage to Louisiana, 1803–1805* (New Orleans: Pelican, 1966), 239; Solomon Northup, *Twelve Years a Slave*, eds. Sue Eakin and Joseph Logsdon (Baton Rouge: Louisiana State University Press, 1968), 25–26, 118, 196–199.

On sadism and slavery, see Camp, *Closer to Freedom*, 33; Garraway, *The Libertine Colony*; Hartman, *Scenes of Subjection*.

But how did the enslaved peddlers in New Orleans travel upriver to the outlying parishes every day? Perhaps some walked, but others likely allied with the *caboteurs*, or river traders, who also moved goods up and down the Mississippi River and built cosmopolitan networks in the process. One observer wrote: "People in this country are so accustomed to travel by water that the generic term *'voiture'* is always applied to a boat. If a Louisianian says to you 'I brought my *voiture*'; 'Can I give you a lift in my *voiture*'; he is referring to his pirogue or skiff as a Parisian using the same word would mean his coach."[36] Riverine travel was an everyday part of life in New Orleans, which expanded the physical and figurative "streets" that these peddlers used to circulate. These boatmen and their passengers collapsed the distance between urban New Orleans and its rural surrounding parishes. The boaters were a diverse crew, which included free white men, free (or self-liberated) black men, and indigenous traders. Though the majority of them were not themselves enslaved, these river traders nonetheless allowed bondspersons to access information, desirable goods, and escape routes.[37]

Like the goods they bartered, the river traders followed global tributaries into Lower Louisiana. Camille Filhe and Joseph Wouters both arrived to Louisiana from Cuba in 1809, perhaps part of the larger influx of Francophone refugees. Other boatmen might have been runaway slaves who cultivated their navigation skills when they labored for their masters. One slave sale advertisement from 1803, for example, listed "A Negro about 35 years old, strong, without defect, boatman (*canotier*)."[38] Officials in St. Charles Parish complained that "coasting traders" employed such men without first verifying their free status, a practice that allowed "runaway slaves [to] intrude themselves into the negro gangs of the plantations." Like the larger ships that docked at the New Orleans port, the subsidiary network of dugouts and pirogues that transported people and goods across southern Louisiana were also quite diverse.[39]

Officials complained that the boatmen's (the available sources show no evidence of women) circulations across Louisiana's rivers and bayous

---

[36] Robin, *Voyage,* 100.
[37] On similar boatmen, black and white, in coastal North Carolina, see David S. Cecelski, *The Waterman's Song: Slavery and Freedom in Maritime North Carolina* (Chapel Hill: The University of North Carolina Press, 2001).
[38] "A Vendre," *Moniteur,* October 15, 1803, my translation.
[39] Daniel H. Usner, *Indians, Settlers, and Slaves in a Frontier Exchange Economy: The Lower Mississippi River Valley before 1783* (Chapel Hill: University of North Carolina Press, 1992).

fostered illicit exchanges with "negroes for stolen goods." In the process, these boatmen were undoubtedly conduits of information between the city and rural slave quarters. According to official intelligence, these traders waited until night to "go into the different huts or cabins, or receive the negroes on Board their craft, and purchase of them for Taffia, all the clothes, plate, fowls or other things, which they may have stolen." Another observer noted the caboteurs "maintain an illicit trade with Negroes that is much more lucrative [than their trade with masters]. [Slaves] steal chickens from their masters, and whatever else they can take, and trade them for tafia, sugar, canvass, handkerchiefs and knick-knacks." Perhaps, as this observer argued, masters benefitted from the caboteurs, as the competition between sellers resulted in lowered prices and increased the assortment of products that masters would otherwise have to travel to town to buy.[40] But the enslaved persons might have benefitted more, as the river traders' circulations allowed bondspersons to secure taffia, or low-grade rum, and other prohibited goods and allowed rural slaves to maintain "simultaneity" with the world beyond the plantation.[41]

More than that, *caboteurs* sometimes helped enslaved persons escape. In 1813, Antoine Doriocourt Jr. complained before the New Orleans mayor that "a certain *caboteur* ... seized a *negre* named Ouanil" who belonged to his father. According to an act of sale, Juan Luis was born in Guinea or the Guinea Coast and the elder Doriocourt purchased him in 1794. Twenty years later, when he was about forty-four years old, Juan Luis ran away with the help of a river trader. The trader refused to inform on the fugitive, and Juan Luis had been missing for one month at the time of Doriocourt's deposition.[42] That same year, an official in St. John the Baptist Parish reported "a young negro girl, aged 12 or 13 years, who had been found on board of an Indian canoe" (an ambiguous term that could have referred to the specific type of canoe or signaled that it was the possession of an indigenous person). She claimed to belong to

[40] Robin, *Voyage*, 119.
[41] Search Warrant, Girod, New Orleans, February 5, 1813, my translation, NYHS NOC 8:11; Louis Toussard, French Consulate, to Claiborne, New Orleans, January 6, 1804 [*sic*], War of 1812 Series (MC 541), Folder 17 (though dated "1804," Toussard had to have written this letter in 1814, because he cites events in 1809 and beyond); Bazile, "Notice"; Report, John Watkins to Claiborne, New Orleans, February 2, 1804, *Letter Books*, II: 9–10.
[42] Deposition, Antoine Doriocourt before Girod, New Orleans, June 12, 1813, my translation, NYHS NOC 8:11; Act of Sale, Maria Elizabeth Destrehan Favre Daunoy to Antonio Doriocourt, Narcisse Broutin, Notary, New Orleans, December 16, 1794, pages 321–322, NANO. The seller was a relative of the woman that enslaved nurse Charlotte accompanied to Bordeaux.

a Mr. Laroge or Larose. This young woman may have been a runaway, a product on the illegal slave market, or any number of other possibilities. Whatever the case, she was on a boat outside of the immediate possession of her legal owner, which captures in microcosm the routine intersection of commerce and community on Louisiana's rivers.[43]

One decade later, in 1828 the bondwoman Agnes engineered a riverine escape from an Assumption Parish plantation with the assistance of a boatman. For days leading up to her escape, Agnes "manifested several times . . . her wish to go to town." This is no small point, as it demonstrates that even people held as slaves on rural plantations remained aware of their proximity to nearby urban spaces. It also reveals that Agnes shared her subversive desire for mobility with her enslaved confidants. At about nine o'clock on the appointed morning, other bondspersons saw her cleaning fish at the river's edge. Within an hour and a half Agnes vanished. "A man known by the name of Chabee, was seen passing by in a pirogue at that time," one witness recalled. Chabee may or may not have been a *caboteur*, but he might have conspired with the bondwoman to transport her along the river. Whether she sailed in the direction of Baton Rouge or New Orleans is unclear, as is the nature of her relationship to Chabee. Whatever their entanglement, Agnes fled her plantation in broad daylight by coordinating a riverine escape.[44]

"I KNOW YOU ARE A MAN & I AM ONE ALSO"

Runaways like Agnes used paths smoothed by trade to engage in the transformational act of escape. When bondspersons stepped outside of their designated places, they transformed their relationship to their bodies and to society, including their masters, fellow bondspersons, and the state. Truancy and flight allowed bondspersons to deprive masters of valuable labor and to reclaim the flesh reduced to chattel in the New Orleans slave market. But such movements also left runaways vulnerable to assault, kidnapping, and even murder. Such illicit movement not only changed the ways that runaways viewed their own bodies, but it also shifted the ways masters viewed them. For masters, flight masculinized some bondspersons even as it feminized others, a trend that is detectable in the runaway advertisements masters published in their efforts to recapture these fugitives. Finally, though truancy and flight allowed runaways to reunite families

---

[43] Eugene Barre, "Notice," *Louisiana Courier*, May 3, 1813.
[44] *Louisiana Courier*, August 15, 1828.

and communities, sometimes even to the point of reversing the routes of the domestic slave trade, complicated community dynamics meant such assemblages carried their own hazards. In short, enslaved persons routinely appropriated and resituated their bodies; what came next was an open question.[45]

When Louisiana's slaves improvised communities in the rival geography, they engaged in a practice as old as New World slavery. From Brazil to Cuba, Panama to Jamaica, St. Augustine to Louisiana's cypress swamps, diverse groups formed autonomous communities. In colonial Louisiana, indigenous and African peoples built communities together, a practice that French administrators strategically undermined by creating incentives for Indians to capture fugitive blacks. Still, maritime and multinational marronage into the late eighteenth century threatened the lives and power of early white settlers. During the Spanish era, the maroon leader St. Malo, who might have been Bambara (a Senegambian group legendary for its martial prowess), led Indians and Africans in a guerrilla war against Louisiana's Euro-American settlers. Spanish authorities captured and hanged St. Malo and some of his followers in 1784, but others maintained communities in Louisiana, including one in Chef Menteur, a settlement named in honor of French Governor Louis Billouart de Kerlerec, the "Chief Liar" who reneged on a treaty with the Choctaw.[46]

In the late colonial and early American eras, enslaved persons continued to flee to indigenous and maroon communities in the Louisiana swamps. Such collective flights required trust, which escapees built in the immediacy of a shared predicament and eased through common beliefs, cultures, and nationalities. In 1802, three men from the Congo fled a plantation together. That same year, four enslaved persons, three men and one woman, fled Acadian planter Louis Alexandre Harang's estate (located in present-day Westwego, Louisiana). They included Pierre-Marc, a Senegalese carpenter fluent in Mobilier (a Choctaw lingua franca), Spanish, French, and English; Janvier, a "red-colored" Nar man; Thomas, also Senegalese, deemed "fat and very black"; and Jeannette, a Nago woman described as tall and thin, bearing scarification marks. In addition to shared bondage, this latter group presumably came from regions in West Africa where Islam predominated, so shared

---

[45] Camp, *Closer to Freedom*, chapter 2.
[46] Gwendolyn Midlo Hall, *Africans in Colonial Louisiana: The Development of Afro-Creole Culture in the Eighteenth Century* (Baton Rouge: Louisiana State University Press, 1992), 201–236.

beliefs perhaps fostered the trust necessary for covert actions. And Pierre-Marc's linguistic ability increased their odds for gaining safe haven with native peoples. Harang suspected the four fugitives headed to "the other side of the Lake [Pontchartrain], having stolen a canoe (*une voiture*) in Chef Menteur." Unfortunately the two men did not get far enough away from slavery: Harang's 1808 estate sale included Janvier, Thomas, and eighteen other slaves (though not Jeannette).[47]

In addition to joining maroons, some human chattel reversed the routes of the slave trade to reconnect the communities from which they had been forcibly separated. Bayou St. John, the waterway that connected New Orleans to Lake Pontchartrain, proved a particularly attractive conduit. In 1811, an enslaved carter named Joseph was leased to a person who resided near Bayou Road, and he turned the fortuitously located worksite into a nexus of escape: "It is supposed that he embarked at the Bayou St. John to go to Chifonte [*sic*] and from thence to Natchez; others say that he has gone to Pensacola." Natchez, named for the indigenous peoples who dominated the region throughout the early eighteenth century, was home to the Grand Village, an important ceremonial mound. The city experienced rapid Anglo-American settlement after the 1783 end of the American revolutionary war, and exploded after Pinckney's Treaty in 1795. Spanish Pensacola was home to significant indigenous populations and maroon communities. The heterogeneity in Natchez and Pensacola offered Joseph an opportunity to transform himself into a free man.[48]

Masters used their understanding of enslaved people's geographic literacy to recapture runaways. In so doing, they acknowledged the expansive social networks to which their bondspersons belonged. When the blacksmith Abraham ran from the Smith plantation in the German

---

[47] "Esclaves Marons," *Moniteur de la Louisiane*, March 19, 1803, my translation; "Esclaves Marons," *Moniteur de la Louisiane*, September 11, 1802, my translation; Raron, Jr., "Runaway Negroes," *Louisiana Courier*, March 12, 1813; Estate Sale, Alexandre Harang, Pierre Pedesclaux, Notary, New Orleans, June 8, 1808, volume 56, pages 235–237, NANO.

"Mobilier" was the "Choctaw jargon used for the purposes of intertribal communication among all the tribes from Florida to Louisiana, extending northward on the Mississippi to about the junction of the Ohio ... also known as the Chickasaw trade language." Frederick Webb Hodge, *Handbook of American Indians North of Mexico* (Washington, DC: Government Printing Office, 1907), 916.

[48] "Runaway Slave," *Louisiana Courier*, October 9, 1811. On Natchez, see Clark, *New Orleans*, 184; Anthony E. Kaye, *Joining Places: Slave Neighborhoods in the Old South* (Chapel Hill: The University of North Carolina Press, 2007).

Coast, his master suspected that he and an accomplice named Jerry escaped to Bayou St. John and then north across Lake Pontchartrain. The two men, he suspected, had assistance: "both [Jerry] and Abraham having made acquaintances at Mobile and St. Stephens, on their route from Baltimore to this place a year ago." These two men used their time on the coffles of the overland slave trade to cultivate relationships, so when they attempted an illicit northeastward journey they likely activated regional networks to do it. In consequence, their master published runaway notices in the *Orleans Gazette, Mobile Gazette, Blakely* [Alabama] *Sun,* and *Mississippi Republican.*[49] Similarly, when the bondwoman Sally of St. Charles Parish ran away, her owner noted, "She is well known in town, especially by Mr. S. Meilleur, who has had her twice in jail." Sally's rebelliousness might have been the reason her former master sold her to the country to begin with, and now she likely headed back into town to reunite with her urban community.[50]

Such movements alternately severed and created community for enslaved persons, but it also transformed the ways that owners gendered and sexualized them. A runaway advertisement for the "negro wench" Anna listed her as "much marked with the small-pox, 25 or 30 years of age and very ugly." Her rebelliousness rendered her grotesque. Had she been on the auction block instead of a runaway advertisement, Anna's countenance might have merited a more favorable assessment. Traders might have packaged her scars, for example, as evidence of immunity, a trait that prospective buyers would have valued.[51] "Ranaway ... a griffe-woman born in Virginia named Nancy, 26 or 27 years old," an 1810 Louisiana runaway advertisement declared. "Her bubbies (*les seins*) are very small and she walks rather as a man than as a woman." Perhaps Nancy troubled gender by refusing to conform to dominant (and dominating) ideas about black slave womanhood, but it is equally possible that this description of Nancy was but one instance of the general defeminization of black women during slavery. Former bondswoman, antislavery activist, and woman's

---

[49] "$50 Rewards," *Mobile Gazette & Commercial Advertiser*, May 26, 1819 and June 2, 1819.
       On the domestic slave trade, see Steven Deyle, *Carry Me Back: The Domestic Slave Trade in American Life* (New York: Oxford University Press, 2005); Walter Johnson, *Soul by Soul: Life inside the Antebellum Slave Market* (Cambridge, MA: Harvard University Press, 1999).
[50] "Ten Dollars Reward," *Louisiana Courier*, April 15, 1828.
[51] "Runaway Slave," *L'Ami des Lois*, May 4, 1813; June 1, 1813.
       On race, gender, and aesthetics, see Taylor, *The Mask of Art*.

rights pioneer Sojourner Truth would later display her breast to prove her sex to a skeptical audience. Then again, the act of flight itself transformed Nancy's gender in the eyes of her owner. In his masculinization of Nancy's movement, Nancy's owner may have unwittingly associated her with the most dominant people he knew – men.[52]

Conversely, escapes feminized other slave women, as masters imagined them to have been seduced away by treacherous black men. When Isabelle fled in September 1803, her owner suspected it was to meet a mulatto bondman named Honoré. In another case, the "negro wench" Felicité fled and took her two children with her. She allegedly intended to meet a "quarteroon" man named Montalvo, and from there the family of fugitives planned to leave the country aboard a vessel. In another instance, Jacques Guillé of the Castillon plantation swore that two bondmen, one Negro and the other mulatto, "entered my camp last night and stole from her bed by force one of the negresses against her will." To be sure, slave stealing was a profession, so it is possible that these men kidnapped the woman. On the other hand, this could also be read as Guillé's erasure of the woman's agency. Her flight with the two men might have been voluntary. In a final example, Martin Gordon suspected Cilas Robertson, a mulatto man presumed to have been free, of convincing a bondwoman to abscond. Gordon vowed "if the said Robertson can establish the fact of his freedom [Gordon] intends to prosecute him before a competent tribunal." In each of these cases, masters assumed female slaves absconded under the influence of a male mastermind.[53]

Some enslaved women, however, fled by themselves or with their children. As discussed in the first chapter, the enslaved woman Finette ran away in the third trimester of pregnancy.[54] Louise, a twenty-two-year-old Igbo woman, fled her owner's Faubourg Marigny residence in 1811. She "was in the habit of going to Gravier's field," so she may have headed back to her usual haunt. In 1815, Julia "a mulatto ... about 22 years of age, tall and slender made, rather down look" ran from her master, and

---

[52] "Runaway," *Louisiana Courier*, October 29, 1810. The ad was printed in both French and English translations. On reading Nancy's gender performance, see Jack Halberstam, *Female Masculinity* (Durham: Duke University Press, 1998); Judith Butler, *Gender Trouble: Feminism and the Subversion of Identity* (New York: Routledge, 1990).

[53] *Moniteur de la Louisiane*, vol. 362 [date missing], September 1803; Deposition, Jacques Guillé before James Mather, New Orleans, October 4, 1808, NYHS NOC 1:8; Deposition, Martin Gordon before Nicholas Girod, New Orleans, August 31, 1813, NYHS NOC 8:11; Henriette Villascousas, "Notice," *Courier*, August 9, 1811.

[54] *Louisiana Courier*, July 29, 1811.

she took her eight-year-old daughter Fanny with her. These women's stories of flight with children highlighted the endurance of maternal love even in the context of slavery and the desperation that drove mothers to flee with their young children in tow.[55]

Local laws ensured that such flights remained dangerous for slaves who dared to steal themselves. "All slaves killed while run away," the Black Code declared, "shall be at the loss of the owner only." A dead runaway posed no cost to the state, so its patrolling agents had little economic incentive to protect a runaway's life. Sometimes officials in New Orleans hired men to catch runaways. As Solomon Northup, the Louisiana slavery survivor, explained decades later, "Catching runaways is sometimes a money-making business." In 1810 Mayor Mather hired Jacques Guesnon and his gang of white men and free men of color to patrol the woods adjacent to Faubourg Marigny (a neighborhood discussed in the next chapter). According to their testimony, members of the posse spotted one of Mr. Lavigne's runaways. "They gave chase, and the negro finally fell once wounded." Then they spotted "two other Negroes in the woods ... working together for Philippe, the negro of Eugène Macarty" (the nature of their sub rosa work is unclear). The other black men included one of Mr. Livaudais' Negroes named L'eveillé and Adonis, a thirty-year-old African-born man who belonged to Thomas Saulet. Their leader Philippe, described as "very insolent, threatening towards his master," taunted Guesnon in French: "You are not a woman. I know you are a man & I am one also." Despite this dramatic confrontation and subsequent adjudication before the mayor, Philippe remained a slave and Guesnon continued to patrol: Twelve years later the city treasurer paid him thirty piastres "for monitoring the Marigny Levee."[56]

---

[55] Ay. LaMarlere, "Ranaway," *Louisiana Courier*, October 21, 1811 (Louise); *Louisiana Gazette*, May 6, 1815 (Julia).

[56] An Act to Repeal All Laws or Provisions of Laws Prescribing the Manner of Remunerating the Owners of Slaves Sentenced to Death or Killed Whilst Run Away, January 8, 1813, *General Digest*, Black Code, §1; Northup, *Twelve Years a Slave*, 118, 183; "*Vous n'ete pas une femme. Je sais que vous etes un homme & je suis un aussi*," Deposition, Jacques Kernion to James Mather, New Orleans, August 13, 1810, NYHS NOC 8:8, my translation; *Mandat de Paiement* [Order to Pay], City Treasurer to Jacques Guesnon, New Orleans, January 14, 1822, NYHS NOC 7:1. On Adonis' age and birth-place, see Act of Sale, René Baudeau to Thomas Saulet, Narcisse Broutin, Notary, New Orleans, May 30, 1805, volume 9, page 424, NANO. In that transaction, Saulet purchased three African-born men: Quashy, Philipe [*sic*], and Adonis, all of whom had been in the United States for about sixteen months.

These men engaged in a skirmish with slave patrollers, but conflicts in the rival geography sometimes resulted in violence among enslaved persons. The notion of a harmonious "slave community" countered once-dominant understandings of slavery's negative effects on individual bondspersons and their families. A collectivism rooted in ethnic affiliations, spiritual practices, and shared oppression were thought to have inspired bondspersons to resist slavery by building families and institutions that operated outside of the individualistic profit-seeking of Euro-Americans. In this conception, women who were enslaved played a particularly important role in maintaining slave unity. Due to the erasure of slave fatherhood, the matrilineal heritability of slave status, and the transience of enslaved men due to labor and escapes, bondwomen became centers of biological and fictive kinship networks for their larger communities. Yet ideas about, contests for, and disputes over property made and remade community in specific times and places in the black Atlantic. First, slave owners' labor demands originally brought these communities together, and everyday actions depended as much on day-to-day survival needs as on shared histories. Second, notions of individual property did not necessarily sever slave solidarities. Across the Americas bondspersons just as readily used the property that they owned through custom if not right to cement community through acts of generosity, for example. The relationship between property, place, and community, then, was subject to the contingency that governed just about everything else.[57]

On one plantation in St. John the Baptist Parish, a bondwoman's decision to cross plantation borders to confront another culminated in the death of another bondwoman, an episode that highlights the contingent nature of movement among bondspersons. The chain of events began between two women on Justin Vicner's plantation. Peggy claimed that she loaned two dresses to twenty-nine-year-old Madelaine, who returned the garments in tatters. This was no small matter. As historian Stephanie Camp argues, enslaved people used adornment, pleasure, and

---

Eugène Macarty, a white man, became the romantic partner of Eulalie Mandeville, a woman of color. Mandeville was the daughter of the wealthy Philip Mandeville de Marigny and half-sister of Bernard Marigny (discussed in Chapter 4). See Thompson, *Exiles at Home*, 194–195; Clark, *The Strange History of the American Quadroon*, 226.

[57] Penningroth, *The Claims of Kinfolk*, 6–10; Smallwood, *Saltwater Slavery*, Chapter 4. On women's role in the slave community, see Deborah Gray White, *Ar'n't I a Woman? Female Slaves in the Plantation South*, rev. edition (New York: W. W. Norton & Company, 1999 [1985]).

sensory enjoyment to resist commoditization and domination and to assert control over their own bodies. Through clothing, enslaved women in particular resisted the "androgynous appearance imposed on some" of them by masters and instead used cotton, dye, and other materials to create stylish and artistic garments. These dresses were valuable, as they required costly investments of time, labor, and material resources, and they also became a point of enormous pride for enslaved women.[58]

On Sunday, January 9, 1820 at about 10:30 p.m., Peggy stole a hunting knife and walked to the widow of Antoine Vicner's neighboring plantation to confront Madelaine about the destroyed dresses. Testimonies conflict over what happened next, but at the end of the altercation the bondwoman Catherine lay dead from a wound under her left breast; Charles, a slave who attempted to apprehend Peggy, had a wounded left hand; and Peggy held the bloodied knife. Peggy fled the carnage she caused at Widow Vicner's plantation and walked to a nearby bar, where she allegedly confessed to Charles Guerin, a white man with whom she and the other bondspersons had a social relationship. In what was likely a rural "cabaret and billiard parlor," Peggy told him that her conflict had been with Madelaine, not Catherine, and that the latter woman's death was accidental, since the deceased woman fell onto Peggy's bosom unaware that the knife was there.[59]

Back at the Vicners' neighboring plantations, Pierre Adam Jacob heard the commotion, learned about the killing, and called the sheriff. Local officials collected depositions from several Vicner men, Jean-Baptiste and Jean-Pierre Folse (brothers and free men of color), Charles Guerin and Lastie Cuviller (white residents), and the Vicners' bondspersons. Madelaine, Peggy's initial target, swore that Peggy had intentionally killed

---

[58] Camp, *Closer to Freedom*, 78–87, 79. See also Shane White and Graham J. White, *Stylin': African American Expressive Culture from Its Beginnings to the Zoot Suit* (Ithaca, N.Y.: Cornell University Press, 1998).

[59] Several documents from this trial are included in the Slavery in Louisiana Collection (MSS 44), Folders 45–54, HNOC. These folders include summonses for enslaved persons to testify, depositions from various witnesses, and the court's final sentence. Recorded in French, these sources illuminate the legal proceedings against bondspersons accused of crimes against one another in Lower Louisiana. Magdalaine, a Louisiana Creole and the mother of one child, had been sold to Jean Vienar [*sic*] on April 1, 1817. See Hall, *Database*.

While such watering holes are generally associated with urban areas, rural Louisiana also featured such entertainment areas, and their numbers increased during the nineteenth century. For example, in 1804 in neighboring St. Charles Parish, "François Lucy and Pierre Fleury called Risquetout" (a nickname that literally means "risk it all," or rash, audacious) formed a partnership to open one such establishment. See Glenn R. Conrad, *The German Coast: Abstracts of the Civil Records of St. Charles and St. John the Baptist Parishes, 1804–1812* (Lafayette: University of Southwestern Louisiana, 1981), 6.

Catherine. "Moi piquer toi!" ("I will stab you!"), Peggy allegedly yelled right before she knifed Catherine. The sheriff brought Peggy to jail where she awaited a trial by jury. Just under five days after the killing, the court found Peggy "not guilty of feloniously and of malice aforethought stabbing the said Catherine." The court ruled the death unintentional – "The said Peggy having then improvidently and to no purpose a knife in her bosom or at her hand, with which … the said Catherine staked herself" – and sentenced Peggy to thirty-nine lashes and three years of hard labor "with a chain and ring around her leg" on the Widow Vicner's plantation.[60]

This murder trial illuminated a heterogeneous and interconnected plantation world in rural Louisiana. The Wichner-Vicner-Vicnairs, for example, descended from some of the earliest European migrants to Louisiana, many of them recruited by John Law from Alsace, the Rhineland, and Switzerland. Nikolaus Wichner, his wife Therese, and their son Gratien (or Christian) as well as Francois Wichner, his wife Charlotte and their two children all journeyed on the same vessel, *L'Elephant*, to Louisiana in 1720. After the death of his first wife, the Wichner patriarch married Barbara Friedrich, widow of Friedrich Merkel. Barbara and Francois Wichner had two sons: Antoine and David. In 1772, Antoine Vicner married Perinne Cuvillier, which meant that the witness Lastie Cuvillier was likely Vicner's in-law.[61] In the colonial era, German migrant families consolidated their landholdings, but by the 1790s the estates fragmented as children subdivided the plots. This splintering of family lands explains in part the contiguity of the Vicner holdings and the interchanges between their respective bondspersons across property lines.[62]

Peggy's was not the only border transgression that night. Madelaine testified that on Sunday afternoon, hours before the confrontation, Marianne, Peggy, Madelaine and Charles Guerin all gathered inside Madelaine's cabin, where they lay across the bed ("couché sur le lis"). Guerin's social if not sexual intimacy with slave women perhaps explains Peggy's willingness to speak freely with him over drinks at a bar. Though certainly unequal, Peggy and Guerin belonged to the same social network,

---

[60] Madelaine's testimony: MSS 44, Folder 51, HNOC. Peggy's sentence: MSS 44, Folder 54, HNOC.

[61] J. Hanno Deiler, *The Settlement of the German Coast of Louisiana and the Creoles of German Descent* (Philadelphia: Americana Germanica Press, 1909), 98–99.

[62] On July 31, 1808, for example, Adam Vicner sold to Jacques Vicner for $1,000 some 2.25 arpents of land "located on the right bank of the [Mississippi] river when ascending about 30 miles above New Orleans" and immediately north of Jacques Vicner's other holdings. Conrad, *The German Coast*, Introduction, 162.

and Peggy likely reasoned that he could serve as an ally to her in the aftermath of this killing. For his part, Guerin neglected to mention his time on the bondwoman's bed in his testimony. The significance here goes beyond prurience. First, the story about a white man sprawled on a bed in a slave woman's quarters showed up in the bondwoman's testimony, but not in Guerin's. His selective silences illuminate the ease with which white men erased their routine but unseemly acts from official testimonies and, by extension, archives. This testimony highlights the critical perspectives that black women's voices offered on this period.

Further, this evocative episode illuminates interracial fraternization and conflict in rural Louisiana. As will be discussed in the next chapter, in New Orleans slaves and free persons drank together in local watering holes regularly enough to prompt laws, surveillance, and contestation. The extreme visibility of such assemblages on the urban frontier, however, must not detract attention from their occurrence, if on a smaller scale, in rural Louisiana as well. A conflict between slave women over a tattered dress illuminated the overlapping diasporas and interlocking social worlds present in the plantation south as well as in its urban cores.[63]

The geographic situation that left New Orleans poised to become a capital of global commerce also made it dependent on and conducive to multidirectional slave journeys and heterogeneous assemblages. As goods themselves, slaves ferried and followed goods across New Orleans, Lower Louisiana and beyond, and their movements built the political and economic infrastructure of their enslavement even as they used their knowledge and circulations to chart alternate geographies for themselves and their loved ones. As with much else, these dynamics that were present across the region became all the more acute in New Orleans itself, and the contest to keep slaves in their place in a diverse capital of commerce and pleasure proved quite the undertaking.

---

[63] Guerin may also have feared social stigma or legal troubles if he admitted to such behavior in sworn testimony. "The legal process exhibited a degree of toleration for white males who had sexual relations with black females, as long as the liaison was kept casual and discreet." Peter W. Bardaglio, "'Shamefull Matches': The Regulation of Interracial Sex and Marriage in the South before 1900," in *Sex, Love, Race: Crossing Boundaries in North American History*, ed. Martha Hodes (New York: New York University Press, 1999), 112–138, 113.

3

Neighborhood Spaces

One night in December 1813, the "Negresse Libre" Jane Right hosted a New Orleans block party. Her guests played music, danced, socialized, and likely drank in and around her home in Faubourg St. Marie. This reclamation of black bodies outside of the designated time and place for such activities – Sunday afternoons in Congo Square – so irked Right's neighbors that they summoned local authorities. Two responding officers, one the police commissioner and the other a watchman from the City Guard, claimed to have observed "a gathering of slaves who were dancing in the street" (*un rassemblement d'esclaves qui dansaient dans la rue*). As the lawmen expelled the presumed slaves from the party, Right supposedly "resisted [the officers] in the performance of their duty" and "responded to them in an insolent manner." Right went to jail, her guests dispersed, and an ephemeral silence descended on the New Orleans street.[1]

---

[1] The officers assumed the status of these revelers based on black phenotype, but it is not possible to know their status. The officers cited Article 40 of the *Code Noir* to justify her arrest: "Free people of colour ought never to insult or strike white people, nor presume to conceive themselves equal to white; but, on the contrary, they ought to yield to them in every occasion." Deposition, Louis Nicolas and Martin Bonseigneur before Mayor Nicholas Girod, New Orleans, December 10, 1813, NYHS NOC 8:11, my translation; An Act Prescribing the Rules and Conduct to be Observed with Respect to Negroes and other Slaves of this Territory, June 7, 1806, §40, Lislet, *A General Digest*.

    This scenario is strikingly contemporary, as the gentrification of historic neighborhoods like Faubourg Tremé (which accelerated post-Hurricane Katrina) pits largely, though not exclusively, working-class and poor black secondline processional devotees against more

In New Orleans and across the modern Atlantic, dense neighborhoods became battlegrounds on which elite and working-class residents
contested their visions for the city. From Liverpool to London, Boston
to New York, port cities' economies depended on mobile and transient
laborers – immigrants and slaves, sailors and merchants – who were
unable or unwilling to establish the patriarchal households associated
with more privileged residents. These transient residents crammed into
boarding houses, and in their spare time they played in the brothels,
bars, and sports fields that formed "an expanding urban network of
commercial enterprise and entertainment."[2] Those in power regulated
this network of places to produce hierarchies of race, class, gender, and
sexuality even as the so-called lower orders used such sites as a theater
in which to challenge those efforts.[3]

Because New Orleans rested at the intersection of early republican
imperial expansion and the growing Atlantic plantation complex, its
neighborhoods were caught between the compatible and contradictory
elements of both developments. Leaders in the early republic considered the moral elevation of the urban working classes in cities like
Boston, New York, and Philadelphia a central part of the national
project. "By the mid-1780s," one historian writes, "many political
leaders complained that ... the common citizens ... were asserting
unacceptable upward social mobility without embracing the virtuous
moral character required in a republic." Separated from the sobering

---

recent, predominately white residents. See Katy Reckdahl, "Culture, Change Collide in
Treme" [New Orleans], *Times-Picayune*, October 2, 2007.

[2] Timothy J. Gilfoyle, *City of Eros: New York City, Prostitution, and the
Commercialization of Sex, 1790–1920* (New York: W. W. Norton & Co., 1992), 20.

[3] The actual theater in New Orleans became a site of contestation and cultural transformation. Theater, music, literature, and fashion benefited from the influx of refined
Saint-Dominguans. "When I arrived in the city, I had the pleasure of assisting to
several comedies, dramas, and musical operas of second class order," one observer
wrote in the 1830s. "The troupe was composed of a dozen actors and actresses who
had real talent, as they were attached to the theatre 'Cap-Francais' in the Island of San
Domingo and took refuge in Louisiana after the insurrection of the negroes in that
Island." For New Orleans, the observer writes, this influx was a net gain: "Louisiana
received great advantages from that unfortunate event in the Island, the great insurrection and upheaval in San Domingo brought many good things to Louisiana, things of
greater importance than the matter referred to above." Augustin-Wogan-Labranche
Family Papers, Manuscript Collection 223, Folder 13, Manuscripts Department, TU.
For a similar observation concerning the theater's debt to Saint Domingue, see
Berquin-Duvallon and John Davis, *Travels in Louisiana*, 25. See also Roach, *Cities
of the Dead*.

influences of family, church, and monarchy that purportedly structured rural life during the colonial era, migrants flocked to cities, worked for wages, and reclaimed their bodies through pleasurable amusements. Early reformists sought to temper the temptations of leisure and to compel the urban working classes to become productive workers and moral citizens. But the so-called lower orders envisioned and implemented their own visions. As a result, leaders and reformers worked to contain and eliminate vice from the urban landscape even as entrepreneurs profited from its increasing appeal to residents and transients alike.[4]

Such contests in New Orleans were distinctive because, unlike Boston or New York, Havana or Liverpool, it underwent occupation by the republican "empire of liberty" as it was becoming a premier site of slavery. While slavery – and slave populations – were on the decline in industrializing European capitals and urban centers of the northern United States, in New Orleans, as in Havana, the social disruptions that attended the rise of the early market economy occurred alongside the expansion of slavery and staple production. Working-class Anglo-American migrants and European immigrants as well as enslaved persons from Africa, the Caribbean, and the Eastern Seaboard converged on the emergent city. But, in the first decade of American rule, free black and slave population increases outstripped those of whites. These demographics prompted local authorities to classify and regulate white workers *and* an exploding free black and enslaved population at the same time. New Orleanians of African descent took part, however unequally, in urban amusements, and as leaders struggled to maintain order they deemed the regulation of neighborhood activities the perfect place to do it.[5]

This chapter begins by examining the place of enslaved people in the heterogeneous households of Faubourg Marigny, a New Orleans suburb immediately downriver from the oldest part of the city. In this

---

[4] Clare A. Lyons, *Sex among the Rabble: An Intimate History of Gender & Power in the Age of Revolution, Philadelphia, 1730–1830* (Chapel Hill: The University of North Carolina Press, 2006), 225; Lola Gonzalez-Quijano, *Capitale de L'Amour: Filles et Lieux de Plaisir à Paris au XIXᵉ Siècle* (Paris: Vendémiaire, 2015); Gilfoyle, *City of Eros*; Linebaugh and Rediker, *The Many-Headed Hydra*; W. J. Rorabaugh, *The Alcoholic Republic, an American Tradition* (New York: Oxford University Press, 1979).

[5] John G. Clark, *New Orleans, 1718–1812: An Economic History* (Baton Rouge: Louisiana State University Press, 1970), chapter 14.

diverse neighborhood, slaves lived in close proximity – though not political or material equality – to their diverse owners and neighbors. The second section explores the tavern culture that emerged inside of and adjacent to the households of early national New Orleans. The line between private and public dwellings was not sharply defined since households also served as boarding houses, taverns, brothels, and gambling dens. Such establishments undermined bourgeois norms of morality and respectability even as they exposed the most vulnerable participants to arbitrary violence, disease, and exploitation. The final section explores the spectacular amusements held on Sundays on the racquette field and in Congo Square. In contrast to the illegal (if routine) participation of slaves in urban nightlife, their Sunday amusements were part of the social fabric that locals and tourists enjoyed. In both sites, the gatherings and exertions of slaves allowed them to assemble, compete, and trade, but they also entertained masters and non-slaveholders alike.

One white Louisiana resident stated in 1940, "The nigger was not allowed no pleasure as long as slavery lasted."[6] His declaration resonates with dominant perceptions of slavery and violence. But perverted amusements defined New Orleans slavery. On the one hand, enslaved Africans reclaimed their bodies and participated in the nightlife that attracted many urban residents. Households, taverns, and public streets all hosted interracial fraternization and intimacy, violence, and drunkenness, all of which concerned local leaders who prized worker productivity and social control. Those same masters and local leaders tolerated and even encouraged other forms of play, such as the Sunday activities on the racquette field and in Congo Square, which allowed locals and tourists to consume the spectacle of black amusement. As one scholar argues, the "investment in and fixation with Negro enjoyment" reflected masters' egocentric desire to "grant the observer access to an illusory plentitude of fun and feeling." While these activities might have been restorative, such activities also functioned as "safety valves" in which leaders allowed some pleasure and latitude to prevent resistance and preserve society. These public scenes in which enslaved people entertained free audiences highlight the predicament of African diasporic cultural

---

[6] Interview, B. M. Dietz by Flossie McElwee, June 5, 1940 in Clayton and Louisiana Writers' Project, *Mother Wit*, 50–51.

production during chattel slavery even under seemingly permissive conditions.[7]

"HOUSING WAS BECOMING SCARCER AND SCARCER"

In 1800, eccentric socialite Bernard de Marigny (1785–1868) inherited a massive plot of land immediately downriver from the French Quarter. During the colonial era, that plot had been a brewery, then a sawmill, and finally a brickyard. Upon reaching his majority in 1805, the young heir decided against turning the massive plot into a sugar or cotton plantation, which would have left him subject to the booms and busts of global commodities markets. Instead Marigny speculated in urban real estate by transforming his land into a "faubourg," or suburb. In 1803, 8,056 people lived in the city (3,948 whites, 2,773 slaves, and 1,335 free blacks), and, as one traveler observed, "the city every day acquired new population."[8] Only they had nowhere to live: "Housing was becoming scarcer and scarcer. A small cottage in an isolated neighborhood, rented for ten to twenty piastres a month and a shop or store, advantageously placed[,] rented for from 25 to 80 piastres."[9] Like colonial leaders nearly a century before him, Marigny also hired French engineers to transform his plot into gridded streets and numbered lots. The new neighborhood featured a public park – Washington Square – and streets to which Marigny gave distinctive names: Rue d'Amour (Love Street), Rue des Bons Enfants (Good Children Street), Champs Elysée (Elysian Fields), Desire (its streetcar line playwright Tennessee Williams later made iconic), and, in honor of the game that Marigny is credited with introducing to the United States, Craps. By 1810, the city's population had nearly doubled to 17,224 (6,316 whites, 5,961 blacks, and 4,950 free persons of color), which increased housing demand as well as the cosmopolitanism for which Marigny's eponymous neighborhood became known.[10]

---

[7] Hartman, *Scenes of Subjection*, 34–35. See also Morrison, *Playing in the Dark*; Rothman, *Slave Country*.

[8] Robin, *Voyage*, 32. See also Campanella, *Bienville's Dilemma*, 26.

[9] Robin, *Voyage*, 32.

[10] An Act, Bernard Marigny and Solomon Prevost before William C. C. Claiborne, April 19, 1805, NYHS NOC 8:3.

On Faubourg Marigny, see Powell, *Accidental City*, 346–351; Campanella, *Bienville's Dilemma*, 28, 149–150; Scott and Hébrard, *Freedom Papers*, 71. In the same decades, DeWitt Clinton, then mayor of New York, appointed the planning commission that created Manhattan's grid. On urban real estate in this era, see Elizabeth Blackmar, *Manhattan for Rent, 1785–1850* (Ithaca, NY: Cornell University Press, 1989).

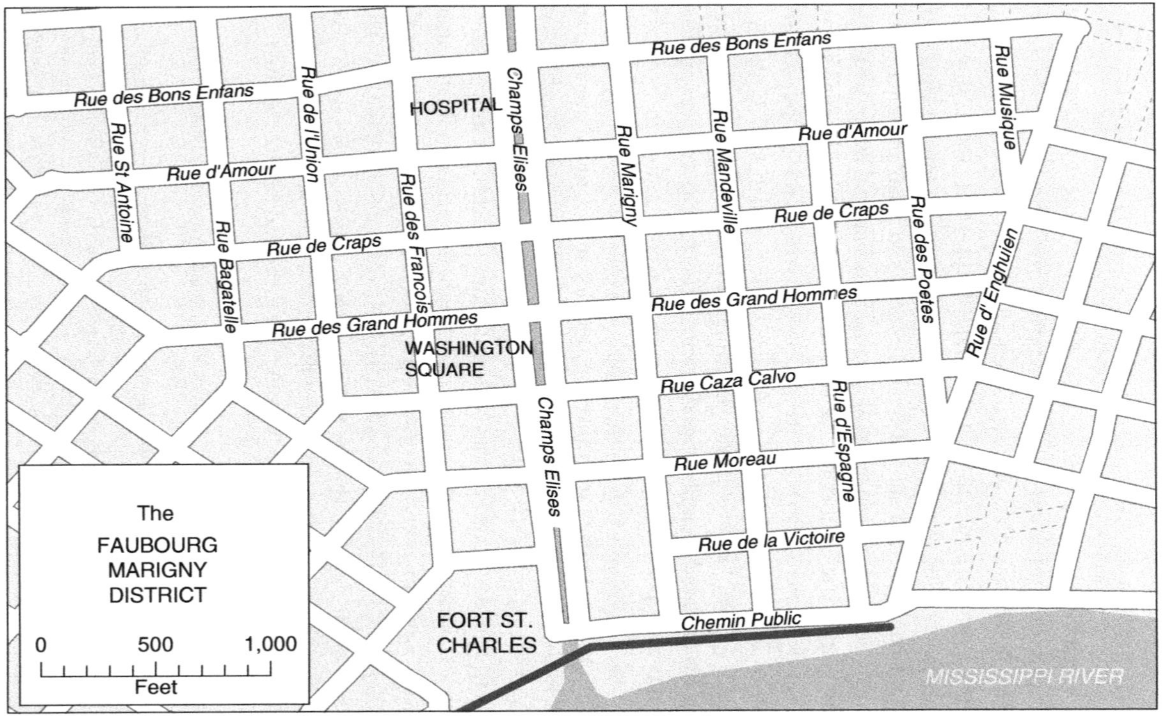
The
FAUBOURG
MARIGNY
DISTRICT
0
500
1,000
Feet
Rue des Bons Enfans
Rue St Antoine
Rue d'Amour
Rue Bagatelle
Rue de Craps
Rue de l'Union
Rue des Grand Hommes
Rue des Francois
HOSPITAL
WASHINGTON
SQUARE
Champs Elises
Champs Elises
FORT ST.
CHARLES
Rue des Bons Enfans
Rue Marigny
Rue Mandeville
Rue d'Amour
Rue de Craps
Rue des Grand Hommes
Rue Caza Calvo
Rue Moreau
Rue de la Victoire
Rue d'Espagne
Rue des Poetes
Rue Musique
Rue d' Enghuien
Chemin Public
MISSISSIPPI RIVER

MAP 3.1 Faubourg Marigny.

Marigny's development was primarily a financial investment, but he also used his profit-seeking venture to counterbalance Anglo-American imperial and demographic power. After the Louisiana Purchase, Anglophone settlers moved to the diverse Faubourg St. Marie (later the American Sector) immediately upriver from the French Quarter. For his neighborhood, Marigny encouraged the settlement of a heterogeneous and relatively less-privileged population of French Creoles and immigrants from Saint-Domingue, Ireland, and Germany. He subdivided his large estate into small, relatively affordable lots, and he extended credit to those who could not pay upfront. These policies attracted working-class and Francophone settlers. Of the nearly 2,000 residents listed in the 1810 federal census, about one third were deemed "white," almost half were free people of color, and almost one quarter were slaves. Faubourg Marigny also featured a concentration of houses headed by free women of color. As Marigny envisioned, his neighborhood became a diverse, worldly counterweight to the American Sector a few strokes upriver.[11]

Diversity and dilapidation went hand in hand throughout the city, but especially in the new subdivision, which led homeowners to organize for infrastructure improvements. With its humid subtropical climate, New Orleans was the least healthy city in the United States for much of the nineteenth century. An 1802 visitor described the city's streets as "flat, [and] the filth from the houses remains where it was thrown; and, during a great part of the year, they are a common sewer; a sink of nastiness, dirt, and corruption." The city's army of mosquitos and transient population fostered the profusion of contagious diseases. Consequently, early Faubourg Marigny residents petitioned local authorities to attend to neighborhood infrastructure. In 1808, J. Macarty petitioned Mayor James Mather to compel other property owners in the suburb to construct drainage ditches to allow the egress of the standing water that threatened to "infect the environment." In 1813, another group of Marigny property owners petitioned the city to maintain the neighborhood's ditches and sidewalks, channels that were critical commercial and cultural spaces in a walking city like New Orleans. Many of those petitioners had French surnames that included Maurin, Etienne, Guerin, Ménière, and Robery (or Roberie), but one man had the Anglo-American surname Pollock, which

---

[11] 1810 US Census as digitized on www.ancestry.com, accessed April 6, 2009. See also Powell, *Accidental City*, 348; Campanella, *Bienville's Dilemma*, 150.

FIGURE 3.1 J. L. Boqueta de Woieseri, *View of New Orleans taken from the Plantation of Marigny, New Orleans,* November 1803 (Chicago History Museum). This image, dated months after the Louisiana Purchase, shows the bald eagle, a symbol of the US nation, hovering above Faubourg Marigny. Presumably, New Orleans was destined to prosper "under [the] wings" of its new empire.

highlights the Euro-American diversity that defined the neighborhood and New Orleans from the colonial era into the early American period.[12]

The diversity of the neighborhood also permeated its individual households, many of which consisted of some permutation of biological family members and renters, free people and slaves. As an international entrepôt, New Orleans attracted capital and the migrants who follow it. These settlers were generally unable to purchase homes, so, as the working classes did across the Atlantic world, the laboring classes, vagabonds, and the unemployed congregated in rented rooms in crowded boarding houses. The 1810 federal census lists an estimated 1,943 residents of the faubourg, including 578 white residents (320 males, 258 females), 854 free people of color, and 511 enslaved persons, a number that included Bernard Marigny's seventy-five bondspersons. Officials did not count enslaved and free persons of color by gender or age as they did for the white population, but free persons of color composed about forty-four percent of the Marigny population, while slaves represented about one quarter of the Marigny's population. As of 1810, people of African descent made up about seventy percent of the neighborhood's population.[13]

Slaves were a critical if vulnerable part of many diverse households. Mathurin Pacaud's domestic arrangements present one instructive example. Pacaud worked as a clerk for the Banque de la Louisiane and served as Grand Orator of the Grand Convention of Ancient York Masons. In August 1808 he purchased from Bernard Marigny two plots of land near Washington Square. He presumably lived in one dwelling and leased the other to tenants. According to the 1810 US Census,

---

[12] Berquin-Duvallon and Davis, *Travels in Louisiana*, 19, 24; J. Macarty to Mather, New Orleans, June 20, 1808, my translation, NYHS NOC 1:8; The Owners of Lands Sold by the City of New Orleans at the Border of the Faubourg Called Marigny before Girod, January 25, 1813, my translation, NYHS NOC 1:9.

On disease in the newly acquired territory, see Conevery Bolton Valencius, *The Health of the Country: How American Settlers Understood Themselves and Their Land* (New York: Basic Books, 2002). On the gridded neighborhood, see Kate Brown, "Gridded Lives: Why Kazakhstan and Montana Are Nearly the Same Place," *The AHR* 106 (February 2001): 17–48.

Oliver Pollock (1737–1823), an Anglo settler, planter, and merchant, settled in British West Florida in 1769. He cultivated economic relationships in Spanish Louisiana, and during the American Revolution he used his commercial ties to Cuba and Spain to supply George Washington's army with gunpowder. On his business dealings, see Light T. Cummins, "Oliver Pollock's Plantations: An Early Anglo Landowner on the Lower Mississippi, 1769–1824," *Louisiana History* 29, no. 1 (Winter 1988): 35–48.

[13] I derived these numbers from the 1810 US Census as digitized on www.ancestry.com, accessed April 6, 2009.

Pacaud's household consisted of one white male, seven free persons of color, and six slaves. In other words, Pacaud was a prominent citizen who likely lived with a free woman of color, their mixed-race children, and their bondservants.[14]

Propertied free women of color, some of them former slaves, also headed Marigny households. Agnes, for example, began her life in bondage upriver from New Orleans in 1759. Owing to slaves' right to self-purchase under Spanish law, a French Louisianan male partner, and her own efforts, by the end of her life she had become an entrepreneur, wife, and slaveholder.[15] In March 1806 she sold two "negresses" named Margueritte and Marianne to a Mr. De La Rodres, and in October she married a free man of color (and father of her newborn daughter) named Joseph Mathieu.[16] Two years later Agnes, described as a resident of Faubourg Marigny, bought from Bernard Marigny a slave named Bimby. The purchase price was 355 piastres, which Mathieu promised to pay Marigny in three installments over the same number of years.[17] About a week later, she purchased from Marigny a plot of land on Rue de Craps for 400 piastres.[18] Since she was already a resident of the

---

[14] Act of Sale, Bernard Marigny to Mathurin Pacaud, Narcisse Broutin, Notary, New Orleans, August 26, 1808, volume 18, page 330, NANO. The sale price was 1,400 piastres.

On Mathurin Pacaud's freemasonry activities, see Walter Parker, "Secret Orders," in *Standard History of New Orleans, Louisiana*, ed. Henry Rightor (Chicago: The Lewis Publishing Company, 1900), 315–325. Pacaud may have been married to or in some way connected to Marie-Louise Pacaud, sister of Pierre Toussaint, the noted Saint Dominguan ex-slave who became quite wealthy in New York City in the early nineteenth century. As his biographers noted, Pierre Toussaint's sister emigrated from Saint-Domingue to Cuba and then New Orleans. She resolved never to go back to Saint Domingue, describing the island as "a country of disorder and tyranny where there is continued fighting." Arthur Jones, *Pierre Toussaint* (New York: Doubleday, 2003), 169.

[15] A French Louisianan named Mathieu Devaux used the right of *coartación* granted under Spanish law to purchase her freedom. Despite her owner's refusals, which extended the process for nearly one year, Agnes eventually left that owner and began a domestic relationship with Devaux. At his death, he bequeathed his property to the children and grandchildren born to him and, in his words, to "my slave Agnes." See Clark, *The Strange History of the American Quadroon*, 97–100.

[16] Act of Sale, Agnes Mathieu to Mr. De LaRodres (or De Larose), Pierre Pedesclaux, Notary, New Orleans, March 21, 1806, volume 51, documents 259 and 260, NANO. On her relationship with Mathieu, see Clark, *The Strange History of the American Quadroon*, 97–100.

[17] Act of Sale, Bernard Marigny to Agnes Mathieu, Narcisse Broutin, Notary, New Orleans, September 2, 1808, volume 18, pages 345–346, NANO.

[18] Act of Sale, Bernard Marigny to Agnes Mathieu, Narcisse Broutin, Notary, New Orleans, September 9, 1808, volume 18, pages 366–367, NANO.

neighborhood, she likely bought the second plot as an investment. By the 1810 US Census she lived in a Marigny home with Jacques Mathieu, a carpenter; Louis Mathieu, a blacksmith; ten other free persons of color; and three slaves.[19] She was listed as a shopkeeper in the city directory the following year. Her shrewd use of credit, real estate speculation, and retail allowed Mathieu to transform herself from slave to master. Consequently, enslaved and free persons of African descent lived under the roof of her Marigny household.

Such households became sites of labor and violence, especially when transient sailors boarded in them. In 1811, MacKenzie, a white sailor, boarded at the home of Susan, described as "a Negro wench." Apparently he and another sailor "were grumbling bitterly against Susan's not washing their clothes." MacKenzie "threaten[ed] that he would take away Susan's life." A man who overheard the threat ran to tell Susan's employer, a local man for whom she worked as a cook, and her employer ran to the house. There he found the sailor MacKenzie as well as "four other men who were found in bed in Susan's house." Susan's employer had all five men taken to prison. The two depositions consulted do not indicate the exact location or other identifying details about this household. Nonetheless this fracas between sailors and an enslaved woman over laundry reveals the risks that enslaved female service workers experienced inside the global households in which they labored.[20]

Likewise, as a sustained consideration of free woman of color Mélanie Drouet's household reveals, the Faubourg Marigny dwellings inhabited by

---

[19] 1811 New Orleans City Directory, NOPL. Agnes Mathieu owned several bondspersons prior to 1810, including Bimby, Eufrosine, Louison, Marianne, and Pierre. See Hall, *Database*.

[20] Deposition, Peter Cunningham before Macarty, New Orleans, February 19, 1811, NYHS NOC 8:9; Deposition, Bartholomew Mahon before Macarty, New Orleans, February 19, 1811, NYHS NOC 8:9.

It was not unprecedented for an enslaved woman to keep a house of her own. According to this testimony, she worked as a cook for MacKenzie but was enslaved by another (whose name is difficult to read in the document – perhaps Belonge). Some enslaved persons supported their masters. One famous example was Pierre Toussaint, who fled with his mistress to New York during the course of the Haitian Revolution and became a well-regarded hairdresser. With his profits, Toussaint provided for his mistress as well as others. Jones, *Pierre Toussaint*. The 1820 Census counts sixty-five unnamed persons as residents of New Orleans boarding houses, but the number was likely far higher. The census captures their marginality to bourgeois visions of the city, as they are listed on one of the last pages of the census under "Names of persons forgotten in the census." Even then, however, the record does not list them by name. 1820 US Census, New Orleans, page 109; NARA Roll: M33_32; Image: 122, www.ancestry.com.

diverse locals of mixed statuses could be just as violent. The absence of family ties in church records suggest that Drouet was born into slavery and later freed, though this is not certain. Then in 1810 Melanía Drouet, "cuarterón libre," gave birth to Gustav Frederic Drouet, classed as a "tierron libre." The baptismal record does not identify the child's father, but that uncommon racial categorization suggests the man was considered white. In May of the following year, Drouet gave birth to another son, Joseph Harman Drouet, listed as "mestizo libre," a term used to indicate Spanish and Indian ancestry specifically or mixed ancestry more broadly. Father Antonio (Père Antoine) de Sedella noted the absence of Joseph Drouet's father, whom he listed as "an unknown father" (*un padre descon-cido*). Both sons' names suggest an association with German-American migrants, but the man's (or men's) identities went unrecorded. Consequently, both sons received a "natural" – not "legitimate" – status in church records. This spiritual illegitimacy resulted from the hierarchies of race, sexuality, and reproduction that defined family and household formation for Drouet and countless others in New Orleans and across the Americas.[21]

Though Drouet experienced racism and sexism, as a free person she could accumulate property, and she, like many others, used slave ownership to increase her personal wealth. On February 1, 1812 Drouet purchased from Louis Labourdette "a negresse named Charlotte, aged 16 or 17 years and creole of Maryland." This young woman had been "taken from Baltimore by Samuel Hoyt" on July 11, 1811.[22] One week later, Drouet bought a house and land on Rue D'Amour (present-day Rampart Street) from Eulalie Foucher, an affluent woman of color who had purchased the lot from Marigny. Far from showing a race- or gender-based solidarity with the bondwoman Charlotte, Drouet instead used ownership of the woman to maximize her own financial position. When Drouet took out a mortgage about one month later, she used her house and her slave

---

[21] "Drouet, Joseph Harman," *St. Louis Cathedral Baptisms* (hereafter SLCB), volume 15, part II, record 680, June 7, 1817, my translation, AANO; "Drouet, Gustav Fred.," SLCB, volume 16, part II, February 12, 1820, my translation, AANO. The Harmann-Harmon-Herman surname was common in the German Coast, and a Frédéric family lived in New Orleans. However, I cannot find evidence of a connection to Drouet. On illegitimacy in the colonial Spanish Americas, see Ann Twinam, *Public Lives, Private Secrets: Gender, Honor, Sexuality, and Illegitimacy in Colonial Spanish America* (Stanford, CA: Stanford University Press, 1999).

[22] Act of Sale, Louis Labourdette to Mélanie Drouet, Michel De Armas, Notary, New Orleans, volume 7, pages 26–27, my translation, NANO.

Charlotte as collateral.[23] Not even a year later, she sent Charlotte back to the auction block.[24] Charlotte's serial forced displacement via the slave markets of at least two Atlantic ports cities, Baltimore and New Orleans, became the means by which Drouet expanded her own household.[25]

Drouet used the wealth that home and slave ownership offered to support her expanding family with her partner, François St. Germain, and sacramental records of their children's births reflect the challenges of regulating reproduction, race, and legitimacy in a diverse yet deeply stratified society. In 1808, the legislature outlawed marriages between "free white persons" and "free people of color" and those between "free persons and slaves," so Drouet and St. Germain, a carpenter born to an Acadian (or "Cajun") mother and a French father, could not marry.[26] Still the couple had five children between 1813 and 1822: Margarita, Josephine, Adelaida, Manuel, and Francois Jr. Though clerics listed St. Germain as each child's father ("the father of the baptized, present at her baptism," one priest wrote at Josephine's 1816 ceremony), each bore his surname, and his relatives served as godparents, the couple's inability to marry before the law rendered their children "natural" rather than "legitimate" before the Lord. These so-called illegitimate children also received different racial categorizations: priests listed Josephine as "quarteronne libre"; Adelaida, "tiezzerona libre"; and Manuel "tíerzeron libre." Francois, who was baptized two months after his father's September 1822 death, was simply listed as "libre" without any racial designation. Finally, in death, as in life, the family unit remained invisible before the church: Burial records listed thirty-nine-year-old François St. Germain as "single, unmarried" (*Soltero no se marié*).[27]

---

[23] Mortgage Promissory Note, Valery Avart to Mélanie Drouet, Michel De Armas, Notary, New Orleans, March 6, 1812, volume 7, page 139, NANO. That act of sale refers to the February 8 purchase before the same notary.

[24] On December 29, 1812, Drouet sold Charlotte to Pierre (Pedro) Feu, party to at least twenty slave sales between 1801 and 1819. Hall, *Database*.

[25] On female slave ownership, see Thavolia Glymph, *Out of the House of Bondage: The Transformation of the Plantation Household* (Cambridge: Cambridge University Press, 2008).

[26] St. Germain was the son of Marie Blanche Bergeron and Pierre Joachim Rene de St. Germain. "St. Germain, Francois," *St. Louis Cathedral Burial Records*, volume 13, page 61, record 666, AANO; Patrick Davis, email message to author, May 22, 2014. I am grateful to Davis, a descendant of François' older brother Martial St. Germain, for pointing out this relationship between Drouet and St. Germain. On the legislature's 1808 law and people's efforts to circumvent it, see Spear, *Race, Sex, and Social Order*, 201–206.

[27] "le toute soira d'apres l'ordre du pere de la baptisée, present a son baptisme," "St. Germain, Josephine," *SLCB*, volume 15, part II, page 49, my translation, AANO; "St. Germain, Adelaida," *SLCF*, 7:1, December 2, 1819, AANO; "St. Germain, Manuel

Even as Drouet confronted the challenges of race, status, and legitimacy before the church, a June 1822 incident literally brought home to
her the conflicts between the exploding number of free, freed, and unfree
people in Faubourg Marigny. The expansion of Drouet's family paralleled
that of the larger city. After 1820 its population exceeded 27,000 (with
some estimates as high as 41,000), and Orleans Parish was home to nearly
15,000 bondspersons.[28] The Faubourg Marigny population expanded at
an average 6 percent annually, from just fewer than 2,000 residents in
1810 to over 3,200 ten years later. About 1,200 of the neighborhood's
residents were white (645 males and 561 females), while free persons of
color made up about 44 percent of the population, a proportion virtually
identical to that of the 1810 Census. The gender imbalance among free
blacks – 878 females to 546 males – meant free females of color constituted just over one-fourth of the neighborhood's population. Finally,
slightly fewer than one in five residents in the neighborhood – 370 females
and 220 males total – were enslaved. This population boom pushed
diverse people from different social strata in ever-closer proximity.[29]

To profit from that demand for housing, Drouet shrewdly (or despe-
rately) rented out rooms in her Rue d'Amour residence, and as a result the
house became the setting for community and conflict. According to subsequent testimony from a white tenant named Joseph Mitchell, he came
into conflict with his fellow boarder, "a free negro woman named Victoire
L'esperanza." Mitchell reportedly observed "the Negro Louis[,] a slave of
Mr. Stais" walk into L'esperanza's room. Louis stood accused of robbing
his master of $400, so Mitchell hoped to capture Louis and collect the
reward money. Mitchell barged into L'esperanza's room, a trespass that
certainly violated the free black woman's personal space. But when
Mitchell entered the woman's bedroom, Louis' mother, "a free negro
woman named Esther," restrained Mitchell long enough for her son to
escape. As Esther held him, Mitchell claimed, he saw in her bosom "a big

---

Pablo," SLCB, 17:I, November 5, 1821, AANO; "St. Germain, Francois," SLCB,
November 20, 1822; Nolan, *Sacramental Records*. Adelaida's baptism was erroneously
recorded in the funeral book and later transferred into the baptismal records. For
St. Germain's burial record, see "St. Germain, Francois," *SLCF*, September 7, 1822,
61, AANO. On death as a window into social life during slavery, see Brown, *The Reaper's
Garden*.

[28] Campanella, *Bienville's Dilemma*, 29; University of Virginia's Historical Census Data
Browser, http://mapserver.lib.virginia.edu/.

[29] Population numbers taken from 1820 United States Federal Census, www.ancestry.com.
[database on-line], Provo, UT: Ancestry.com Operations, Inc., 2010. Images reproduced
by FamilySearch.

and heavy load like money wrapped in a kind of white linen," a bundle that Mitchell assumed was the money that Louis had stolen. L'esperanza, Mitchell concluded, "appear[ed] to be a concealer of thieves and stolen things."[30]

The scene that unfolded inside of the bedroom that a free black woman rented from a free woman of color implicated people from every social station. Though Mathieu Charles Staes was physically absent, the presence of his bondman Louis and the wealth that he embodied meant that Staes had a material interest in what happened in that room. Staes' rise and fall in New Orleans paralleled that of many others. In 1810, Staes, an "ironmonger and storekeeper," lived with his wife Mary on Levée Street (present-day Decatur Street). Between that year and 1817, he traded several slaves, including Maria, a twenty-three-year-old purchased in June 1810 (it is unclear when Staes purchased Louis).[31] Staes' finances suffered during the Panic of 1837, and a few years later the septuagenarian died insolvent.[32]

That bedroom became a safe space for two women of African descent, both of whom were likely born into slavery and later freed, to nurture a close friendship. By 1820, Orleans Parish was home to over 3,000 free black women and girls due to *coartación* (the right to self-purchase) in the Spanish period and Caribbean migrations. However, *partus sequitur ventrum*, the doctrine that held that the status of the child followed that of the mother, ensured that enslaved women gave birth to enslaved children. Louis' bondage, then, suggests that Esther was enslaved at the time of his birth. The names "Victoire," "L'esperanza," and "Esther" were all common among the city's bondswomen. And Mitchell described Victoire L'esperanza as a "free negro woman," which indicates

---

[30] Deposition, Joseph Mitchell before Mayor Joseph Roffignac, New Orleans, June 21, 1822, MSS 44, Folder 13, HNOC. Mitchell committed an act of dubious legality. On the one hand, Section 32 of the Black Code of 1806 authorized any "freeholder" to "seize and correct" any slave who was "absent from his usual place of working or residence." Section 37, however, empowered masters and their deputies to pursue runaways "wherever they may be, without prior notice, *except* in the principal dwelling house" (emphasis added). An Act Prescribing the Rules and Conduct to be Observed with Respect to Negroes and Other Slaves of this Territory, June 7, 1806, in Lislet, *A General Digest*, 107.

[31] Hall, *Database*.

[32] In *Bertoli v. The Citizens' Bank* (1846) before the Louisiana Supreme Court, the Citizens' Bank, which had given Staes three different mortgages on his house and lot, disputed the liquidation of his estate following his death. In the 1850 US Census, Mary Staës, his widow, is listed as owning six slaves. See *Bertoli v. The Citizens' Bank* (1846), 1 La. Ann.119, 1846 WL 3368 (La.).

that he did not believe her to have been of mixed racial ancestry. Such shared experiences perhaps drew these women into a close friendship.[33]

Finally, L'esperanza's bedroom offered a free mother and her enslaved son a safe harbor in which they nurtured kinship ties in a society determined to exploit if not sever such bonds. By the 1820s, New Orleans was becoming the capital of the US domestic slave trade. Every coffle that passed from the port, through the city's streets, and onto auction blocks reminded passersby of the fragility of black family. Yet rather than repress their bond for fear of an eventual separation, mother and son defended it. Esther reportedly harbored her son, hid his plunder, and subdued a white man long enough to open for her son an ephemeral path to liberty. Though such actions might not conform to bourgeois notions of respectability often rendered unavailable to the impoverished, Esther engaged in a potent act of resistance when she defended her son within a system of domination.[34]

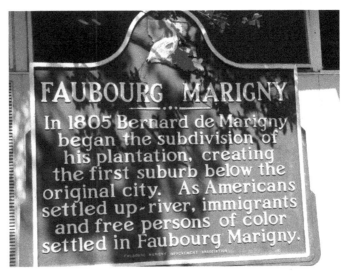

FIGURE 3.2 Historical marker for Faubourg Marigny, New Orleans. It makes no mention of enslaved residents in that neighborhood's history
(photograph by the author).

[33] University of Virginia's Historical Census Data Browser, http://mapserver.lib.virginia .edu/. On manumission, see Schafer, *Becoming Free, Remaining Free*, Prologue.
[34] On slavery and motherhood, see Morgan, *Laboring Women*; Hartman, *Scenes of Subjection*.

"PLACES OF RIOT AND INTOXICATION"

One question about the altercation in Drouet's home remains: If Louis and Esther did steal the money, how did they plan to launder such a large sum? A glimpse into the dynamic underworld of neighborhood taverns reveals bustling centers of cross-racial commerce where any commodity – alcohol, sex, chance, and even illegally imported slaves – could be purchased for the right price. The tavern was a cultural and commercial institution, a place of opportunity and exploitation for enslaved men and women, free people of color, and white people of varying national backgrounds and class positions. Some taverns were licensed commercial spaces, while others were private residences rendered public to those who sought amusements. In both cases, they were a central part of the neighborhood fabric across the early city. In some instances, the interracial intimacies housed under the tavern's roof defied the hardening lines and hierarchies imposed by dominant society and allowed enslaved persons to participate in the material culture that their labor produced. But every such asymmetrical encounter contained systemic risk, and participants quarreled in such houses even as local authorities subjected these spaces to surveillance. Such surveillance held potentially dangerous implications for all participants, but especially for slaves.

In 1802 a visitor to New Orleans recorded the following:

> The city abounds with tippling houses. At every cross street of the town and suburbs, one sees those places of riot and intoxication crowded day and night. The low orders of every colour, white, yellow, and black, mix indiscriminately at these receptacles, finding a market for their pilferings, and solacing their cares with tobacco and brandy. Gambling is practised to an incredible excess. To dancing there is no end. – Such a motley crew, and incongruous scene![35]

Like the Mississippi River and the auction block, taverns and public houses defined the physical and social cityscape of early New Orleans. Licensed coffee houses, cafés, and taverns predominated on Royal and Chartres Streets, but they also operated with varying levels of visibility across the entire French Quarter. Jean Lafitte's Blacksmith Shop (Figure 3.3), located on the corner of Bourbon and St. Phillip Streets, allegedly functioned as a front for the privateer's lucrative illicit trade – including contraband slaves. The Café des Améliorations, located on the edge of the old city at the corner of Rampart and Toulouse Streets, catered primarily to French Creoles, while the Cafés des Refugiés (or Café des

---

[35] Berquin-Duvallon and Davis, *Travels in Louisiana*, 53–54.

Exiles) catered to Saint Dominguan émigrés. In addition, in 1814 the *Courrier de la Louisiane* announced the opening of another establishment, Maspero's Exchange, formerly Bernard Tremoulet's Exchange Commercial Coffee-House. Located at the intersection of Chartres and St. Louis Streets, this two-story building became a preeminent bar, gambling parlor, and slave auction block. According to its initial advertisements, owners shared a "determination to spare neither pains nor expense, to conduct it in a style of elegance never before witnessed in this place, and to render the house really and permanent [*sic*] useful to commercial gentlemen and the public in general." In exchange for a $5 subscription fee, members enjoyed a reading room stocked with the latest political, geographic, and commercial publications, enviable access in an international city.[36]

Much to the displeasure of some local gentlemen, not all bars catered exclusively to local gentlemen. Indeed, these establishments proved so popular that the 1811 New Orleans City Directory listed nearly twice as many publicans as it did doctors. Men and women, including a Widow Schmidt, described themselves as "cabaretiers."[37] These tavern keepers bought operating licenses from the city government. In *Ramozay et al. v. The Mayor &c. of New Orleans* (1811), "grog-shop" owners complained that the mayor required an annual licensing fee of $100 for an inclusive license that authorized them to sell alcohol, operate a pool table, and keep an inn or boarding house. The plaintiffs sought less expensive licenses that authorized the sale of alcohol only. The Court found in favor of the City.[38]

Interestingly, when slaves illegally patronized licensed taverns, they indirectly funded the government charged with oppressing them. Local officials did not recognize such indirect support from slaves, who could not legally purchase alcohol from these shops. The *Code Noir* stated:

intoxicating liquors shall not be sold to slaves, without a written permission from their master ... any person violating that provision shall incur a penalty; and moreover, be answerable to the owner for all damages which the master may suffer in consequence thereof.

---

[36] *Louisiana Courier*, November 18, 1814. Roulhac Toledano, *The National Trust Guide to New Orleans* (New York: John Wiley, 1996), 19–21.

[37] 1811 New Orleans City Directory.

[38] *Ramozay et al. v. The Mayor &c. of New Orleans* (1811), 1 Mart. (o.s.) 241, 1811 WL 1028 (La.Terr.Super.Orleans).

FIGURE 3.3 Lafitte's Blacksmith Shop, ca. 1960. Lafitte's Blacksmith Shop gained national fame in the twentieth century as one of Tennessee Williams' favorite nightspots. The site was added to the National Register of Historical Places in 1970 for its "briquet-entre-poteaux" ("brick-between-post") architecture (Getty Images).

As James Pitot, the city's second mayor, complained, "Hundreds of licensed taverns openly sell to slaves, and, in making them drunk, become throughout the day and night receivers of stolen goods from their masters." Parties given by free people of color, he complained, attracted "the scum of such people and of those slaves who, eluding their owner's surveillance, go there to bring their plunder."[39] Governor Claiborne shared Pitot's revulsion. In 1804, he learned "that the Holders of Slaves complained generally of the negligence of the Police," whose inability to keep slaves out of taverns reportedly resulted in low productivity and therefore increased labor costs to their owners. And as the visitor quoted at length above noted, "The low orders of every colour, white, yellow, and black, mix indiscriminately." Local leaders feared that these "incongruous scenes" in a slave society would lead to social instability, illegal trade, and radical politics. They called for increased regulation.[40] In 1808, the New Orleans City Council Orleans passed an ordinance to regulate "inns, public boarding houses, coffee-houses, billard-houses [*sic*], taverns, and other places of entertainment in the City, Suburbs and Liberties." It imposed a fine of $10 on any establishment that sold alcohol without a license. It forbade the selling of liquor to "any Indian," and allowed alcohol to slaves only with the written permission of their masters (soldiers in the garrison faced the same limitation, as they required written approval from an officer). Likely in an attempt to prevent theft from their owners, slaves were required to purchase alcohol "in coin"; barter was expressly prohibited unless the slave could produce written authorization from a master. Tavern keepers who disobeyed risked fines and civil suits from disgruntled slave owners.[41]

---

[39] An Act Prescribing the Rules and Conduct to be Observed with Respect to Negroes and other Slaves of this Territory, §28, in Lislet, A General Digest, 105. James Pitot and Robert D. Bush, *Observations on the Colony of Louisiana, from 1796 to 1802* (Baton Rouge: Published for the Historic New Orleans Collection by the Louisiana State University Press, 1979), 29.

[40] WCCC to John Watkins, New Orleans, July 8, 1806, Claiborne and Rowland, *Letter Books*, III:357; Berquin-Duvallon and John Davis, *Travels in Louisiana*, 53–54.

In colonial New York City, for example, John Hughson's waterfront tavern allowed socializing among the "lower orders" – slaves, free blacks, and poor whites – who allegedly master minded the Great Negro Plot of 1741. Linebaugh and Rediker, *The Many-Headed Hydra*. On the Great Negro Plot, see Jill Lepore, *New York Burning: Liberty, Slavery and Conspiracy in Eighteenth-Century Manhattan* (New York: Knopf, 2005); Thomas J. Davis, *A Rumor of Revolt: The "Great Negro Plot" in Colonial New York* (New York: Free Press, 1985).

[41] New Orleans City Council, "An Ordinance Concerning the Police of Inns, Public Boarding-Houses, Coffee-Houses, Billard-Houses, Taverns and Other Places of

Even still, "all types of men came to New Orleans," and a culture of drinking tied them into a diverse if hierarchic fraternity. New Englanders and Germans, Irishmen and Africans congregated in the city's spaces, and alcohol provided the social lubricant that set their social betters on edge.[42] Tavern keepers had every incentive to let market demand, not laws or racist ideologies, govern their trade. José, "a Spanish negroe," ran away from his master on New Year's Day of 1810. Since three of his fingers had been chopped off, it is likely that this escape was not José's first effort at disobedience. "It is supposed that he has sold his clothes and a blanket to buy liquors," his owner reasoned, "which prevents him to come back to his master."[43] In his case, it is hard to know whether his owner or his possible addiction was the more brutal master, though the latter burden likely helped him to cope with and temporarily escape the former. In 1816, a serviceman named Dr. Will Williams complained that "Abner Vuissoz, tavern keeper, holds a riotous and disorderly house, at the Faubourg Marigny behind [four] St. Charles and further [sells] liquors to the soldiers of the Garrison, contrary to the Police regulations."[44] Such disregard for the law prompted new legislation: An 1818 Louisiana law stated, "Whoever shall be guilty of keeping any disorderly inn, tavern, ale house, tipling [*sic*] house, gaming-house or brothel, shall suffer fine or imprisonment, or both."[45]

Still, slaves continued to purchase alcohol from these establishments, and the consequences proved deadly for them and costly for their owners. This was the case in *Delery v. Mornet* (1822), which reached the Supreme Court of Louisiana. According to one witness, the plaintiff's bondman named Jasmin entered Mornet's house, purchased alcohol, drank it, and stayed for about fifteen minutes. Jasmin then left Mornet's residence and boarded a canoe. Accounts differ over what came next. In one version of events, a drunken Jasmin accidentally fell overboard. In a competing narrative, Jasmin quarreled with another drunken slave on the boat, and when

Entertainment Within the City, Suburbs and Liberties of the City of New-Orleans," in *Police Code, or Collection of the Ordinances of Police Made by the City Council of New Orleans* (New Orleans: J. Renard, Printer of the Corporation, 1808). Early American Imprints, Series 2, no. 15740. March 28, 2014, http://infoweb.newsbank.com.

[42] Clark, *New Orleans*, 279. On drunkenness in the early republic, see Gilfoyle, *City of Eros*, chapter 4; Rorabaugh, *The Alcoholic Republic*.

[43] De Bellegarde [owner], "Run Away," *L'Ami des Lois*, January 18, 1810.

[44] Deposition, Will Williams before Macarty, New Orleans, May 22, 1816, NYHS NOC 8:12.

[45] An Act to Amend the Penal Laws of this State, §7, March 19, 1818, in Lislet, *A General Digest*, 388.

a white man threatened to flog both of them as punishment. Jasmin dove into the water to escape. Whatever the precipitating events, Jasmin drowned, and the plaintiff sought compensation from Mornet. The court ruled in Delery's favor. Since Jasmin was Negro, the court reasoned, the defendant should have known that Jasmin was a slave who could not legally purchase alcohol under his own authority. Judge Martin declared, "the presumption being, that a black man is a slave; as by far the greatest proportion of persons of that color are, in this state, held in slavery." The presumption that all blacks were enslaved was necessary to govern: "There would be no possibility of punishing illegal acts relating to that species of property, if the knowledge of the actual slavery of the negro was essentially to be proven in the trespasser." Jasmine's blackness should have been enough to impute slave status. When Mornet failed to presume Jasmine's enslavement and sold him alcohol, the vendor started a chain of events that ended with the death of Delery's human property. The court ordered Mornet to pay and, in so doing, reinforced the connection between blackness and slavery.[46]

The drunkenness that taverns facilitated precipitated violence within tavern walls and in the public streets. One man watched from his window near the corner of Bourbon and Ursulines Streets as two "Negres" quarreled at about 8:30 in the morning. They fought for about five or six minutes before a Mr. Schmidt (perhaps a relative of the widowed barkeep) separated them. It is unclear why the two men fought or whether or not they were drunk from the night before, but an account of their fracas reached the mayor's office.[47] In another instance, Jean Baptiste Voiro testified that he and a group of friends had gathered at a watering hole named the Lobri Causant when a certain Lambert barged in and began insulting Voiro, calling him "a slave trader, fool (*coyon*), coward (*capon*), and other equally insulting names." That these men considered "slave trader" an insult on par with fool and coward speaks to the uneasy relationship between southern ideologies of paternalism and global economic shifts toward capitalism. Indeed, "trader" at times carried anti-Semitic connotations as well. In launching those insults, Lambert challenged Voiro's manhood. Voiro and his friends hustled Lambert out of the bar, but the latter returned with two sabers intent on stabbing Voiro. The group eventually overpowered him, but this vignette illuminates the ways that insults, ideologies, and alcohol could prove a deadly

---

[46] *Delery v. Mornet* (1822), 11 Mart. (o.s.) 4, 1822 WL 1268 (La.).
[47] Deposition, Antoine Lavergne before Mayor Mather, New Orleans, August 19, 1811, my translation, NYHS NOC 8:9.

combination in taverns filled with intoxicated people.[48] Finally, drunken sailors made easy targets for local criminals. An unknown assailant shot John Palmer, a white workman aboard the *Two Friends*. Palmer testified that the night before, "a moment before gunfiring," he walked along the levee toward the market. He "stopt for easing himself" when "he was struck on the back of his head with a billet, then he rose and went on the levee where he was shot." When unable to secure medical attention, he went back to his Faubourg Marigny boarding house.[49]

As in speakeasies and shebeens across the world, house parties and taverns brought people together, and those heterogeneous mixtures relied on person-to-person networks of trust. Though slaves were most vulnerable in those spaces, the need for secrecy around illicit activities pervaded several segments of society. Those who enjoyed same-sex intimacies, for example, could become subject to prosecution. In 1805 Governor Claiborne, under the advisement of the Legislative Council, decreed the following: "Every person who shall hereafter be duly convicted of any manner of rape, or of the detestable and abominable crime against nature, committed with mankind or beast, shall suffer imprisonment at hard labour for life." Conceivably, queer desires could turn even privileged white men into prisoners.[50]

Similarly, slaves in all gatherings, even those dominated by free persons of color, could become subject to prosecution, punishment, and ostracism. Arnaud Fonvergne, a free man of color, testified that while attending a house party on Jefferson Street, he noticed an enslaved girl (*une fille de couleur esclave*) on the dance floor. According to his testimony, Fonvergne

---

[48] "le declarant qu'il a traite d'esclaves, de coyon, de capon et d'autre denominations aussi insultante." Deposition, Jean Baptiste Voiro before Macarty, New Orleans, July 6, 1818, my translation, NYHS NOC 8:14. On anti-Semitic connotations associated with "slave trader," see Johnson, *Soul by Soul*, 24–25.

  For an online dictionary of Cajun slang, see SugieBee, "Cajun French Language Dictionary," http://sugiebee.blogspot.com/p/cajun-french-language-dictionary.html, accessed September 21, 2012.

[49] A sympathetic bystander took Palmer to Charity Hospital. The doctor was not in, so Palmer went to the Faubourg Marigny house where he boarded. Later that night when guardsmen investigated barges near the crime scene, "everybody there seemed or pretended to be asleep, only one voice answered, being roused, they had heard nothing." Deposition, John Palmer before Macarty, New Orleans, June 5, 1818 NYHS NOC 8:14.

[50] An Act for the punishment of Crimes and Misdemeanors, May 4, 1805, *General Digest* §2. See also George Chauncey, *Gay New York: Gender, Urban Culture, and the Makings of the Gay Male World, 1890–1940* (New York: Basic Books, 1994).

  As Chauncey cautions, such laws notwithstanding, 20th-century binaries between heterosexuality and homosexuality did not necessarily apply to earlier periods, and men (and likely people of other genders as well) created a more fluid sexual environment than such laws might suggest.

expressed "concern that it was against the law for a slave to dance with
free people, and told one of his friends as much." Perhaps Fonvergne
feared that the presence of a slave woman jeopardized his own safety
from her master and from local authorities. Or perhaps the young woman
hoped to pass for free that night and the privileged man publicized her
status to shame her. Whatever the case, Marseille, also a free man of color,
overheard Fonvergne's remark and grew incensed. Marseille "hit
Fonvergne on the head with a stick," and Marseille's friends finished the
job. "Marseille is the one who brought the slave to the party," Fonvergne
groused. "[Marseille] had one of his friends dance with her, and escorted
her out." This story illustrates the complexities of intersecting hierarchies
of race, status, and gender in New Orleans by the 1820s. This young
woman gained entry to the party because of her relationship to Marseille
and his friends, presumably free black men, but another man from the
same caste wanted her excluded. The young woman's relationship to
Marseille is unclear. They might have been acquaintances, relatives, or
lovers. He might have been her owner. Whatever the case, diverging
opinions on the legitimacy of this slave woman's presence at the party
sparked a violent conflict between free men of color.[51]

In addition to dancing and fisticuffs, New Orleans taverns also teemed
with commercial sex. As female sex workers advertised their bodies before
the public, they marked their houses and neighborhoods as part of
a disreputable sexual geography – much to the dismay of their ostensibly
respectable neighbors. Two white men complained that Laurent Boussard
(or perhaps Broussard), also presumably a white man, ran a "house of
prostitution" (*un maison de prostitution*) on the corner of Julia and
Baronne Streets in Faubourg St. Marie. On a Saturday afternoon
in July 1818, four to six presumably white "femmes prostituées" who
lived at Boussard's dwelling allegedly attacked another female boarder in
a neighboring residence. The deponents also complained about the
women's attire, which the men described as "skirts that stop just below
the belt" (*les jupes jusqu'au dessus de la ceinture*) or even skirts "without
front or back" (*leurs jupes pas derrière et pas devant*). The display of these
women's bodies constituted "a public scandal," the men argued, one that
brought disgrace to the entire neighborhood.[52]

[51] Deposition, Arnaud Fonvergne before Roffignac, New Orleans, March 23, 1822, my
translation, NYHS NOC 9:3.
[52] Deposition, Jean David Laizer before Macarty, New Orleans, July 13, 1818, my translation
NYHS NOC 8:14; Deposition, Joseph Taboury before Macarty, New Orleans, July 14,

Most free, working-class women who engaged in sex work did so in response to limited earning power in the wage labor market. Enslaved women, on the other hand, labored as sex workers at their masters' bidding or to earn money for themselves. Traveler C. C. Robin alleged that masters encouraged their enslaved women "to use their free time in prostitution and to report back each day the amount they have taken." Supposedly, these women sought "generous lovers" who visited these enslaved women, not in brothels, but in their masters' homes. The women then brought some or all earnings to her owners. "The lady of the house, who ordinarily has charge of the matter, grows accustomed to seeing lovers come and go to her Negro servant and she arranges to have them let in at night." While this account encompasses three of Robin's favorite themes – misogyny, French Creole libertinage, and African hypersexuality – his vignette nonetheless expands the concept of hiring out beyond the artisanal work of skilled bondmen, conventionally defined as blacksmiths, coopers, and so on. Domestic slave labor could include sex work, and in the process the master's house could become a site in the geographies of New Orleans prostitution.[53]

It is challenging to document prostitution among enslaved women in the early nineteenth century, but travel narratives reveal the ways white males gazed on and consumed the bodies of women of African descent. Over the nineteenth century Americans created a hypersexualized image of New Orleans, a trope that they reproduced in literature.[54] During the transition

---

1818, my translation NYHS NOC 8:14. Even as Laizer used local authorities to discipline these women's sexualities he took advantage of the sexual availability of women of color and white women. Laizer fathered children with his white wife, Hélène Ségoire, and with free woman of color Justine Bacquié. The latter relationship resulted in The Toucoutou Affair, one of antebellum New Orleans' greatest race-making scandals. In that case, Laizer and Bacquié's daughter Anastasie Desarzant unsuccessfully sued a woman for slander for having called the former woman a person of color rather than white. See Thompson, *Exiles at Home*, chapter 2. On prostitution in early New Orleans, see Judith Kelleher Schafer, *Brothels, Depravity, and Abandoned Women: Illegal Sex in Antebellum New Orleans* (Baton Rouge: Louisiana State University Press, 2009); Alecia P. Long, *The Great Southern Babylon: Sex, Race, and Respectability in New Orleans, 1865–1920* (Baton Rouge: Louisiana State University Press, 2004). See also Cynthia M. Blair, *I've Got to Make My Livin': Black Women's Sex Work in Turn-of-the-Century Chicago* (Chicago: The University of Chicago Press, 2010); Philip Howell, *Geographies of Regulation: Policing Prostitution in Nineteenth-Century Britain and the Empire* (Cambridge: Cambridge University Press, 2009); Christine Stansell, *City of Women: Sex and Class in New York, 1789–1860* (Urbana: University of Illinois Press, 1982), 172–175.

[53] C. C. Robin and Stuart Landry, *Voyage to Louisiana, 1803–1805* (New Orleans: Pelican, 1966), 246.

[54] Emily Clark, *The Strange History of the American Quadroon: Free Women of Color in the Revolutionary Atlantic* (Chapel Hill: The University of North Carolina Press, 2013).

to United States authority, United States Major Amos Stoddard accused Spanish settlers in Louisiana of preferring "a fat black wench to any other female!"[55] Though sex with black women and the beating of black men were common enough to be entitled twin "Virginian Luxuries" in a contemporary oil painting, Stoddard used the sexual preference for the allegedly grotesque black woman's body as shorthand for Spanish deviance. Timothy Flint, a Congregational missionary from New England, recorded observations of his travels to the Lower Mississippi River Valley in the 1820s. He complained about the absence of religion (he compared its level of heathenism to that of "Hindostan") and the surfeit of vice. Natchez he thought "full of boatmen, mulattoes, houses of ill fame ... in short, the refuse of the world." And if Natchez was Sodom, then New Orleans was Gomorrah. Even still, the missionary praised the city's "yellow women ... remarkable for the perfect symmetry of their forms, and for their fine expression of eye." These exotic "nurses" attended any sick "stranger ... brought up by prevailing fever." Yellow women assisted the male migrants who suffered from yellow fever, a disease both epidemiological and ideological. "Yellow" women belonged to a host of racial and economic categories, including slave, free, and freed. Whatever the case, Flint valued these women based on the services that they offered to men.[56]

Sex work perhaps yielded wages, but it also carried risk. Customers could refuse to pay, and sex workers had little protection from the routine sadism that underpinned slave societies. Sex workers also risked contracting sexually transmitted infections. A visitor to New Orleans described the arrival of a shipment of "Universal Regenerator," a syphilis cure: "What even the most unabashed libertine would not have done in Paris, here was done by the ladies, who queued up openly in the streets to buy the Regenerator." "Ladies," he suggested, would not publicly admit that they had ever had sex, let alone give tacit acknowledgement of a sexually transmitted infection. But those who had limited access to health care faced an even greater risk. In 1813, the surgeon Chevalier charged LaRonde for the treatment of the latter's bondwoman's

---

[55] Amos Stoddard, *Sketches, Historical and Descriptive of Louisiana* (Philadelphia: Matthew Carey, 1812; reprinted New York: AMS Press, 1973), 283.

[56] Timothy Flint and James Flint, *Recollections of the Last Ten Years, Passed in Occasional Residences and Journeyings in the Valley of the Mississippi, from Pittsburg and the Missouri to the Gulf of Mexico, and from Florida to the Spanish Frontier: In a Series of Letters to the Rev. James Flint, of Salem, Massachusetts* (Boston: Cummings, Hilliard, and Co., 1826), 295, 300. It is not accidental that Flint chose "Hindostan" as the headquarters of godlessness. See Edward W. Said, *Orientalism* (New York: Pantheon Books, 1978).

afflictions, which included persistent coughs, a bronchial infection, and an advanced sexually transmitted infection (*un vice vénérien bien prononcé*). Her symptoms might have included sores, rashes, fatigue, headaches, hair loss, muscle aches, or even dementia. However she contracted the infection, whether from a fellow bondsperson, an owner, or a client, this woman undoubtedly suffered.[57]

Like sex work, gambling also brought diverse crowds into public houses and taverns, and people of African descent labored and perhaps participated in those arenas. Bernard Marigny is believed to have introduced the game of craps to the United States, a pastime he loved so much he named a street in his suburb for it (it was later renamed Burgundy). He was not alone. What one historian argues about New Orleans during the later Jacksonian era applied just as well to the earlier period: "The region's entire economic environment required a gambler's sensibility." In a city where a bet over the outcome of the 1824 gubernatorial election prompted a lawsuit before the Supreme Court of Louisiana, speculators gambled on commodity futures, slave productivity, real estate, and even the city itself. New Orleans also attracted professional gamblers. Like sailors and boatmen, gamblers also spent significant amounts of time on the riverboats that traveled the Mississippi. The men were known for that mobility as well as their masculinity, and they participated in a vibrant underworld in the city.[58]

Testimonies from observers offer a glimpse of the diverse commercial and social worlds in these gambling establishments. Migrant Joseph Pryor spent a great deal of his six weeks in New Orleans touring the city's houses

[57] Robin, *Voyage*, 41; Invoice, Chevalier (surgeon) to M. LaRonde, New Orleans, June 29, 1813, *Chevalier v. LaRonde*, MC 532, Folder 12, TU. On the sadistic violence of slavery, see Doris Garraway, *The Libertine Colony: Creolization in the Early French Caribbean* (Durham: Duke University Press, 2005).

  "Universal Regenerator" is a curious phrase also mentioned as part of an advertisement on the walls of the gentlemen's restroom in a downtown hotel in New York City. "Our Downtown Hotel," *New York Times*, January 31, 1853. Around the same time, the phrase gained currency as a synonym for Jesus, who through salvation became the "Universal Regenerator" for mankind. By the 1860s, the phrase applied to a divinity, a health supplement, and a cure for sexually transmitted infections.

[58] *Montillet v. Shiff* (1825), 4 Mart.(n.s.) 83, 1825 WL 1350 (La.). In that case the plaintiff and defendant gambled on the outcome of the gubernatorial election between Bernard Marigny and Jacques Villeré. On gambling in the early republican and antebellum south, see Joshua D. Rothman, *Flush Times and Fever Dreams: A Story of Capitalism and Slavery in the Age of Jackson* (Athens: University of Georgia Press, 2012), 184, chapters 5 and 6. Thomas C. Buchanan, *Black Life on the Mississippi: Slaves, Free Blacks, and the Western Steamboat World* (Chapel Hill: The University of North Carolina Press, 2004); Ann Fabian, *Card Sharps, Dream Books, & Bucket Shops: Gambling in 19th-Century America* (Ithaca, NY: Cornell University Press, 1990).

of chance. In Laurent Boussards's house he spied "several persons ... playing there equally," a group that included "adventurers from the western country." Pryor visited other houses in which people "gambl[ed] at the roulette." The night before his testimony he visited Richard McFarland's, where he saw "the wheel of fortune a going." At Wyatt's establishment, "the gambling was kept by a mulatto of about ten or twelve years," thought to have been the proprietor's son. Other persons of African descent, both slave and free, likely worked in similar capacities in the city's houses of chance.[59]

Whether persons of African descent entered these establishments as gamblers or as laborers, they nonetheless encountered unsavory and violent characters. One witness described a white man named Macarty who "frequents grogshops, gaming houses, and is generally known for a gambler." Macarty, the witness claimed, "though he be able to work, has neither profession nor trade, nor any property wherewith to maintain himself." Macarty "lives idle," the witness continued, "without following any honest occupation to procure himself the means of subsistence." Rather than enter the labor market, sell his sweat, and accumulate property in the boomtown that attracted so many profiteers, Macarty, like many other investors, chose to gamble instead.[60] Those efforts were filled with the thrill of uncertainty and the threat of ruin. Intense, violent conflicts over gambled goods sometimes involved the authorities. Free man of color Valcroix Allain testified that he took part in "a game of chance" hosted by a cabaret keeper adjacent to the levee. At some point Allain and the proprietor had a disagreement, which prompted Allain to complain before the mayor. Gambling attracted a diverse crowd, but it is unclear the extent to which slaves patronized those establishments. In whatever capacity they entered, however, they stood in close proximity to financial ruin and violence.[61]

"AT THE OLD PLACE DOWNTOWN AND IN PRESENCE OF THE USUAL ... CROWD OF SPECTATORS"

The flows of diverse people of all statuses through the confined spaces of boarding houses and taverns, for example, undermine overly neat

---

[59] Deposition, Joseph Pryor before Mather, New Orleans, March 20, 1811, NYHS NOC 8:9.

[60] Deposition, William Cook before Mather, New Orleans, August 14, 1811, NYHS NOC 8:9.

[61] Valcroix Allain before Girod, New Orleans, March 19, 1813, my translation, NYHS NOC 8:11.

distinctions between public and private. Though privately owned, they attracted diverse crowds and were subject to state surveillance. These establishments flourished as the state tolerated the transgressions that made the city infamous. The racquette field and Congo Square, by contrast, were public grounds where the gambler's money fever intersected with African diasporic sport and culture for public amusement. On Sundays, as Anglo-American Protestants in New England attended church services, many New Orleanians followed morning mass at the St. Louis Church with more worldly amusements. Even as these licit activities fostered social heterogeneity, cultural creativity, and economic opportunity, both of them – one forgotten, the other memorialized – turned people of African descent into raced objects on display for public consumption. On Sunday afternoons, spectators in New Orleans gazed on the burdened practice of African diaspora.

Long before European settlers arrived in North America, native peoples played a game similar to stickball that became the antecedent to lacrosse. As one historian writes, "there is little doubt from descriptions emanating from . . . tribal records east of the Mississippi that the ancestor of modern lacrosse – the name derives from the French word for the stick – was widespread." Those matches held social and sacred significance, so participants engaged in extensive physical preparation and they sought the ritual expertise of spiritual leaders. The extensive wagering that accompanied matches reallocated material resources, and the frequently violent contests also served diplomatic functions between nations.[62]

By the time Pierre Clément de Laussat, Napoleon's appointee to the governorship of Louisiana, described it, the game of racquette had much in common with its pre-colonial predecessor – with the key exception that the athletes he observed were of African descent. Laussat described the heady atmosphere of a Sunday match:

The Negroes and mulattoes, in groups of four, six, eight – some from the city, others from the country – challenged each other to *raquette des sauvages* . . . where bets rose from five to six hundred piastres fortes. Each team distinguished itself by ribbons of motley colors. The game was dangerous. Rarely did it happen that there were no accidents, no arms or legs broken. Metairie, more commonly called the Plaine Labarre, usually served as a tilting ground. The road was full with an unbroken line of traveling coaches, cabriolets, horses, carts, spectators, and players. The escorted winners retired triumphant. By a strange inconsistency,

[62] Anthony Aveni, "The Indian Origins of Lacrosse," *Colonial Williamsburg Journal* (Winter 2010), available at www.history.org/Foundation/journal/winter10/lacrosse.cfm, accessed March 2, 2014.

only too common, the spectators cheered and encouraged the skill and triumph of those very athletes whom they dreaded having to fight someday.[63]

Described by one scholar as "a lacrosse-like Choctaw Indian game," native and white men also played racquette, but only the matches between black men attracted this level of enthusiasm. Regardless of the sexual practices of individual participants or spectators, the entire performance was rooted in a racialized homoeroticism. What Laussat called an "inconsistency" was instead quite consistent with the enactment of white supremacist power: free spectators trained a homoerotic gaze upon the desired and feared black male body from the safety of the sidelines. In the era of the Haitian Revolution and the 1811 Deslondes Revolt, Laussat's remark about "dread" conjured visions of Toussaint L'Ouverture, Henri Christophe, and Jean-Jacques Dessalines. Virile black male bodies pitted against one another on this field confirmed the dominant society's conceptions of black masculinity – as well as their ability to contain it.[64]

The violent choreography of these ritualized games was part of its appeal, but it extracted a high physical and likely psychic cost from the men who competed before the jeering crowds. As twentieth-century novelist Ralph Ellison details in *Invisible Man*, black men's violent jousts for the pleasure of white male viewers proved physically and psychically costly. In the Battle Royal, the unnamed protagonist undergoes public sexual humiliation, a bloody group fight, and a frenzied competition for money. Ellison's fictional description of the Battle Royal sits quite close to the historical events on the racquette field. Laussat acknowledged that broken bones were a matter of course. In the absence of protective gear, other visible and invisible injuries were likely just as common. The men likely suffered

[63] Pierre-Clément de Laussat, *Memoirs of My Life to My Son during the Years 1803 and after, Which I Spent in Public Service in Louisiana as Commissioner of the French Government for the Retrocession to France of That Colony and for Its Transfer to the United States* (Baton Rouge: Published for the Historic New Orleans Collection by the Louisiana State University Press, 1978), 54. In the pejorative name for the game – "racquettes des sauvages" – the French acknowledged the game's debt to native peoples. By the early nineteenth century when Laussat wrote, the "noble savage" trope had been in use throughout Europe for centuries.

[64] Jerah Johnson, *Congo Square in New Orleans* (New Orleans: Samuel Wilson, Jr. Publications Fund of the Louisiana Landmarks Society, 1995), 36. On the intersections of race, sexuality, and sport, see Kevin Hylton, "'Race,' Sport and Leisure: Lessons from Critical Race Theory," *Leisure Studies* 24, no. 1 (January 2005): 81–98; Thadious M. Davis, *Games of Property: Law, Race, Gender, and Faulkner's Go Down, Moses* (Durham: Duke University Press, 2003); Brian Pronger, *The Arena of Masculinity: Sports, Homosexuality, and the Meaning of Sex* (New York: St. Martin's, 1990), 128.

concussions and other traumatic brain injuries, dislocations, sprains, and bruises. And the long-term effects of such Sunday activities, especially when coupled with the rigors of slave labor during the week, undoubtedly took a cumulative toll on their bodies. And the psychic costs of engaging in a brutal sport for others' pleasure are perhaps indescribable.[65]

Despite legislation in the 1830s that forbade them, these games continued in plain sight until the Civil War. In New Orleans, they were held in the Third District near Claiborne Circle (near present-day Hunter's Field), and by the 1850s reporters covered the matches in local sports columns. In August 1858, the *Daily Crescent* reported on what at that point had become a thirty- or forty-year rivalry between two raquette teams: "the Laville party, composed of city negroes, and the Bayou party, made up of the negroes living out back of town." The use of the term "negroes" suggests that these men were enslaved, but it is also possible that the teams consisted of some combination of free and bound blacks. The men wore regalia: "The Laville donkeys sported blue colors and all wore blue caps; the Bayou boys' colors and caps were red." The atmosphere at the games became so raucous that spectators interfered with the actual match. Once the voyeurs "crowded the field so much, that the darkeys were [loath] to begin, being fearful that the crowd would prevent fair play." The men played for two minutes, realized the crowd was too dense, then took down their targets. Two "public spirited white men" intervened, being "of opinion that the darkeys ought to have fair play – Sunday being their only good day." The "negro" men played their game, "marched off the field," and then thanked the spectators for allowing them to play. Like stickball among native peoples and cricket in the Caribbean, racquette for enslaved players in Louisiana allowed participants to compete and demonstrate their masculinity. On the other hand, the theatrical aspects of this game revealed as much about the spectators as it did the participants. The largely male audience's titillation at this gladiatorial performance sublimated and sated their desire to consume black male bodies even as it affirmed dominant ideologies of white masculinity. Indeed, even the anticipation sent the free spectators into such frenzy that the two white men had to police them. As the sports columnist reflected, "It does us good to see the darkeys at 'racket,' and we hope to see them have a clear field hereafter."[66]

---

[65] Ralph Ellison, *Invisible Man* (New York: Random House, 1952).

[66] *New Orleans Daily Crescent*, August 16, 1858, August 30, 1858, September 20, 1858. (emphasis added) On the outlawing of the sport, see Johnson, *Congo Square*, 45. On

Still, the racquette field provided at least one financial benefit for women of color. "One whole side of the field was flanked by the refreshment booths of turbaned wenches," one observer recorded. As the previous chapter shows, enslaved women belonged to vast commercial networks. Women of color also earned money through commerce on Sundays in the stalls and booths located on the periphery of the sports field. These "turbaned wenches" may have been enslaved women peddlers who sometimes wore *gélés* or *dukus* (West African head wraps), or perhaps they were free women of color who wore *tignons* (hair coverings that ostensibly protected white men from the seductive charms of fair-skinned women of partial African descent). Whatever their status, these women profited from white male spectators in the most American of ways – free trade.[67]

The asymmetrical power relationship between subjects and objects notwithstanding, some of the bondmen likely found on the racquette field some measure of value in their opportunity to compete and win on Sunday afternoons. They could demonstrate athletic prowess, socialize with fellow slaves and other residents, and impress prospective sexual partners. In addition, they sometimes earned money with which they could purchase any number of goods. Sports such as racquette or cricket held regenerative power in the creation of black manhood and, by extension, nationalist ideologies. It is impossible to know exactly what these men derived from the events on the field, but whatever the case, they nonetheless appeared each Sunday to meet the boys on the battlefront:

Racket: The darkeys had their usual Sunday battle at racket last evening at the old place downtown and in presence of the usual multitudinous and excited crowd of spectators. On this occasion, the eagle of victory perched on the banner of the La Villes, and great was the excitement of that party's partizans [*sic*]. The Bayous are

conducting ethnography on the spectators of the performance of Otherness, see Coco Fusco, "The Other History of Intercultural Performance," *The Drama Review* 38, no. 1 (Spring 1994): 143–67. I thank Eng-Beng Lim for this connection between sport and performance.

[67] *The New Orleans Daily Crescent*, August 16, 1858.

Spanish colonial governor Esteban Miró addressed the alleged seduction of white males and interracial concubinage by ordering free women of color to cover their hair with a *tignon*. See Thompson, *Exiles at Home*, 175.

On West African head wraps in antebellum New Orleans, see Evans, *Congo Square*, 59. Evans also mentions enslaved persons' preferences for "oriental and Indian attire," including "Turkish turbans." Such references call to mind the relationships between African and Southeast Asian diasporas worldwide. See Bald, *Bengali Harlem and the Lost Histories of South Asian America*.

now behind; but "never say die" is their motto and there are plenty of Sundays coming on ahead.[68]

Place Congo

If, as Toni Morrison argues, the imagined "blackness that African peoples have come to signify" provided the materiel of American self-fashioning, then Congo Square might be considered a birthplace of this nation. As one of the few sites in the United States where law and custom permitted enslaved persons to drum and dance publicly, Congo Square now represents an early transcendent site of African diasporic cultural production. But Congo Square was no exception to the racist regime in New Orleans or even the plantation Americas; it was constitutive of it. Though some scholars call attention to the way that Congo Square functioned as a safety valve that defused tensions in a hierarchical society, I argue that the site furthered the slave system in a far more fundamental way. Instead of viewing it as a curious coincidence that the burgeoning capital of the US slave economy became known, then and now, as a headquarters of slave music and dance, I view them as inextricably bound. In "blackness *and* enslavement," Morrison writes, "could be found not only the not-free but also, with the dramatic polarity created by skin color, the projection of not-me. The result was a playground for the imagination." Congo Square, I argue, was a physical playground for imagined blackness that, like the slave markets and racquette fields only steps away, gave free persons an opportunity to enjoy a curated and contained blackness. In the

---

[68] *New Orleans Daily Crescent*, September 20, 1858. Hazel Carby expresses the link between sport, gender, and anticolonialism for Trinidadian scholar C. L. R. James: "ideologies of black masculinity, whether conscious or unconscious, were already shaping his understanding of the performative politics of cricket *and* his idea of how colonialism should be opposed." See Hazel Carby, *Race Men* (Cambridge, MA: Harvard University Press, 1998), 120. The song "Meet De Boys on The Battlefront" appears on a record by the Wild Tchoupitoulas, one of New Orleans seventy-plus Indian tribes, in collaboration with the Meters and released in 1976.

Hunter's Field remains an important site for the city's Mardi Gras Indians, who use the site as a "battlefront" every year. Some "tribes" process along Bayou St. John, others come from Faubourg Tremé and Uptown New Orleans, but on Mardi Gras Day those who process downtown meet at Hunter's Field, where they compete not with fists, but with the beauty of their suits. See Ned Sublette, *The World That Made New Orleans: From Spanish Silver to Congo Square* (Chicago: Lawrence Hill Books: Distributed by Independent Publishers Group, 2008); Roach, *Cities of the Dead*; Reid Mitchell, *All on a Mardi Gras Day: Episodes in the History of New Orleans Carnival* (Cambridge, MA: Harvard University Press, 1995).

simultaneous observation of, participation in, and distancing from blackness, Americans in Congo Square defined themselves as white and free.
Even as the music, dance, and rituals solaced the oppressed, those same
exact actions simultaneously deepened and destabilized the divide
between blacks and whites, slaves and free persons, objects and subjects.[69]

The five or so acres that made up *Le Place Congo* brought an Atlantic
assembly to Rampart Street, the northern border of the Old City that
extended from Canal Street past the French Quarter. Initially the space
was thought to have been a sacred site, market, and transportation hub
for the Houma nation, though it is also likely that other indigenous
peoples, such as the Bayougoula, Tunica, and Acolapissa nations, also
gathered there. During the French period, it continued as a market and
thoroughfare. African captives, many of them experienced traders taken
from urban West and West Central Africa; indigenous persons, both
slave and free; and Euro-Americans of diverse backgrounds produced a
multiracial market culture in the city. Consistent with Catholic beliefs,
the 1724 *Code Noir* specified Sundays as a non-laboring day, and by the
following decade parsimonious masters encouraged bondspersons to
grow crops for their own sustenance for sale in Congo Square's weekend markets. By 1812, after two major changes to the built environment – the dismantling of the Fort St. Ferdinand and the integration of
land purchased from plantation owner Paul-Claude-Joseph Tremé into
the city grid – officials preserved Congo Square for public gatherings.
As will be discussed in the following chapter, such events included
public floggings and executions. A few years later an 1817 city

---

[69] Morrison, *Playing in the Dark*, 6, 38. See also Katrina Thompson, *Ring Shout, Wheel
About: The Racial Politics of Music and Dance in North American Slavery* (Urbana:
University of Illinois Press, 2014), chapter 5.
   Certainly the events at Congo Square can be seen as evidence of African cultural
"survivals" or "retentions" in the Americas. It was one of the few sites in the United
States where African peoples legally congregated, drummed, danced, and practiced
spiritual traditions. As such, it illustrated the cultural connections that united people of
African descent across the Caribbean, Latin America, and the Atlantic World. Yet an
anthropological approach to describing the events relative to their African antecedents
elides the ways that the activities in that place helped to both create and subvert the
historical processes in which it occurred. To be blunt, I am less interested in the transcen-
dence of black belief and more interested in the historical hell in which blacks believed.
Vincent Brown, "Social Death and Political Life in the Study of Slavery," *AHR* 114, no. 5
(December 2009): 1231–1249; Patterson and Kelley, "Unfinished Migrations"; Fabian,
Time and the Other. On the African roots of Congo Square, see Evans, *Congo Square*.
On Congo Square as safety valve, see Rothman, *Slave Country*.

ordinance confined the Sunday gatherings to that one site. There, people from diverse backgrounds produced "a citywide institution."[70]

On the one hand, enslaved and free persons used Sundays at Congo Square to create a local culture that remains distinctive even today. The barrel drums of various sizes and the rhythms they produced, most notably the "bamboula" or "secondline" beat, lay at the heart of the weekly experience. They also played the *banza* (or *banja*), a forerunner to the banjo. The music was accompanied by song, with lyrics drawn from a mixture of French, Spanish, and English as well as African diasporic languages including Ki-Kongo, Haitian Kreyòl, and other *patois* forms from the circum-Caribbean. Finally, as shown in Figure 3.4, enslaved persons danced. And as they arranged their bodies in a rhythmic circle, they took their place within the cosmic communities that crossed the borders of living and dead, past, present, and future.[71]

By extension, Congo Square belonged to the larger Afro-diasporic spiritual geographies of early New Orleans, which stretched from the Saint Louis Church to the bayous outside of the city where some devotees of *Vodun* practiced their rituals. People of African descent, both slave and free, dominated the Catholic church in the colonial and early American periods. Under French and then Spanish administrations, Ursuline nuns accepted pupils of African descent, and Father Antonio ("Pere Antoine") de Sedella, pastor of the Saint Louis Church, enjoyed popular support due to his commitment to the lower orders of believers, including enslaved persons.[72] But after Sunday mass, many Afro-Catholics, like their white counterparts, then congregated in Congo Square. As one editorialist complained in an 1813 edition of the *Louisiana Courier*, local Catholicism "has not in the opinion of the northern preachers a teint sufficiently dark and religious, and notwithstanding the example of the

---

[70] Evans, *Congo Square*, 35; Johnson, *Congo Square*. On Faubourg Tremé, see Michael E. Crutcher, Jr., *Tremé: Race and Place in a New Orleans Neighborhood* (Athens: University of Georgia Press, 2010).

[71] For more technical treatments of music and dance at Congo Square, see Evans, *Congo Square*, and Sublette, *The World That Made New Orleans*. On the ring shout and the African diasporic significance of the circle formation, see Sterling Stuckey, *Slave Culture: Nationalist Theory and the Foundations of Black America* (New York: Oxford University Press, 1987), chapter 1.

[72] Emily Clark, *Masterless Mistresses: The New Orleans Ursulines and the Development of a New World Society, 1727–1834* (Chapel Hill: The University of North Carolina Press, 2007), 5, 230–231; Mary Bernard Deggs, Virginia Meacham Gould, and Charles E. Nolan, *No Cross, No Crown: Black Nuns in Nineteenth-Century New Orleans* (Bloomington: Indiana University Press, 2001).

THE BAMBOULA.

FIGURE 3.4 African Americans dancing and singing the Bamboula, New Orleans, 1800s, © North Wind Picture Archives/Alamy Stock Photo. The skyline for the city center is visible in the distance.

Israelites who were in the habit of dancing before the holy arch, they cannot conceive how it is possible to lift up one's heart to the creator by dancing on a Sunday." For this unnamed yet elite author, Sunday dances were not a distraction from Catholic rituals, but a conduit for them.[73]

Congo Square also lent itself to the practice of voodoo, which one scholar calls "one of the signal achievements of people of African descent in the western hemisphere: a vibrant, sophisticated synthesis of the traditional religions of Dahomey, Yorubaland, and Kongo with an infusion of Roman Catholicism."[74] As historian Rachel Harding writes of Salvador and the Recôncavo in Brazil, Congo Square also became "sacred ground, a place made holy in trauma." The sensationalism associated with voodoo and Congo Square should not obscure the ways that actual people used music, song, and dance to connect with an Atlantic geography of belief and succor with parallels in Candomblé in Brazil, Santería in Cuba, and Shango in Trinidad.[75]

As on the racquette field, in Congo Square people of African descent reclaimed their bodies and created communities even as free, predominately white spectators gazed on them with a mixture of desire and repulsion. Though persons of African descent formed a nucleus, Congo Square attracted people of different backgrounds, locals and tourists alike. In 1819, one observer claimed to have seen 500 people gathered, while subsequent visitors numbered the participants and observers in the thousands. And their numbers only grew into the later antebellum period. Local white residents attended, as did thousands of tourists. Local newspapers encouraged "every stranger" to view the spectacle "once at least, no one will ever regret or forget it." Edward (E.P.) Christy used his observations of songs, music, and dance at Congo Square to create materials for his eponymous performance group. Christy's Minstrels, which he founded in 1843, became popular across the nation and in Europe. Stephen Foster, considered a father of American music, composed songs for the troupe's shows. Similarly, the pianist and composer

---

[73] *Louisiana Courier*, April 14, 1813.
[74] Robert Farris Thompson, *Flash of the Spirit: African and Afro-American Art and Philosophy* (New York: Random House, 1983), 163.
[75] Rachel E. Harding, *A Refuge in Thunder: Candomblé and Alternative Spaces of Blackness* (Bloomington: Indiana University Press, 2000), xiii.

Louis Moreau Gottschalk also found in Congo Square uncompensated inspiration for what became profitable cultural productions.[76]

What were the psychic costs of praying and partying in front of tourists and in walking distance of auction block row? Ex-slave testimonies from the early twentieth century convey two possibilities. Marie Brown, a descendant of Saint-Dominguan émigrés, lived in Faubourg Tremé. Her initial reaction to the interviewer – "No, I ain't tell my secrets to nobody" – reflected wise dissemblance in the Jim Crow era. Brown, a Christian – "I reads my Bible first thing in the morning and last thing at night" – considered Congo Square a site of "devilment." "I never went with hoodoo peoples, but once I saw them dance at Congo Square," pointing to it as she spoke. Of course many self-professed Christians also practiced African-derived beliefs, so Brown's interior world could have been more complicated than she suggested. On the other hand, spirituality in the African diaspora became "an emblem of divergence": Relatively privileged blacks associated themselves with Christianity and left African-derived spiritual systems to the lower orders (at least in public). Brown's discursive distance from hoodoo affirmed her own respectability in Jim Crow Louisiana.[77]

By contrast, Nathan Hobley reveled in the opportunity to narrate exotic aspects of black culture and amusement. Born in 1858, he claimed to know everything about Congo Square. "I always attended the Congo Square functions," he stated. "I was too young to take any active part, but I learned everything." Like Marie Brown, he also distanced himself from voodoo, but he referred to himself as a "Divine Healer … who heals all

---

[76] Evans, *Congo Square*, 34–36, 40. Christy's Minstrels' performances in Mechanics' Hall, for example, became foundational to the creation of a white, working-class male class identity in New York in the years before the Civil War. Eric Lott, *Love & Theft: Blackface Minstrelsy and the American Working Class* (New York: Oxford University Press, 1993), chapter 3.

[77] Interview, Marie Brown to Zoe Posey, May 29, 1940, Clayton and Louisiana Writers' Project, *Mother Wit*, 33–36.

On religion and stratification among persons of African descent in the antebellum South, see Gomez, *Exchanging Our Country Marks*, 228.

On black women, Christianity, and the politics of respectability in the early twentieth century, see Michele Mitchell, *Righteous Propagation: African Americans and the Politics of Racial Destiny after Reconstruction* (Chapel Hill: The University of North Carolina Press, 2004); Evelyn Brooks Higginbotham, *Righteous Discontent: The Women's Movement in the Black Baptist Church, 1880–1920* (Cambridge, MA: Harvard University Press, 1993); Darlene Clark Hine, "Rape and the Inner Lives of Black Women in the Middle West: Preliminary Thoughts on the Culture of Dissemblance," *Signs* 14 (Summer 1989): 912–920.

bodily, temporal, and spiritual ills by prayer, faith, the laying on of hands, and the use of certain herbs and vegetation; also [by] Christian Science, ritualism of the Catholic Church, and occult reasoning." With such varied expertise, one would expect from him a vivid account of Congo Square, which he delivered. He shared stories about noted voodoo practitioner Marie Laveau and the people who could "dance the bamboula," or the African dance named for the drum used in rituals in West Africa, the Caribbean, and Louisiana.[78]

But Hobley's story about his father's experience in Congo Square had little to do with cultural expression and everything to do with the chattel principle. Though he perhaps intended it to be a heartwarming story about the paternalistic affection that tied masters to slaves and thereby held slave families intact, the tale nonetheless represented a "leakage" of the ever-present threat of separation that defined slave life in the era of the domestic slave trade.[79] Reportedly, Hobley's parents belonged to a Mr. Cunningham who owned a plantation downriver from New Orleans. "My parents told me that their master and missis treated them fine, and were good to all their slaves, whom they always spoke of as 'my servants.'" Perhaps this was the case, but it is equally likely that at the height of Jim Crow and the Great Depression Hobley thought it best to narrate the dominant society's romanticized version of antebellum history. Whatever his intentions, he immediately undermined his disclaimer: "Down in what they called Congo Square, slaves were bought and sold." Hobley continued, "So it happened that old master sent down a batch in which my father was included." Hobley's word choice – "batch" – reflected the endurance of the market logic that turned black people into commodities. Upon recognizing the imminent separation, Hobley's father begged Cunningham, "'Master, you ain't goin' to sell me, are you'?" to which Cunningham replied, "Sell you, the finest man I know! Of course not." Cunningham "brought [Hobley's father] home and said that as long as he lived, he would never be sold." Presumably, this was a happy ending, since Hobley's family remained intact. Yet, the story also reveals the

---

[78] Interview, Nathan H. Hobley to Zoe Posey, New Orleans, January 1941, in Clayton and Louisiana Writers' Project, *Mother Wit*, 111–121. Hobley and his wife, Mary Sagasta, maintained a lucrative spiritual commerce, so he may have considered this interview a marketing opportunity. Mary Sagasta, whom Hobley described as "dark-complexioned and ... often taken for a colored woman," was the niece of Práxedes Mateo Sagasta, Prime Minister of Spain during the Spanish-American War of 1898. On Práxedes Mateo Sagasta, see Henry Cabot Lodge, *The War with Spain* (New York: Arno Press, 1970).

[79] On "leakages," see Painter, "Three Southern Women and Freud," 93–111.

everyday horrors of the slave trade in Congo Square and across antebellum New Orleans. Hobley's father might have been spared, but the other, unnamed members of the "batch" did not receive a reprieve from the auction block. And, despite the Hobley family's ability to remain together, they did so as slaves. Cunningham did not free Hobley's father; he put the slave man back "in his pocket," where Cunningham could decide to sell the man at any moment. And the memory of the capriciousness of the Congo Square slave market traveled through the decades into the mid-twentieth century.[80]

"As we spent time in New Orleans," an influential twenty-first-century visitor observed, "we realized how truly it is a melting pot." Americans have long struggled to find the appropriate metaphor to describe the historical meetings and cultural mixtures in the city and nation. In New Orleans, the "gumbo" metaphor emphasizes the diverse influences that, under certain conditions, meld into something new. But such melding did not happen in an egalitarian vacuum. Stark inequalities defined the neighborhoods of early New Orleans. Those sites did not transcend or operate outside of the violence and material inequalities of an urban slave society. As these prismatic scenes from an urban landscape reveal, multiracial gatherings did not by definition preclude or eliminate racism. On the contrary, heterogeneous gatherings intensified racist ideologies and the socio-economic stratifications that they facilitated. Power structured every aspect of early New Orleans society, even a little Sunday afternoon fun. And, as Jane Right learned firsthand, when that fun threatened local order, the police hauled troublemakers off to jail.[81]

---

[80] On slave sales as being "put in a master's pocket," see Johnson, *Soul by Soul*, 19.

[81] Peter Del Vecho, quoted in Brooks Barnes, "Her Prince Has Come. Critics, Too," *New York Times*, May 29, 2009. Del Vecho produced the Disney film "Princess and the Frog." That film, which features Tiana, the multinational conglomerate's first black princess, is set in early twentieth-century New Orleans.

4

Penal Spaces

This negro has been found guilty and sentenced to be hanged in the usual place of execution in this city with a writing on his back with the words "for having assaulted and beaten his master with shedding of blood."

Complaint against the Negro Azi (1810)

There is a line of demarcation, which it would be rash in the extreme to destroy even in punishments; and the sight of a freeman performing the forced labour, or suffering under the stripes usually inflicted on the slave, must give rise to ideas of the most insubordinate nature.

Edward Livingston (1833)

In an 1812 deposition before the mayor, Blas Puche lay bare the body of his former bondswoman Celeste. The twenty-three-year-old woman had run away from her subsequent owner, so Puche shared his knowledge to facilitate her capture. Puche described Celeste as having "a beautiful black complexion, below-average size and well constituted." Puche's appraisal of the bondwoman was an informed one. Puche was a slave owner and, as warden of the New Orleans jail, slaveholder for the state. Every day, Puche and his subordinates inspected, classified, warehoused, and exploited runaway slaves, criminals, debtors, and others accused of stepping out of place. Leaders in cities across the Atlantic World birthed modern prisons, but the wardens in New Orleans had to do it in slavery's metropolis.[1]

---

[1] "d'une complexion d'un beau noir, taille au dessous de la commune et bien constituée," Deposition, Blas Puche before Mayor James Mather, New Orleans, May 6, 1812, NYHS NOC 8:10, my translation. Puche purchased Celeste in 1805 from Jean-Baptiste Davis of New Orleans, "the said Negro wench belonging to me for having being ordered to be delivered to me by his Excellency William C. C. Claiborne on the twentieth of December

In the late eighteenth and early nineteenth centuries, reformers in England, France, and the United States imagined and then built a novel structure – the penitentiary, a site designed to use physical confinement to rehabilitate errant subjects and citizens. The reasons for this transition remain contested. Some see in the concomitant rise of capitalism and the penitentiary evidence that bourgeois reformers designed the institution to turn the rabble into reliable wageworkers. Others see the prison's emergence as part of the "new humanitarianism" of the eighteenth century in which antislavery reformers deemed corporal punishment uncivilized and instead called for a more humane, rational system of punishment. In his influential *Discipline and Punish: The Birth of the Prison,* theorist Michel Foucault argues that one marker of modernity in the Age of Enlightenment was the transition from corporal punishment, such as public floggings and beheadings, to "the gentle way in punishment," the penitentiary.[2]

Yet as reformers deemed corporal punishment barbaric, chattel slavery – a system reliant on bodily torture – expanded across the Americas from New Orleans to Havana, Kingston to Rio de Janeiro. As one historian of Cuba writes, "Masters feared that any limits placed upon their ability to inflict physical punishment would be perceived by slaves as a sign of weakness, resulting in resistance." For example, the public workhouses and jails of Jamaica, historian Diana Paton argues, existed not to transform criminals into good citizens, but to turn rebellious inmates into obedient slaves through physical and mental coercion. Paton concludes, "that body and mind cannot be separated from each other, that modern power works on both, and that violence and pain are fully part of modern power." Atlantic slavery contradicted Foucault's distinction between pre-modern bodily punishment and modern incarceration.[3]

last part, in virtue of the documents I then manifested." Puche sold her to Manuël Dominguez, described as a resident of Pensacola who was present in New Orleans ("vecino de la Hare de Pensacola actualement en cita Ciudad"). Perhaps Celeste found respite in the multinational maroon communities of Spanish Florida, or else she hid somewhere in Louisiana. Act of Sale, Jean-Baptiste Davis to Blas Puche, Pierre Pedesclaux, Notary, New Orleans, March 29, 1805, volume 49, page 306, NANO; Act of Sale, Blas Puche to Manuel Dominguez, Pierre Pedesclaux, Notary, New Orleans, May 13, 1809, volume 58, Folder 10, page 208, NANO. For thirty-four other transactions to which Puche or his heirs were party, see Hall, *Database,* accessed November 15, 2012.

[2] Michel Foucault, *Discipline and Punish: The Birth of the Prison,* trans. Alan Sheridan (New York: Vintage Books, 1995), 104.

[3] Childs, *Aponte Rebellion,* 36; Diana Paton, *No Bond but the Law: Punishment, Race, and Gender in Jamaican State Formation, 1780–1870* (Durham: Duke University Press, 2004), 12.

In the slaveholding Americas, both urban and rural, slavery and incarceration worked in tandem to produce modernity. Studies of penal reform in the United States typically focus on the Northeast, where the political and social transformations of urbanization, industrialization, and immigration prompted two waves of prison construction, one in the 1790s and the other in the 1820s.[4] But in New Orleans, where the economy depended on staples produced by slaves, the penal system existed not simply to turn errant members of the working class into productive citizens, but to remove from the urban landscape those persons who threatened the interests of the local planter and merchant elite and to use their labor to build local infrastructure. The jail's employees categorized, housed, and exploited suspected runaways; inflicted corporal punishment on recalcitrant slaves at their masters' request; incarcerated whites and free blacks who, among other offenses, violated the regime of private property; and exploited slave and free inmates' labor to build the city. There was nothing post-slavery about mass incarceration; those institutions created one another.

This chapter charts the contested change over time story of confined cosmopolitanism inside the New Orleans jail. It reconstructs the shifting literal and figurative place of inmates of varied backgrounds from the late colonial era to the construction of a modern penitentiary in 1837. On the literal level, what in the colonial era was a site at the heart of the city, one as socially heterogeneous as it was physically dilapidated, local leaders in the 1830s replaced with a hygienic facility on the city's edge, one designed to segregate inmates by their social position. Figuratively, this categorization and manipulation of people inside the jail did the symbolic work of creating imperial and then national subjects during Louisiana's transition from a European colony to an occupied territory to a state in the US Union. When individuals entered the jail, they became "legible" to

---

[4] Rebecca M. McLennan, *The Crisis of Imprisonment: Protest, Politics, and the Making of the American Penal State, 1776–1941* (New York: Cambridge University Press, 2008), chapter 1; Michael Meranze, *Laboratories of Virtue: Punishment, Revolution, and Authority in Philadelphia, 1760–1835* (Chapel Hill: The University of North Carolina Press, 1996); Adam Jay Hirsch, *The Rise of the Penitentiary: Prisons and Punishment in Early America* (New Haven: Yale University Press, 1992); Michael Stephen Hindus, *Prison and Plantation: Crime, Justice, and Authority in Massachusetts and South Carolina, 1767–1878* (Chapel Hill: The University of North Carolina Press, 1980); David J. Rothman, *The Discovery of the Asylum; Social Order and Disorder in the New Republic* (Boston: Little, Brown, 1971). A key exception is Edward L. Ayers, *Vengeance and Justice: Crime and Punishment in the 19th Century American South* (New York: Oxford University Press, 1984).

the state through intake interviews and bodily inspection, and jailers used this information to situate them inside the jail.[5] In so doing, wardens also situated these people within the "body politic," or the "power and knowledge relations that invest human bodies and subjugate them by turning them into objects of knowledge."[6] For people of African descent, slave-owning municipal employees like Puche drew on a collective body of knowledge that stretched from the travel narratives of early European explorers to the slave forts of West Africa, from the race-thinking of early modern intellectuals to slave traders' ledgers.[7] They used that information to attribute and then reinforce race, gender, and class positions onto them before exploiting their labor. In the process, they manipulated people inside of the jail to deepen the chasms between whites and blacks, slaves and free persons in the larger society.[8]

Incarcerated people "talked back" to state power. Many of those held behind the jail's walls – vagabonds, insubordinate sailors, pirates, and runaways – landed there because they had allegedly violated laws or norms. That willingness to challenge authority did not end at intake. Inmates had their own designs for the prison, and they used everything from armed resistance to collaboration with authorities to challenge or manipulate state power. Those struggles reverberated beyond prison walls. The geographies of punishment offer a rich lens for investigating the interplay between state power and the tactics that slave and free inmates used to challenge it. More than that, contests that governed the arrangement of people inside of this jail provide a barometer for the contingent construction of modernity in the city, empire, and Atlantic world to which it belonged.[9]

---

[5] On legibility, see James C. Scott, *Seeing Like a State: How Certain Schemes to Improve the Human Condition Have Failed* (New Haven: Yale University Press, 1998).

[6] Foucault, *Discipline and Punish*, 28.

[7] Stephanie Smallwood, *Saltwater Slavery: A Middle Passage from Africa to American Diaspora* (Cambridge, MA: Harvard University Press, 2007); Morgan, *Laboring Women*, chapter 1.

[8] Stoler, "Tense and Tender Ties," 829–865.

[9] I take that phrase from bell hooks, *Talking Back: Thinking Feminist, Thinking Black* (Boston: South End Press, 1989). On the radical politics that inspired revolutionary and rebellious activities in the Atlantic World, see Linebaugh and Rediker, *The Many-Headed Hydra*; Scott, *Weapons of the Weak*; Cedric J. Robinson, *Black Marxism: The Making of the Black Radical Tradition* (Chapel Hill: The University of North Carolina Press, 2000 [1983]).

INCARCERATION IN THE EMPIRE OF LIBERTY

From Massachusetts to New York, Pennsylvania to Virginia, officials in the early republic created and confined criminals. The post-revolutionary economic downturn amid increased immigration and urbanization led to social upheaval, and officials contained those tensions by confining persons they deemed troublemakers. By the 1780s, officials in various US states reduced the number of capital crimes and experimented with public labor and solitary confinement. In Philadelphia, Quaker-inspired leaders at the Walnut Street Prison favored solitary confinement over hard labor based on the belief that solitude would compel inmates to reflect on their crimes, undergo an internal transformation, and become productive members of society. "By the turn of the century," one historian writes, "eight of the sixteen American states had instituted some sort of program for criminal incarceration." The prison was part of the national fabric.[10]

Long before it became a territory of the early republic, Louisiana served as a penal colony for France. In 1729 colonial authorities built the first New Orleans civil prison. It was located in the city center and only steps away from the Saint Louis Church (in the Spanish era it became known as the Cabildo complex and later Jackson Square). Officials gradually shifted their efforts from controlling unruly French colonists to policing enslaved indigenous and African peoples. An extant journal from 1766 provides a glimpse into the colonial jail's operating costs. Itemized purchases included candles, paper, bread, and chairs, which suggest functional (if bare) accommodations.[11] Executions were carried out by Louis Congo, a "negre" who secured freedom for himself and his wife by taking on the "infamous occupation" of putting to death persons of all backgrounds. Imprisonment and executions continued throughout the eighteenth century, when fires, partial renovations, and makeshift additions left the physical structure in disrepair.[12]

---

[10] Hirsch, *The Rise of the Penitentiary*, 11; Meranze, *Laboratories of Virtue*; Myra C. Glenn, *Campaigns against Corporal Punishment: Prisoners, Sailors, Women, and Children in Antebellum America* (Albany: State University of New York Press, 1984), 10–11.

[11] Mr. Monteil, *Journal des dépenses de la colonie de la Nouvelle Orléans*, January 2–December 31, 1766, MssCol 2038, NYPL.

[12] Dawdy, *Building the Devil's Empire*, 189–218. French Guiana provides a fruitful comparison of a French penal colony during the Age of Revolution. See Miranda Frances Spieler, *Empire and Underworld: Captivity in French Guiana* (Cambridge, MA: Harvard University Press, 2012).

During the Spanish era, administrators exploited slave and convict labor toward the improvement of municipal infrastructure, a practice that put prisoners in the streets. In the 1790s, slave laborers expanded the levees to protect the city from flooding. In 1794 Barón de Carondelet ordered convicts and 150 slaves to construct the Carondelet Canal (later known as the Old Basin Canal), which wound about one and a half miles from the edge of the French Quarter to Bayou St. John. This diverse crew of the dispossessed – fugitive slaves, criminals, and vagabonds – was housed inside of the police jail, but their labors on the public works made them visible to the larger society. According to James Pitot, mayor of New Orleans from 1804 to 1805, the Spanish governor had ensured the following: "drainage of the city, street cleaning, reliability of its patrols, surveillance of gambling houses, inspections of dance halls and theatres, and immediate imprisonment of vagrants and fugitive slaves."[13] Since they labored on the public works, the spectacle of multiracial punishment was part of everyday life in Spanish New Orleans.[14]

In the era of the Louisiana Purchase, champions of empire legitimized their rule based in part on the relative advancement of their criminal justice systems. Protestant Anglo-Saxons in particular perpetuated the Black Legend, or the myth that the predominately Catholic Spaniards were exceptionally tyrannical and inherently unstable, a tendency displayed most vividly during the Inquisition.[15] Major Amos Stoddard, Territorial Governor William C. C. Claiborne's second in command, claimed that during the Spanish period Louisiana's residents feared "the terrors of the … magistrate, the frightful apprehension of Mexican mines, and the dungeons of Havana" as well as "the supposed antipathy of the government to all strangers." The threat of such punishments "awed the settlers from the United States into submission," Stoddard continued, which in turn "produced an uncommon degree of subordination among them."[16] Paul Alliot, an immigrant from Saint-Domingue, complained about the corruption endemic to

---

[13] Pitot and Bush, *Observations on the Colony of Louisiana*, 27.

[14] Lawrence N. Powell, *The Accidental City: Improvising New Orleans* (Cambridge, MA: Harvard University Press, 2012), 205–207.

[15] Pitot and Bush, *Observations on the Colony of Louisiana*, 8. On the Black Legend, see Chris Schmidt-Nowara, "'This Rotting Corpse': Spain between the Black Atlantic and the Black Legend," *Arizona Journal of Hispanic Cultural Studies* 5, no. 1 (2001): 149–160; J. N. Hillgarth, *The Mirror of Spain, 1500–1700: The Formation of a Myth* (Ann Arbor: University of Michigan Press, 2000), chapter 8.

[16] Amos Stoddard, *Sketches, Historical and Descriptive of Louisiana* (Philadelphia: Matthew Carey, 1812; reprinted New York: AMS Press, 1973), 283.

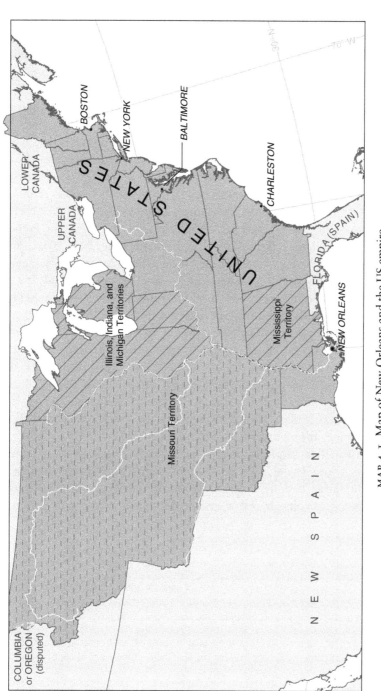

MAP 4.1 Map of New Orleans and the US empire.

the Spanish criminal justice system: "The rich murderer is quit of it for money, while often he who has no money to give, is sent to the galleys or to the mines for the rest of his life." In England, free "mulata" Louisa Calderon's 1801 sentence to a device called the "picquet" in Trinidad, a Crown colony recently acquired from Spain, sparked an outcry and made her a cause célèbre. Many in England feared that such tortures in the colonies reflected poorly on their civilization and undermined the legitimacy of their empire.[17] Neither British nor American reformers wanted their respective empires to be linked to the tortures they associated with the Spanish justice system.[18]

The Louisiana Purchase extended US authority over a criminal justice system charged with disciplining a population far more multi-ethnic – and enslaved – than just about any other US city. One French Creole in Louisiana reflected, "I visited Philadelphia, New York, and Baltimore ... where it was a crime to be a Frenchman."[19] If French Creole Catholics felt criminalized in the northeastern United States, they were the dominant group in metropolitan New Orleans. Other residents included Spaniards, the descendants of colonial-era Anglo settlers, free persons of color, slaves (many of them African-born), and indigenous peoples. Even more recent Anglo-American settler-imperialists were fractured by region, as New England upstarts, for example, hoped to outshine the "saucy Virginian and supercilious Carolinian." The need for hierarchy amid such heterogeneity undermined colonial leaders' ability to institute the "rational" punishment that reformers adopted in other states.[20]

More than that, despite reformers' increasing emphasis on non-corporal punishment, local leaders inflicted sensational, public, and corporal punishments on slaves and free persons of African descent during that era of antislavery revolts. In French Saint-Domingue and British Jamaica,

---

[17] "[Calderon] was tied by one wrist to a scaffold," James Epstein writes, "her other wrist tied to her ankle, she was then lowered by means of a pulley onto a wooden spike, the full weight of her body resting on her naked foot." This torture went on for fifty-three and fifty-four minutes the first day, then twenty-four minutes on the second. James Epstein, *Scandal of Colonial Rule: Power and Subversion in the British Atlantic during the Age of Revolution* (Cambridge: Cambridge University Press, 2012), 21.

[18] Paul Alliot, *Louisiana under the Rule of Spain, France, and the United States, 1785–1807*, 2 vols., trans. James Alexander Robertson (Cleveland, OH: The Arthur H. Clark Company, 1911), I: 73. On the Havana jail, see Childs, *Aponte Rebellion*, 31–32.

[19] Pitot and Bush, *Observations on the Colony of Louisiana*, 17.

[20] Levi W. Weeks to Ephraim Hoyt, Esq., September 27, 1812, Weeks Family Papers, Manuscript Collection 198, Box 1, Folder 6, Manuscripts Department, TU.

planters routinely inflicted sadistic tortures on bondspersons, with levels of violence consistent with the fear of a vastly outnumbered ruling class in a slave society. Cuba became legendary for its vicious man-eating dogs, some of which were exported to revolutionary Saint-Domingue.[21] With such a diverse yet stratified population on the southwestern frontier, authorities – Territorial Governor William C. C. Claiborne (a Jefferson appointee), the mayor (a Claiborne appointee), City Council, and the court system – regulated a territory that seemed so distinct that many suspected it could not become American.[22]

New Orleans was a frontier town filled with frontier violence, and the lawlessness made it seem ungovernable. In 1808, Pierre Francois Missonet, Judge in the City Court of the Territory of Orleans, admitted as much when he complained to Mayor Mather: "It is very difficult to police a city filled with individuals who, for the most part, do not have any respect for the laws and for the authorities."[23] This lack of respect for authorities permeated all levels of society. "Aggression flourished most democratically where gambling and drinking flourished," one historian writes, and New Orleans had both. In the city and across the region, white men generally settled disputes between themselves in duels and the like rather than bring such matters before the state.[24] But even those who, like French traveler C. C. Robin, had a low estimation of the local population generally had an even lower estimation of the judicial system. Robin lambasted the "venal and ignorant magistrates, stained with every vice ... and clouds of jack-leg lawyers ... dispersed

---

[21] Sara E. Johnson, *The Fear of French Negroes: Transcolonial Collaboration in the Revolutionary Americas* (Berkeley: University of California Press, 2012), chapter 1; Brown, *The Reaper's Garden*; Garraway, *The Libertine Colony*; Paton, *No Bond but the Law*.

On the violence of scholars' reproducing the descriptions of torture, see Hartman, *Scenes of Subjection*.

[22] Strife between the United States and France, for example, inspired Federalists to pass the controversial Alien and Sedition Acts of 1798, which threatened to deport anyone whom the president deemed "dangerous to the peace and safety of the United States, or shall have reasonable grounds to suspect are concerned in any treasonable or secret machinations against the government." The Quasi-War between the United States and France (1798–1800) over these issues only heightened Federalists' suspicions of French Louisianans. Alien and Sedition Acts, 1798 [Online version, www.ourdocuments.gov/doc.php?flash=true&doc=16, National Archives and Records Administration, November 15, 2012].

[23] [Pierre Francois] Missonet to Mather, New Orleans, December 5, 1808, NYHS NOC 1:8, my translation.

[24] Ayers, *Vengeance and Justice*, 13; Dessens, *Creole City*, 58–67.

through the land like reincarnated harpies ... feasting on the blood and flesh of the cowed inhabitants."[25] Some of Robin's vivid vitriol may have stemmed from his resentments of Spanish administrators in Louisiana and lawyers and other members of the Third Estate responsible for the overthrow of the *ancien régime* in France. Even still, Robin was not alone in his low regard for local society and the local officials charged with policing them. Imperial subjects-turned-citizens in Louisiana constantly contested the imposition of laws from Spanish and then American administrators.

"THE LAWS ('LES DROITS') OF THE JAIL REMAIN FIXED"

In the early republican era, slaveholding citizens used the legal system to tighten constraints on slaves. Louisiana's 1806 Black Code stated that arrested "negroes" could be put to hard labor "on the condition that the said city council and sheriffs shall provide for the maintenance, house room, clothing and medical attendance of said negroes, at the expense of the city." The law required jailers to advertise the incarcerated "negroes" in the newspaper to facilitate the return of runaways to their owners.[26] That same year, New Orleans' leaders agreed on the need for "surveillance of slaves of both sexes who are arrested by the police or suspected runaways." After negotiations, Mayor Mather and the City Council jointly approved the "Rules for the Police Prison" on August 3, 1807. In these two acts – the 1806 passage of the Black Code and the 1807 adoption of policies to govern the local prison – local legislators prescribed punishment geographies. This section uses the "Rules for the Police Prison" to explore the judicial proceedings that brought slaves to the central jail, the intake process, material conditions inside the facility, and the chain gangs on which inmates labored. In the halting effort to transform penal theory into everyday practice, we see the intertwined construction of class, race, gender, and status alongside the creation of a modern penitentiary.[27]

---

[25] Robin and Landry, *Voyage to Louisiana, 1803-1805*, 179.

[26] An Act Prescribing the Rules and Conduct to be Observed with Respect to Negroes and other Slaves of this Territory, June 7, 1806, §28, in Lislet, *A General Digest*, I: 106.

[27] Conseil de Ville, "Règlement pour la Prison de Police," New Orleans, August 3, 1807, NYHS NOC II:4, my translation. On slavery and French colonial laws, see Ghachem, *The Old Regime and the Haitian Revolution*.

The larger carceral landscape in New Orleans certainly included many other sites. The pens that held the slaves to be sold, for example, were often called "slave jails." I am interested in this particular site because of its centrality, but I do not intend to suggest that there are not other sites that could be fruitfully explored.

One critical function of the criminal justice system was to punish disobedient slaves. Enslaved persons could not testify against white people, but, as bondspersons Maria Redas and Azi learned, they could stand trial in criminal cases. Insurrection, for example, was a capital offense, one for which accused bondspersons were to "be indicted and tried without appeal by the judges of the place." In 1792, Angelica Monsanto sold a forty-year-old "negra" named Maria Redas to Francisco Luis deFeriet. In 1810, after eighteen years of servitude to that master, the fifty-eight-year-old bondwoman allegedly attempted to murder De Feriet and his family by hiding crushed glass (*verre pillé*) in their food. De Feriet suspected she had acted under the influence of a black man (*un negre*) whom she refused to name. Contrary to this claim that De Feriet swore to in City Court, Marie Rose and other enslaved women did not require male guidance in their efforts to resist bondage. They often used poisoning as a form of resistance because, as cooks and nurses, they had easy access to their owners' food. Whether Marie Rose acted alone or with a conspirator, however, she traded one life sentence for another. In *Territory of Orleans* v. *Marie Rose* (1810), a judge declared Marie Rose "condemned to remain in prison forever" (*condamné à garder une prison perpétuelle*). Two months after her sentence (and one month after the Deslondes Revolt), the legislature instructed the treasury to pay de Feriet $500 compensation "provided [he] execute a transfer and abandon … the said slave to the territory."[28]

---

[28] Act of Sale, Angelique [Monsanto] Dow and Robert Dow to Francisco Luis Deferiet, Pedro Pedesclaux, Notary, New Orleans, July 4, 1792, volume 15, page 224, NANO; Affidavit, Louis de Feriet before Pierre Colsson, New Orleans, December 3, 1810, Louisiana Purchase Bicentennial Collection of the Louisiana Digital Library, http://loui sdl.louislibraries.org, accessed January 29, 2010, my translation; *Territory of Orleans* v. *La Negresse Mary* (1810), Louisiana Purchase Bicentennial Collection; Territory of Orleans Legislature, "An Act to Authorize Lewis de Feriet to Claim from the Treasurer of the Territory the Estimated Value of a Negro Woman Condemned to Perpetual Imprisonment," in *Acts Passed at the First Session of the Second Legislature of the Territory of Orleans* (New Orleans: Bradford & Anderson Printers, 1808), 18–19. On poison as a common method of resistance among enslaved women, see Deborah Gray White, *Ar'n't I a Woman? Female Slaves in the Plantation South*, rev. edition (New York: W. W. Norton & Co., 1999 [1985]), 79.

   Angelique Monsanto was the daughter of Esther Levy, an Ashkenazi Jew, and David Rodrigues Monsanto, a Sephardic Jew born in The Hague in October 1729. Together several of their children migrated to Curaçao before settling in New Orleans in the late 1750s. Angelica's brother Isaac became a prominent storekeeper, merchant, and banker. The transition to Spanish authority, however, resulted in their expulsion. Since Governor Alexander O'Reilly issued a 1769 order that deported English merchants, Isaac's

Such incarceration did not supplant corporal punishment. Rather incarceration and spectacular executions both existed on a spectrum of punishment in early American New Orleans. The Black Code stated that "any slave who shall willfully strike his master, mistress, or his or her child or children, so as to cause a confusion, or effusion or shedding of blood, shall be punished with death." The same year that Maria Redas was sentenced, a twenty-five-year-old African-born man named Azi stood accused of assaulting his master at the bondman's act of sale. Authorities held Azi in jail during his 1810 trial. In the court's transcript, the clerk recorded the proceedings in French, the dominant local language, and Azi purportedly marked the document with an "X." Nine days later, however, the clerk recorded the verdict and sentence in English, the language of US empire:

This negro has been found guilty and sentenced to be hanged in the usual place of execution in this city with a writing on his back with the words "for having assaulted and beaten his master with shedding of blood."

When Azi used violence to contest his own sale, he undermined the sanctity of the free market and the law. Upon execution the display of his lifeless body would bear witness to the power of slaveholders and the empire that empowered them. His execution became a political ritual which was, at once, definitive and incomplete: definitive because Azi would die, incomplete because, despite their theatricality, public executions did not end slave resistance. In the opening days of 1811, not one year after Azi's execution antislavery insurgents staged the Deslondes Revolt, which, as discussed in Chapter 1, was the largest in US history. After the Deslondes Revolt, officials mounted the severed heads on stakes staggered along the Mississippi River as a deterrent. Civilization indeed.[29]

---

expulsion likely owed as much to his activities as a merchant as to his religion. They settled in nearby Pensacola in British West Florida, where in 1772 Angelica married George Urquhart, a Scottish Protestant and one of Isaac's business associates. After Urquhart's 1779 death, she, her two sons, and presumably Urquhart's slaves (including Maria Redas) moved back to New Orleans. Monsanto then married another prominent Scot, Dr. Robert Dow, in 1781. She was a member of the Episcopal Church until her death in 1821. Bertram Wallace Korn, *The Early Jews of New Orleans* (Waltham, MA: American Jewish Historical Society, 1969), 10–56; Bradley, *Interim Appointment*, 10.

[29] An Act Prescribing the Rules and Conduct to be Observed with Respect to Negroes and other Slaves of this Territory, June 7, 1806, §17, in Louis Moreau Lislet, *A General Digest of the Acts of the Legislature of Louisiana* (New Orleans: Benjamin Levy, 1828), I: 100–112; An Act Prescribing the Rules and Conduct, Crimes and Offences, §10, *General Digest*, 116; Complaint against the Negro Azi, a slave of Joseph, City Court, Criminal Case file no. 167, June 9, 1810; *Territory of Orleans v. Cesar, the Slave of Girod* (1811); *Territory of*

If the slave market turned people into products, then the jail turned them into prisoners. Local officials employed state-of-the-art technologies to manage the heterogeneous and expanding population inside the prison. At intake, officials read bodies to render people "legible" before the state. In an inspection process virtually identical to the one that traders and buyers practiced in the slave market, jailers examined physical bodies and conducted interviews to approximate inmate biographies before tabulating that information in municipal reports. The "Regulations for the Police Prison" required the jailer to

keep a bound Register, marked and signed by the Mayor, closed and stopped at the end of each year, in which he will write each day with no blank spaces, the slaves who were brought to prison, whether as runaways not accused of crimes, or whether by way of correction, and specifying their name, that of their master, their age with size and every morning he will deliver to the Mayor a note of the prisoners in the city.

However asymmetrical the circumstances, warden and inmate together constructed biographies of those held captive through a combination of bodily inspections and oral interviews (a difficult feat in such a polyglot town). Corrections officers compiled this information into a grid and then shared it with the mayor and, in the case of suspected runaways, local newspapers. Like the US national census that began in 1790, these grids also created membership in communities, only this time from below. Daily reports from the 1820s and 1830s list blacks in a manner nearly identical to that of slave ship ledgers: names, master's names, and reason for incarceration. Category headings included "*Negres* in chains," "In jail without chains," "Sick," "In the dungeon," and "Negresses." As it was a registry of slaves, only persons of African descent, male and female, were listed in these reports, though the jail housed a broader population (as will be discussed shortly).[30]

Standardized prison ledgers hid in plain sight the global backgrounds of inmates taken from the port city's streets. As such, inmates found themselves locked inside a prison as cosmopolitan as the city in which it was located. Claiborne complained that "Negro's purchased from the Jails of Jamaica, have been smuggled into the Territory." This statement perhaps

Orleans v. the Negro Slave Andre (1811), all available on the Louisiana Purchase Bicentennial Collection of the Louisiana Digital Library, http://louisdl.louislibraries.org.

On the legal standing of enslaved persons in antebellum Louisiana's courts, see Schafer, *Slavery, the Civil Law, and the Supreme Court of Louisiana*.

[30] "Règlement pour la Prison de Police"; Daily Reports, 1820–1839, New Orleans (La.) Police Jail, TX205, City Archives, NOPL, my translation. On the analogous process in the context of the slave market, see Smallwood, *Saltwater Slavery*, chapter 2.

reflects one imperial official's anxieties, but it is altogether likely that some New Orleans inmates had been incarcerated previously in the workhouses and prisons of the British, French, and Spanish Caribbean. In a characteristic *Louisiana Courier* listing from August 1810, Warden Puche advertised custody of the following inmates: Dixon, an Igbo man "about 30 years old, five French feet two inches high, of a robust make"; Sam Jackson, "aged about 27 years size five feet two inches, born in Spotsylvania County, state of Virginia"; and Pierre, known as Petit Capot, "of the Mandinga nation, from 40–45 years, 4 French feet 10 inches high." In 1813, "a Havanna [*sic*] negro named *Juanillo Leonisio*, speaking nothing but Spanish" escaped from the jail, and Puche suspected he would attempt a maritime escape "being a seamen [*sic*] by trade." In recording the different nationalities represented in the jail at any one moment, the ledgers illuminate the diverse social worlds locked into the jail. But in publishing narratives based on the intake ledger, the warden activated his archive toward the practice of recapture.[31]

Suspected runaways nonetheless undermined the intake process and its ledgers, which highlighted the absurdities of expected self-disclosure at the junction of enslavement and imprisonment. Officials in their arrogance trusted captives to tell the truth. Puche's advertisement for the runaway William, a Mandinga man who bore scarification marks on his chest, begins with seemingly authoritative biometric data – William's height was "4 feet and 10 ½ inches high, French measure" – before it exposes the limits of Puche's knowledge: "[William] doesn't know the name of his master, and can't give any information about his residence. He speaks neither French nor English."[32] Because of sales and language barriers, it is possible that William did not know this information. It is equally possible that the runaway intentionally withheld the very information that would hasten his reunion with the master from whom he escaped. A year later Puche advertised Scipion, "about twenty-five years of age, four feet eight inches high, English measure, of the Congo nation, speaks nothing but English and cannot tell the name of his master."[33] Perhaps Scipion, like

---

[31] Claiborne to Robert Smith, New Orleans, November 12, 1809, *Letter Books*, V: 1–2; *Règlement pour la Prison de Police*; "Runaway Negro at the Jail," *Louisiana Courier*, August 20, 1810; Blas Puche, "Runaway from the Jail," *Courier*, December 1, 1813, (emphasis original). Puche further described Leonisio as having "difficulty in separating his upper from his lower jaw" and "very white teeth and a handsome face."

[32] "Runaway Negro at the Jail," *Louisiana Courier*, August 20, 1810. The ad for William appeared again on August 27, 1810.

[33] "Runaway in Jail," *Louisiana Courier*, August 21, 1811.

William, lacked the capacity to communicate his biography. More likely, both men exploited a system that relied on their self-reporting to dissemble about their backgrounds and evade their owners, an action that to some degree made the jail warden complicit in their escape.

Other inmates of African descent used their linguistic and cultural competencies to challenge the attributed slave status that justified their confinement. Indeed in Louisiana, Brazil, and across the slaveholding Atlantic, phenotypic blackness was reason enough to incarcerate and enslave people, and available evidence suggests that a fair number of free blacks landed in the New Orleans jail based on a presumed slave status.[34] "A negro named Frank, of the Ebo nation, about 30 years old, 5 feet high (French measure) having the teeth of the lower jaw filed," one jail advertisement declared. Frank "says he is free, and that he came to this country from New York about 2 years and an half ago, in a vessel commanded by one Mr. Collins."[35] Travel without written verification of their free status could land a free black behind bars. At the same time, freedom claims allowed persons held as slaves to challenge that status. In either case, by insisting on their freedom, such inmates challenged the state's right to classify and confine them. So many other inmates of African descent claimed to be free that they came to have their own abbreviation in the ledgers: "s.d.l.," abbreviated French for "so-called free."[36]

Inmates classed as white were imprisoned alongside black ones on violent and non-violent offenses. Of course, such inmates also underwent an attribution process at intake, in which the jailer determined based on bodily inspection that the person should be considered white. In one case, police arrested and imprisoned an unidentified white man (*un blanc*) for

---

[34] Sidney Chalhoub, "Illegal Enslavement and the Precariousness of Freedom in Nineteenth-Century Brazil," in *Assumed Identities: The Meanings of Race in the Atlantic World*, ed. John D. Garrigus and Christopher Morris (College Station: Published for the University of Texas at Arlington by Texas A&M University Press, 2010), 88–115.

[35] "Negro in Jail," *Louisiana Courier*, September 23, 1811.

[36] "Records of Correctional Institutions," City Archives, NOPL, http://nutrias.org/~nopl/inv/neh/nehtx.htm#tx2, accessed August 5, 2012. The abbreviation likely derives from the French "soi-disant Libre."

As discussed in Chapter 3, the 1810 Superior Court ruling in *Adéle Auger* v. *Frederick Beaurocher et al.* (*Adelle* v. *Beauregard*) placed the burden of proof of documenting a mixed-race person's status as a slave on her master, while it was incumbent upon "Negros" to document their own freedom. Enslaved persons across the slave south "pretended to be free" by using forged passes, relying on white phenotypes, running away, and any other number of tactics. See Camp, *Closer to Freedom*; Graham Russell Hodges and Alan Edward Brown, *"Pretends to Be Free": Runaway Slave Advertisements from Colonial and Revolutionary New York and New Jersey* (New York: Garland Pub, 1994).

allegedly threatening an officer.[37] In another instance, Mayor Mather asked Warden Puche to confine Jacques Pape, "utterly deranged in his senses."[38] In addition to the lashes they routinely received on the seas, unruly sailors regularly landed in jail when at port. The *Ganges* departed New London and arrived in New Orleans in early 1811. During the voyage, the seaman William Colson reportedly behaved with "malicious avarice" and "riotous disobedience," which included threatening to kill his captain. Those charges landed Colson behind bars in New Orleans.[39] The next year, a different captain testified that one of his sailors, Edward Concklin, became so unruly as to warrant imprisonment.[40] Manuel, a free black sailor aboard Capt. Joseph Couthouy's brig *Hazard* "positively refused" to feed a hog when asked, "adding that he would kill [a] mate with an ax if the latter was to touch him." Couthouy sought Manuel's imprisonment "for a number of days or until the vessel sails from this Port."[41] In 1816, seaman Thomas Bracey went to jail for alleged insubordination.[42] John Hendricks, a "coloured man" employed on various ships, spent more time on land than on his vessel, Ralph Jacobs complained. Hendricks allegedly assailed Jacobs "with very abusive language." When Jacobs threatened to call the authorities, Hendricks "bade defiance to the whole Police and City Guard."[43] Terrestrial structures disciplined maritime conduct, which in turn fostered confined cosmopolitanism inside the New Orleans jail.[44]

---

[37] Löeben, "Report du 24–26 December (Xbre) 1808," Police Dept. Reports, NYHS NOC 10:1.

[38] Mather to Puche, February 13, 1811, NYHS NOC IX:10.

[39] Deposition, Henry Crary and Jonathan Spencer before Mather, New Orleans, February 9, 1811, NYHS NOC 8:9. The captain had good reason to fear. An 1811 notice in the local paper declared that a Captain William Hobbet who set sail from New Orleans for New Providence "has been murdered by the crew in the neighbourhood [sic] of Eleuthera." "Notice," *Courier*, November 6, 1811.

[40] Deposition, Henry Hunter before Mather, New Orleans, April 2, 1812, NYHS NOC 8:10.

[41] Deposition, Joseph Couthouy before Girod, New Orleans, April 11, 1813, NYHS NOC 8:11.

[42] Deposition, William Bartlett before Macarty, New Orleans, November 1, 1816, NYHS NOC 8:12.

[43] Deposition, Ralph Jacobs before Roffignac, New Orleans, June 22, 1825, NYHS NOC 9:5.

[44] The US founders authorized flogging as a punishment for sailors as early as 1775, when John Adams penned the "Rules for the Regulation of the Navy." Congress assented to the document in 1797, and from then until 1850 corporal punishment aboard naval vessels remained legal. Fink, *Sweatshops at Sea*, chapter 2; Glenn, *Campaigns against Corporal Punishment*, 9.

Inmates charted any number of paths before they entered the New Orleans jail, but once inside they entered a carceral world controlled by the warden and his staff. The Regulations for the Police Prison of 1807 called for certain spatial and disciplinary practices, but they did not easily translate from the prescriptive level to everyday reality.

The regulations extended the colonial practice of housing the warden and inmates at the center of the city's physical landscape. Fugitives and criminals would be detained "in the main building situated behind the City Hotel" (present-day Jackson Square), a space that itself had a lengthy history as the city's political and spiritual core (the St. Louis Church at the center of the complex). The mayor was to appoint a warden – "a literate man of good moral character" – to oversee the St. Peter Street complex. The successful candidate would also be of means, as the second article required he deposit 1,000 piastres as surety. Finally, the warden would also live on the prison grounds on the first floor of the City Hotel. Mather nominated Blas Puche, whose experience included a post as Corporal of the Night Watchmen under the final Spanish administration.[45] Article 13 of regulations stated: "In addition to the lodgings ... the Warden will be allowed on City funds an annual salary of 500 piastres payable quarterly."[46]

Warden Puche's support staff included a network of watchmen and jailers whose salaries made employment in corrections and law enforcement in general an attractive option, especially for immigrants. In 1811, the French consul in New Orleans wrote to Mayor Mather on behalf of Louis Bainville, a migrant from Saint-Domingue who had been "displaced and ruined by the Catastrophes." He hoped to elevate his personal status by policing those more vulnerable than he. In February 1814, Mayor Girod authorized the city treasurer to pay Joseph Peralta thirty-five dollars for one month's labor as a watchman for the chain gang. A few months later the city treasurer paid Jacques Lamothe 125 piastres for three months of work as a jailer. In addition, the regulations allowed one escalin for each time jailers beat an enslaved prisoner, which created a small but tangible financial incentive (either for the guards or for the jail as an

---

[45] "Règlement pour la Prison de Police"; Acts and Deliberations of the Cabildo, book 4, volume I: 74, NOPL.

[46] "Règlement pour la Prison de Police."

This amount was a significant amount, especially since it included lodging. To compare, modest lodgings could be had in the city for as little as twenty to eighty piastres per month. See Robin, *Voyage*, 32.

institution) for corporal punishment. The jail modernized corporal punishment for slaves not by eliminating it, but by commoditizing it.[47]

The 1807 regulations also required the warden to protect the jail's facility and the inmates by standardizing sanitation procedures, a practice consistent with emerging ideas about the relationship between bodies, health and the environment. Regulations required the warden to keep the facility "in the greatest state of cleanliness." Cells were to be "washed and watered with vinegar at least once a week" and the walls "white-washed twice a year." The warden was also to ensure "that the cells (*les cachots*) were opened from one to one and a half hours each day." In addition, Puche needed to "freshen the air, and ensure the courtyard [was] swept every morning and washed at least twice a week." Puche was to manage the animals kept at the facility for food, and in the case of illness authorities were to quarantine detainees to prevent the spread of communicable disease. Each morning Puche was to send a handful of "*nègres de chaîne*" (with two Watchmen as supervisors) to the Mississippi River each day to secure water for the jail. Then at night he was to inspect the inmates and "order transported to the river all refuse via St. Peter Street and never by the main door of the City Hotel." In the notoriously unsanitary city, the prisoners, like many other residents, disposed of their waste into the river. In those regulations, leaders implemented policies based on their assumptions about the relationship between sanitation, space, and health.[48]

Leaders also prescribed seemingly progressive regulations of particular significance for female inmates. The mayor and police commissioner visited the prison monthly "to ensure that [inmates] are healthy and safe, if the prisoners are provided the quality and quantity of food & necessities; finally that they are not experiencing any abuse."

---

[47] "Mandat de Payment," Girod to Joseph Peralta, New Orleans, February 23, 1814, THC: Collection VII, available at LSA; "Mandat de Payement," City Treasurer to Jacques Lamothe, New Orleans, May 20, 1814, NYHS NOC VI:15, my translation; Jean Baptiste Porée to Mather, New Orleans, October 15, 1811, NYHS NOC I:8, my translation.

On immigrants to the United States who ascended by distancing themselves from or oppressing those beneath them, see Noel Ignatiev, *How the Irish Became White* (New York: Routledge, 1995).

[48] "Règlement pour la Prison de Police." "Watchmen" is the only English word in the document.

On sanitary conditions in early New Orleans, see Powell, *Accidental City*, 205–207. On the connection between bodies, health, sanitation, and settler imperialism, see Valencius, *The Health of the Country*.

According to the seventh article of the regulations, female inmates were to be kept "in rooms separate from the cells of detained men; and the Jailer will watch that [male inmates] do not communicate with them." Since white women were rarely imprisoned in the south, this measure was particularly important for women of African descent, both slave and free.[49] Such a regulation did little to prevent same-sex rape within the prison, but it may have prevented some male inmates from assaulting female ones. Yet, even if this policy was followed to the letter, these women remained vulnerable to the depredations of jail employees. When women such as Betsy, listed in a sale advertisement as "a crazy black wench," entered the jail, the constant threat of sexual assault simply compounded the ongoing traumas of slavery. In December 1813, Blas Puche publicized the incarceration of "a negro wench named PEGGY, who appears to be in a state of insanity." She claimed to have escaped from a nearby sugar plantation, and she entered the jail wearing "an iron collar with three branches." By the time that Puche published the advertisement, Peggy had been incarcerated for at least one month. Plantation abuses perhaps undermined Peggy's mental health, and incarceration deepened her pain.[50]

Physical segregation by sex may have prevented certain abuses, but it also furthered the state's mission to govern society through the regulation of gender and sexuality. When New Orleans officials segregated inmates based on their bodies they created gendered inmates. Such segregation might have alienated queer and transgender bondspersons who might have identified as any number of genders or solidarities. In addition, such segregation might have separated male and female

---

[49] Historian Edward Ayers writes of the antebellum period, "seldom could more than one or two women be found in a Southern penitentiary." This assertion holds for white women, but enslaved women appeared throughout prison ledgers. By the 1850s, however, white women, many of them immigrants, who labored as sex workers in New Orleans became subject to arrest. See Ayers, *Vengeance and Justice*, 62; Schafer, *Brothels, Depravity, and Abandoned Women*.

[50] "Règlement pour la Prison de Police"; *L'Ami des Lois*, January 23, 1816; "Runaway Slave in Jail," *Louisiana Courier*, December 10, 1813. The advertisement does not specify the name of the sugar plantation.

On the psychic traumas of slavery, see Alex Bontemps, *The Punished Self: Surviving Slavery in the Colonial South* (Ithaca, NY: Cornell University Press, 2001); Nell Irvin Painter, "Soul Murder and Slavery: Towards a Fully-Loaded Cost Accounting," in *Southern History across the Color Line* (Chapel Hill: The University of North Carolina Press, 2002), 15–39.

allies who might have offered one another camaraderie, intimacy, and support.[51]

Also in keeping with reformist impulses, the state also segregated inmates by sex to prevent reproduction inside the facility. The monastic deprivation of bodily pleasure toward the redemption of the soul had long been a hallmark of spiritual traditions across the world. Penologists across the Atlantic advocated sex-based segregation to prevent consensual and non-consensual sexual activity between inmates, preclude reproduction, and prevent the spread of sexually transmitted infections. An enslaved female inmate's pregnancy would diminish her ability to labor on the chain gang and perhaps increased her health-care costs, though her master would likely reap the material benefit of her "increase." Consequently, the state had both humanitarian and pragmatic incentives to maintain sex-based segregation inside the jail.[52]

Finally, in addition to the politics of place within the prison, the facility itself was situated inside a larger carceral geography defined by the circulations of the "ateliers," or work gangs, across the urban landscape. These bound circulations were significant for several reasons. First, when these convicts and *"nègres de chaîne"* tended to the levees, paved streets, and removed waste, they literally built the city. More than that, the sweat equity that these men and women invested into the urban infrastructure was the result of a public–private partnership. When slave owners leased their slaves to the chain gang, they delegated the perquisites and responsibilities of mastery to the state in exchange for liquid capital. This alchemical ability to deliver a person to the jailer and then receive public money in the form of bank notes allowed slave owners to hedge their investments in more volatile or less liquid enterprises. Lastly, on a figurative level, the everyday sight of chained workers on the urban landscape created norms and knowledge about the people who were chained and those who were not. Over time leaders established policies

---

[51] I stop short of saying that some black men might have sought to protect black women from rape inside the jail, at the hands of either guards or fellow inmates, though this is certainly possible. As Kimberlé Crenshaw argues, violence against black women's bodies must not be read exclusively in terms of competing patriarchies between black and white men. Kimberlé Crenshaw, "Mapping the Margins: Intersectionality, Identity Politics, and Violence against Women of Color," *Stanford Law Review* 43, no. 6 (July 1991): 1241–1299.

[52] On the relationship between prison geographies and sexual relationships between inmates as well as inmates and guards, see David Sibley, *Geographies of Exclusion: Society and Difference in the West* (London: New York, 1995).

to ensure that, in the public theater of the city's streets, the chained laborers, whether male or female, were all black.[53]

The 1807 "Règlements" called for any enslaved male held in the New Orleans jail for more than twenty-four hours to be "put to work for the city which will pay the price of food for the detained slaves," but women classed as slaves also labored on the public works. Those who resisted risked whippings of "not more than 25 lashes per correction." An extant public works report from two decades later gives an indication of the kinds of tasks public workers performed:

Today's public works consisted of 33 monthly *negres*, 57 *negres* in chains, 29 negresses, and 36 convicts working to clean the streets, the markets, and the levee; helping the carpenters, blacksmiths, the paver, and the gardener ... repaired Magazine Street; took masonry measurements ["mesurer des cailloux"]; stood in position to transport the sick; buried animals; repaired Royal Street.

The blacksmiths made fittings for the lanterns. The carpenters repaired ... the wheelbarrows ... one was watching the store and keeping the tools in good condition.

Twelve dumpers cleaned the street; 37 provided materials to the carpenters, fluters, and pavers; maintained the paved streets; transported materials to the levee from the depots; picked up papers on Tchoupitoulas Street.[54]

The racial composition of the category referred to as "convicts" is unmarked, though there is a compelling reason to assume that at least some convicts were white. First, unmarked humanity in this period tended to be white; persons of color typically merited a racial marker. Second, white men routinely landed behind bars. And third, the interracial chain gang had not yet been outlawed. Nonetheless, this chain gang was overwhelmingly "negre," a term used interchangeably (if at times inaccurately) with slave. An equally significant point is that nearly one in five of the laborers was female. New Orleans Mayor Nicholas Girod even advocated such labor as a gendered embarrassment to prevent the idleness of incarcerated enslaved women and deter disobedience. As he wrote in 1813, "the shame and humiliation [enslaved women] would experience in seeing themselves led to these laborious duties, would serve as a greater punishment, more keenly felt than even the prison or the lash." This punishment, in his estimation, would operate as much on these women's minds as on their bodies.[55]

---

[53] On the intersection of slavery and state on the local chain gangs, see Rothman, *Slave Country*, 99. On the display of black bodies, see Hartman, *Scenes of Subjection*.

[54] Report, Joseph Pilié to Prieur, February 11, 1830, Slavery in Louisiana Collection, Manuscript Collection 44, Folder 7, HNOC, my translation.

[55] Nicholas Girod, May 8, 1813, quoted in Rothman, *Slave Country*, 99.

These predominately black chain gangs performed essential labor that made the city habitable and navigable for everyone. Paved streets facilitated the circulation of people and goods, which benefitted planters, merchants and consumers. Lanterns eased travel for laborers and revelers at night. Sanitation duties exposed the workers to contagions, but improved the public's health. The gardens beautified the cityscape and added European charm to the newly American city. And in emergencies prisoners represented a quick and cheap labor reserve in the face of imminent threats. When the river breached the city's levee in 1828, the mayor "immediately on the receipt of the information, ordered out the jail convicts and chain negroes, together with what other force could be raised at so unreasonable an hour."[56] All residents and visitors benefitted from the arduous labor of the chain gangs – with the exception of the enslaved workers and, at times, their owners.

Though some disobedient bondspersons wound up in jail for "correction," other slave owners sent their slaves, most (though not all) of them male, to labor at the public works for their masters' profit. Like absentee slave owners across the Atlantic World, diverse owners outsourced the work of mastery in exchange for bank notes. Masters left their slaves in the jail for as little as a few days up to nearly one year. In 1811 a "negre" named Lafortune labored on the chain gang from May 29th to June 15th, and his owner, a Mr. Lemarié, received $4.25 in payment. Mayor Nicolas Girod ordered paid to Claude Girod six piastres for twenty-eight days of work by the latter's bondman Harry. Joseph Antoine Peytavin received six piastres for the twenty-four days of labor that his bondman performed. Edouard Forstall received 12 piastres in July 1819 and $13.50 in December for the twenty-four and twenty-seven days respectively that his bondman Benoît labored on the chain gang. Prosper Foy received $13 for twenty-six days of work performed by "his mulatto Casimir." In March 1822, Mr. V. Fitzgerald leased his "negresse" Euphrosine to the chain gang, as did Jean Fisher, who did the same with his bondwoman Clarisse. Masters enjoyed the guaranteed, virtually immediate profit of leasing their slaves to the state.[57]

---

[56] "Crevasse," *Louisiana Courier*, March 25, 1828.

[57] Mandat de payment, Mather to Lemarié, New Orleans, July 5, 1811, THC, Collection VII; Mandat de payment, Girod to Girod, New Orleans, September 26, 1812, THC, Collection VII; Mandat de payment, Girod to [Joseph Antoine] Peytavin, New Orleans, March 12, 1814, THC, Collection VII; Mandat de payment, Macarty to Forstall, New Orleans, July 2, 1819, THC, Collection VII; Mandat de payment, Macarty to Forstall,

White female slave owners also profited from the jail's custodial functions. Mme. V. James, a white woman, sent her bondman Sans Façon to the jail. Between January 1813 and February 1814, he worked 342 days. The city paid her eighty-five piastres for the year of labor with a "deduction for Sundays and for five holidays" (*cinq jours de fêtes*). Mme. André Villamil received $6.75 for the twenty-seven days of work her bondman performed on the public works in June and July 1814. Both women might have had any number of economic or non-economic reasons to leave the bondman with the state. This arrangement might have been the most profitable one, or for any number of reasons they might have simply preferred the enslaved men out of their houses. On the other hand, these women might have used the jail to insulate themselves – and their race-based status – as southern white ladies from performing the unbecoming work of slave ownership.[58]

Free black slave owners in New Orleans also availed themselves of the jail's services, which landed their enslaved men and women inside the jail and on the chain gang. John Johnson, described as a "free Negro" (*Negre Libre*), received $30.50 for 152 days of work by his slave Hector, who worked on the chain gang between March and July 1814. Only a few months later, in October, Johnson received another $30.50 for Hector's work on the chain gangs. Rosette Montreuil, a free woman of color, received $14.50 for labor performed by her mulatto bondman Michel. In a handful of instances from the records surveyed, female slave owners were responsible for the imprisonment of slave women. Madame Paris, a free woman of color, leased her bondwoman Marie Françoise to the prison for February through April of 1822. Significantly, this woman did not work on the chain gang. Instead, she was described as a "Negro at the jail" (*Nègre à la Geole*). Perhaps she worked in some other capacity, perhaps cleaning, laundry, or cooking. Whatever the case, free black slave owners also profited from a system in which the state leased the

New Orleans, December 17, 1819, THC, Collection VII; Mandat de payment, Macarty to Prosper Foy, New Orleans, April 18, 1819, THC, Collection VII; Mandat de payment, Roffignac to Fitzgerald, New Orleans, March 7, 1822, THC, Collection VII; Roffignac to Fisher, New Orleans, March 15, 1822, THC, Collection VII.

The Heartman Collection housed at Xavier University and available on microfilm contains over 1,000 such documents, many of them from later in the antebellum period. I do not fully explore them here, but they offer an invaluable resource on the relationship between slaves and the New Orleans jail well into the 1830s and beyond.

58 Mandat de payment, Girod to Mme. V. James, New Orleans, March 18, 1814, Collection VII, THC, my translation; Mandat de payment, Girod to Mme. André Villamil, New Orleans, July 25, 1814, Collection VII, THC, my translation.

labor of privately owned slaves to build local infrastructure. The presence of these slaves who had not been accused of crimes only added to the diversity of both the jail and the chain gangs.[59]

When slaves labored on the work gangs due to criminal sentences, however, their masters' interests sometimes came into conflict with those of the state. In 1815, Joseph Chardon petitioned the City Council concerning his bondwoman Phibie, a "strong and robust" quadroon. The mayor sentenced her to two years on the public works for an unrecorded infraction. Phibie worked for the city year round, performing labor that Chardon described as "hard and painful" (*durs et pénibles*). Upon her release, Chardon alleged, the jailer, likely Puche's successor John H. Holland, billed Chardon $90.25 for Phibie's meals and $12 for medical expenses. Chardon was enraged that the city enjoyed "the fruits of [Phibie's] labor" for two years and then charged her master for boarding and health care. To support his claim, Chardon cited a case from the previous year in which an enslaved man named Georges labored on the public works and his owner did not have to pay fees to reclaim him. It is unclear whether or not Chardon paid the reclamation fee, but his complaint highlighted the fissures between the interests of some individual masters and the state.[60]

---

[59] Mandat de payment, Girod to Johnson, New Orleans, August 17, 1814, Collection VII, THC (The payment note is addressed to "James Johnston, N/L," but the signature is written "John Johnson"); Mandat de payment, Girod to Johnson, New Orleans, October 21, 1814, Collection VII, THC; Mandat de payment, Macarty to Montreuil, f.d.c.l., New Orleans, June 30, 1819, Collection VII, THC; Mandat de payment, Roffignac to Paris, New Orleans, February 4, 1822, March 7, 1822, and April 18, 1822, all Collection VII, THC.

[60] Complaint, Joseph Chardon before the New Orleans City Council, December 16, 1815, Slavery in Louisiana, Manuscript Collection 44, Folder 4, HNOC, my translation. See also Ariela Julie Gross, *Double Character: Slavery and Mastery in the Antebellum Southern Courtroom* (Princeton: Princeton University Press, 2000), 31–33. Chardon also appeared in a later case, *Chardon's Heirs v. Bongue* (1836). In his will, Chardon emancipated two of his slaves, Jenny and Eugene, and left them $3,000 each. He appointed Pierre Bongue executor. Chardon's biological relatives in France, however, challenged the validity of the will. The Supreme Court of Louisiana upheld the will, thanks in part to Phibie's testimony. Her testimony and that of other witnesses revealed that, during a trip to his native France, Chardon's nephews attempted to kill him. Chardon responded by disinheriting all biological relatives. It is unclear whether Phoebe was free at this point. See *Chardon's Heirs v. Bongue* (1836), 9 La.Rptr 458 (LA 1836), in Louisiana Supreme Court, *Reports of Cases Argued and Determined in the Supreme Court of the State of Louisiana*, eds. Thomas Curry and Branch Walthus Miller (New Orleans: Benjamin Levy, 1836), IX: 458–771.

Similarly, when slave labor on the public works proved deadly, owners lost people and precious capital. Like Phibie, Felix Armand's bondman Apollon was also sentenced to public works, and part of his labor involved the demolition of houses. He sustained an injury, so the city sent Apollon to the hospital. In July 1817, they billed Armand for the fees, which he contested. He reasoned that since the city had enjoyed Apollon's unpaid labor then, according to the Black Code, the city should therefore assume the liabilities. It is unclear whether Felix had to pay for the hospitalization, but he did pay an even higher cost. The city worked Apollon to death: he succumbed to his injuries in early August. This enslaved man lost his life due to unsafe labor conditions on the public works, and in the process his master lost a valuable investment. Though this loss and others like it, if uncompensated by the state, might have devastated an individual owner, the public works more broadly extended the collective slave power in the city. Even in this instance, the harmed master did not threaten slavery as an institution, nor did he give much consideration to the lives of the slaves themselves. Rather master and state contested the rules that should gov-ern – and thereby legitimized – their collective power to extract labor and life from those held as slaves.[61]

Enslaved persons' release from the penal system could prove as con-troversial as their entry. Pardons in particular became yet another point of contention between colonial officials and residents. The governor's ability to vacate or amend sentences for slaves afforded masters and other inter-ested parties a final opportunity to legally contest the decisions meted out by judicial authorities. As Apollon's story reveals, time on the public works could become a death sentence. Masters lobbied to prevent the same fate for their slaves, and sometimes they were successful. In 1806 Claiborne pardoned John Loyd, "a mulatto man and bond servant ... convicted before the Honorable the Superior Court of this Territory, of the crime of Theft, and ... sentenced to two years hard labour."[62] Claiborne pardoned a Native American person named Annetto, who had been found guilty of "having aided and assisted the escape of Negro's – from their masters." Details in this case are elusive, but indi-genous peoples were enslaved during the colonial period, and even after

---

[61] Règlement pour la Prison de Police; Surveyor's Report, Joseph Pilié to Mayor Denis Prieur, February 11, 1830, Slavery in Louisiana Collection, Manuscript Collection 44, Folders 7–9, HNOC; Felix Armand to Macarty, New Orleans, July 30, 1817, NYHS NOC I:10; Armand to Macarty, New Orleans, August 2, 1817, NYHS NOC I:10.

[62] Claiborne to Sheriff of the County of Orleans, May 27, 1806, *Letter Books*, III:292.

slavery became predominately black both groups continued to intermarry and form alliances, so any number of solidarities might have prompted Annetto's actions. It is unclear whether Annetto was enslaved or free. Either way, the governor decided to mete out mercy in this case.[63]

Like most executive decisions, pardons invited dissent, as one person's act of mercy was another's threat to public safety or personal interests. In the aftermath of the Deslondes Revolt of 1811, for example, owners lobbied Claiborne on behalf of their valuable captured slaves. When Francis Rivas of Iberville Parish complained about another of Claiborne's pardons, the governor responded: "The Negro to whom you alude [sic], was pardoned on Condition, that he should remain a Prisoner for life in the Joal [sic] of New Orleans, & employed at hard labor." This was not simply an act of mercy. A "Negre de chaine" was more useful to the state than another black corpse. Claiborne reassured the complainant that the pardon would not imperil the slave system or social control: "There is no ground therefore for [the] uneasiness ... given to yourself & family."[64]

"A COMBINATION ... BETWEEN THE COLOURED AND WHITE PRISONERS"

Even as Claiborne defended the prison's efficacy in 1812, local leaders feared promiscuous alliances inside the prison as much as they feared them in society at large. By then, only a few years after the founding of Haiti and one year after the largest slave revolt in US history, elites in Louisiana and the Atlantic plantation world feared subversive revolutionaries. As the War of 1812 commenced (discussed in the next chapter), political and military leaders feared alliances between the republic's domestic enemies – Native Americans and slaves – and the British. Article 11 of the Règlement anticipated unlawful collaboration between the jail's keepers and its captives: "A Jailer who by negligence allows a detainee to leave will be fined ninety-nine piastres, with half for the owner and half for the city; and if it is found he assisted with the evasion, in addition to the fine he will be dismissed" (notably, "detainees" were assumed to have owners, i.e. to be enslaved). This was no small point, as corruption and insubordination extended to the ranks of law

---

[63] "Return of Civil Appointments, Pardons &c. from the 1st of July 1807, to the 31st December 1807 inclusive – Orleans Territory," October 9, 1807, *Letter Books*, IV: 146.

[64] Claiborne to Francis Rivas, New Orleans, May 16, 1812, *Letter Books*, VI: 99–100.

enforcement: In one instance from 1822, a corporal had a guardsman incarcerated for the use of disrespectful language and other acts of disobedience. The jail's structure created the conditions for illegal cooperation between employees and inmates.[65]

More than that, organized resistance to the prison regime among the inmates themselves proved an equal, if not greater, threat. A famous 1814 jailbreak illuminated the diverse communities that formed inside the jail and the ways that those networks provided the foundation for resistance. In that year, Pierre Lafitte, the pirate and sometime illegal slave trader, "escaped" the jail after his brother Jean Lafitte agreed to enter the War of 1812 on the side of the United States. J. H. Holland, the "keeper of the prison," advertised a $1,000 reward for his recapture. The advertisement noted Pierre Lafitte "took with him three negroes, to wit – Sam, formerly the property of M. Sawza, Ceasar the property of Mr. Pierre Lefebvre, and Hamilcar, the property of Mr. Jarnais." Holland's narrative attributed agency to Lafitte ("took with him"), but it is equally possible that these men became allies and seized this opportunity to escape. If so, this escape implicated a global web of trade. Lafitte's trade networks stretched from New Orleans to Veracruz and Matamoros, and Hamilcar's name suggests he might have been (or descended from) an African-born Muslim. Hamilcar either strategically allied with or became subject to a known slave trader and enemy of state to escape the jail.[66]

In addition to regulating social relations within the prison, the city also invested large sums to police the border between incarcerated inmates and the local population. At the time of the 1820 federal census, the police jail listed 81 inmates as male slaves and ten as female slaves; ninety inmates classed as white men were held in "jail for debt and misdemeanors."[67] Blacks and whites were segregated on paper if not in the actual prison. Ironically, their confinement (and quarantining) may have saved their lives during the yellow fever outbreak in the summer of

[65] Règlement pour la Prison de Police; Deposition, Jacob Hart before Macarty, November 2, 1818, NYHS NOC 8:14.

[66] "1000 Dollars Reward," *Louisiana Courier*, November 18, 1814.
   On African-born Muslims in early Louisiana, see Michael A. Gomez, *Black Crescent: The Experience and Legacy of African Muslims in the Americas* (Cambridge: Cambridge University Press, 2005); Hall, *Africans in Colonial Louisiana*.

[67] 1820 U.S. Census, *New Orleans, Louisiana*, page: 110; NARA Roll: M33_32; Image: 123, www.ancestry.com. Officials did not classify any of the incarcerated as white females or free blacks.

that year, which left over 2,000 people dead.[68] Nonetheless, desperate prisoners broke down the boundary between the inside and outside. Between May and December 1822, Warden Dominique Bellaume billed Mayor Roffignac at least 1,480 piastres for the jail's operating expenses, but money did not buy security.[69] Rumblings of trouble began in April 1823, when six prisoners escaped: "John G. M'Quahe, sentenced to hard labour for burglary; Stephen Tarleton, John Dailey, and John Moore, convicted of larceny; Thomas Bingham, [convicted] of manslaughter; and JM Fremont committed for larceny." The absence of racial markers and the presence of surnames, several of them English and Irish, suggest these men were Euro-American and perhaps working-class immigrants. The escapees exploited the jail's dilapidated infrastructure by "digging under the wall of their cell a hole sufficiently large to let them pass into the yard of the city prison, where they [scaled] the wall and got into the street." They escaped the jail and perhaps used their privilege as white men to disappear into the New Orleans streets.[70]

Mayor Roffignac, Sheriff G. W. Morgan, and a deputy sheriff inspected the prison in the month after the escape. The *Louisiana Gazette* reprinted the sheriff's observations in which he expressed concerns about the work equipment stored onsite. Morgan feared that the tools that prisoners used to build the city could also be used to escape the prison. The relocation of the implements would unclutter the cramped prison yard, strengthen surveillance efforts, and deprive potential escapees of such tools. What Morgan feared most, however, were black–white alliances within the prison: "the city for its own safety would be obliged to enlarge and strengthen the prison; that if a combination took place between the coloured and white prisoners the community would be in great danger." For Morgan, a more spacious prison would preclude multiracial political resistance and thereby create a safer society.[71]

---

[68] In the early nineteenth century, physicians debated the communicability of yellow fever, with some arguing that the disease was not contagious. Governor Villeré, on the other hand, considered the disease contagious, and charged the legislature take precautions. As evidence, Villeré pointed to the absence of yellow fever behind prison walls, where no prisoner contracted the disease. Alcée Fortier, *A History of Louisiana*, 4 vols. (Paris: Groupil & Co., 1904), 189–190.

[69] Invoices, Warden Dominique Bellaume to Mayor Roffignac, May 4, 1822; March 17, 1822; June 7, 1822; July 8, 1822; August, 8, 1822; September 5, 1822; October 3, 1822; November 8, 1822; December 4, 1822, NYHS NOC 6:1.

[70] *Louisiana Gazette*, April 9, 1823.

[71] Deposition, G. W. Morgan before Gallien Preval, New Orleans, May 29, 1823, reprinted in *Louisiana Gazette*, May 30, 1823.

Indeed, one such "combination" occurred in a jail located upriver from New Orleans. A Baton Rouge newspaper reported that in the early evening of Wednesday, September 17, 1823, as the local jailer distributed dinner, four prisoners rushed him, seized his keys, dashed across the prison yard, and scaled the fence. "Assistance was procured," and officials recaptured three men near the prison. The fourth escapee they caught "within six or seven miles of town." The paper's description of the fugitives reveals the contingent making of race and status within prison: "Of these, two were convicts, and one by the name of Wilson is awaiting his trial for slave stealing; the fourth is a negro." The three white men required explanations for their incarceration: two had been convicted of crimes, and the third awaited trial. The fourth, "a negro," needed no such explanation; blackness was presumably reason enough for confinement. As with Lafitte's New Orleans escape nearly a decade before, this prison break also fostered a curious alliance: an accused slave stealer and a negro, likely enslaved, escaped confinement together. On the one hand, there is nothing unusual about a slave stealer's absconding with a slave. Perhaps he hoped to sell the black man on the black market. But, it is equally possible that the black man was not stolen, but actually chose to enter a strategic alliance with these men. Finally, in this one instance, the exigencies of imprisonment inverted the norms of the dominant society: "The two convicts were in irons, but it seems found means to shake them off." The two convicted white men had to break out of fetters, while the "negro" man was not chained. His blackness, perhaps, was shackle enough.[72]

These four men broke out of the Baton Rouge jail on a Wednesday. Five days later, on Monday, New Orleans inmates mounted a full-scale prison revolt. On the morning of September 22, a jail keeper entered one of the three doors leading to the exercise yard, a space of "not … more than about a fifth or sixth of a common lot of 60 by 120 feet." About fifty of the 160 prisoners stormed him, and they nearly gained access to the street. A single door stood between the prisoners and freedom, a door guarded by a "a faithful turnkey (though a black boy and a slave)." He must have been considered faithful, because the regulations insisted the warden "never entrust to one of the slaves … the keys to the prison and the small gates under any pretext." This slave trustee indeed proved trustworthy. He bolted the door and prevented the mass escape (and therefore locked himself inside the prison with the rebels, so he hid inside a chimney).

---

[72] "From the *Baton Rouge Gazette*," *Louisiana Gazette*, September 23, 1823.

The prisoners attempted to use an iron bar to break the lock on the street door, but by then the city guard arrived. The guardsmen drove the prisoners back into the yard – "though not till one of them had received a severe wound from one of the keepers, by a dirk." Undeterred, the inmates moved to the dungeon, where they broke open the locks on the doors, entered the chamber, and took planks from the floorboards, which they then carried to the gallery. There they built scaffolding in hopes of climbing to the roof.[73]

By this time the military and private citizens surrounded the prison. As the prisoners mounted the roof, someone in the crowd began firing on the prisoners, wounding (and likely killing) at least one person. The other rebels retreated, some by cutting a hole through the floor to reach the keeper's quarters. "While at work there," the newspaper described, "one of them was shot from the street window. The ball entered his forehead between the eyes and killed him dead upon the spot; soon after which they were quelled and secured in their proper apartments." The prison went on heightened alert. Those who participated in the revolt were enchained, and guardsmen remained stationed around the prison.[74]

These two incidents – the small escape in Baton Rouge and the larger uprising in New Orleans – both raise the possibility of multiracial "infrapolitics" not only within prisons, but also across prisons. In both cases, prisoners formed a collective bent on resistance. The exact demographics of the insurgents in the New Orleans revolt remain unclear. The revolt implicated about one third of the total inmate population, which suggests a high level of collaboration among individuals from diverse backgrounds, but this is not certain. They might have all been Euro-American, as with the escape in New Orleans five months prior. In that case, the black trustee might have used state power to foil a revolt by lower-class white men. On the other hand, these two episodes raise the possibility of collective resistance over social boundaries inside the jail and spatial boundaries across the state. It is difficult to document this connection, but, the timing and location of the events raise the intriguing possibility that incarcerated persons in New Orleans might have acted either under the inspiration of or in concert with their counterparts in Baton Rouge. Such coordination, of course, would pose an intolerable risk to the leaders in a growing city.

[73] Deposition, Morgan, May 29, 1823; *Louisiana Gazette*, September 23, 1823.
[74] *Louisiana Gazette*, September 23, 1823.

Even as officials went on heightened alert after the riot, individual inmates still resisted incarceration and the public works. In early 1824, not even three months after the dramatic revolt inside the New Orleans jail, a mulatto bondsman named James escaped the chain gang. Local leaders and leading citizens hoped to quell such defiance, but they could not agree on how to do it. Some wanted to strengthen the existing prison's structure, while others wanted a new prison, and debates raged between Jacksonian and anti-Jacksonian factions, fiscal conservatives and those who advocated economic investment in the infrastructure. In May 1824, Roffignac contracted with architect Gabriel Correjoller to renovate the existing jails ("pour l'entreprise & l'augmentation des Prisons"), and Correjoller committed to offering 1,500 piastres as security for starting the process. The fractiousness and corruption of local politics notwithstanding, elected officials decided to prevent such radical resistance by building a modern penitentiary.[75]

Louisiana officials acted in line with the international trend toward penal reform. Brazil's 1824 Constitution outlawed corporal punishment on citizens, though it remained legal for slaves (and members of the armed forces). At about the same time, the Auburn Prison (formerly Newgate Prison) in New York formalized a newer model of prison discipline. The Auburn System's philosophy emphasized the redemptive aspects of hard work. To that end, officials required collective hard labor by day and solitary confinement by night. That plan also introduced other measures, including mandatory silence, military-style marches to cells, and constant surveillance during labor. In 1826, the Massachusetts legislature followed suit, and in 1829 its "New Prison" followed the Auburn example. Officials in many other states followed, and the Auburn Model came into widespread use.[76]

The following year, theoretical arguments and unforeseen material circumstances converged to create the conditions for building a new, modern prison. Edward Livingston, the penal theorist responsible for the Louisiana Civil Code of 1825, encouraged wardens to prevent "the corrupting influence of promiscuous association" inside the prison.

[75] Cardinaud, "Report of the Captain of the Guard, January 3-4," January 4, 1824, Police Department Reports, NYHS NOC 10:1; Promissory note, Gabriel Correjoller before Roffignac, New Orleans, May 17, 1824, NYHS NOC 9:4.

[76] Peter M. Beattie, "'Born under the Cruel Rigor of Captivity, the Supplicant Left It Unexpectedly by Committing a Crime': Categorizing and Punishing Slave Convicts in Brazil, 1830–1897," *The Americas* 66, no. 1 (July 2009): 11–55, 14; Hirsch, *The Rise of the Penitentiary*, 65–66.

Wardens and visitors could not, he argued, observe "the signs of intelligence, or hear the whispers of communication ... between the most abandoned felons, working for years within a few feet of each other. Strict discipline, we are told, prevents this." The proper discipline, of course, was the whip. Jailers "may beat any convict without any kind of restriction," he argued. "He has only to suppose an irreverent look or a sign of intelligence, and it is his duty to apply the whip – there can be no check." That same year, the city suffered a devastating fire that destroyed the Pontalba house on the corner of St. Peter and Levee Streets. Had the fire spread, one local paper reported, it would have damaged the Pontalba buildings, "the buildings on the corner of Chartres and St. Peter streets, the city hall, prison, and rest of the buildings on that square, most probably, would all have been destroyed." The fire necessitated hasty relocations, and in its aftermath, Prieur and Derbigny debated the feasibility of inmate segregation by race in light of the costs of renovation versus new construction.[77]

The following year, Andrew Jackson took national office, and he brought with him a commitment to nation-building through the manipulation of people in space, specifically through the enfranchisement of white men, the removal of indigenous populations, and the expansion of black slavery. In 1830 the champion of white manhood signed the Indian Removal Act, which led to the forcible deportation of indigenous persons from the Deep South to Indian Territory (present-day Oklahoma) and opened millions of acres for white settlers to expand cotton country. He was also an early supporter of the American Colonization Society, an organization dominated by southern planters dedicated to the removal of free blacks from the nation (they would be resettled in Liberia). In other words, Jacksonian Americans understood the relationship between race, space, and the nation on a local and global scale.[78]

On the smaller scale, prisons also allowed individual states to quarantine undesirable people from the body politic. The same year Jackson was

---

[77] Edward Livingston, *Letter from Edward Livingston, Esq. to Roberts Vaux, on the Advantages of the Pennsylvania System of Prison Discipline* (Philadelphia: Jesper Harding, 1828), 8–9; L'Argus, February 4, 1828; Henry C. Castellanos, *New Orleans as It Was: Episodes of Louisiana Life* (New Orleans: The L. Graham Co., Ltd., 1905), 190; "Administrations of the Mayors of New Orleans: Denis Prieur (1791–1857)," Louisiana Division, NOPL, http://nutrias.org/info/louinfo/admins/prieur.htm, accessed February 8, 2010.

[78] Saxton, *The Rise and Fall of the White Republic*; Theda Purdue, "Cherokee Women and the Trail of Tears," *Journal of Women's History* 1, no. 1 (Spring 1989): 14–30; Yarema, *The American Colonization Society*.

elected, Louisiana Governor Pierre Derbigny outlawed interracial public works. The 1830 report quoted at length above included unmarked convicts, presumably white, who labored on the public works alongside blacks. A report from the following year, by contrast, listed "31 monthly nègres, 46 nègres de chaines, & 19 nègresses" who labored by cleaning, assisting tradesmen, measuring stones and sand, and making repairs to the slaughterhouse. After this law took effect, all of the men and women on the chain gang were black.[79]

That same year, Edward Livingston also became minister plenipotentiary to France, at which time he expressed a status-based theory of punishment that hinged on a sharp cleavage based on racialized status:

There is a line of demarcation, which it would be rash in the extreme to destroy even in punishments; and the sight of a freeman performing the forced labour, or suffering under the stripes usually inflicted on the slave, must give rise to ideas of the most insubordinate nature.[80]

As such, corporal punishment remained a key component of social control in the plantation south. Even as northern reformers, abolitionists, and others worked to outlaw the lash for citizens, southerners fiercely defended their right to whip slaves. In an era in which white manhood came to hold intrinsic value, leaders became loath to sentence white men to the same punishments as black men. The assumption was that black women would also work on these gangs and receive these punishments. And if they could not be inflicted upon white men, they definitely would not apply to white women, which would have violated patriarchal notions of white femininity. If the public works represented "hundreds of tiny theatres of punishment" in a punitive city, Edward Livingston wanted its laborers to have black faces. In France, the public works were coming to an end; the last chain gang appeared in 1836. This development did not sway the Francophile Livingston, and the largely black chain gang, then and now, provided cheap labor for public and private profit.[81]

As Livingston theorized Louisiana punishment in France, Frenchmen Gustave de Beaumont and Alexis de Tocqueville visited the New Orleans jail as part of their survey of US prisons. The July Monarchy in France also had a prison problem, and they sent the two Frenchmen to survey best

---

[79] Report, Pilié to Prieur, December 24, 1831, Slavery in Louisiana Collection, Manuscript Collection 44, Folder 9, HNOC.

[80] Edward Livingston, *A System of Penal Law for the State of Louisiana* (Philadelphia: James Kay, Jun. & Co., 1833), 139.

[81] Ibid., 139; Foucault, *Discipline and Punish*, 109, 113.

practices in the United States. What they saw in 1832 left them "unable to describe the painful impression." They continued:

The place for convicted criminals in New Orleans cannot be called a prison: it is a horrid sink, in which they are thronged together, and which is fit only for those dirty animals found here together with the prisoners. It must be observed that those who are detained here are not slaves: it is the prison for persons free in the ordinary course of life.

The visitors emphasized their shock at the sight of free men in the jail, but evidence suggests the jail housed both free and enslaved persons. Perhaps the sight of free men in this facility made a deeper impression on the visitors than the banal degradation of the enslaved. Whatever the case, the two Frenchmen noted one ostensibly positive point amid the penury: conditions were so inhumane in the dilapidated facility that the governor promised funding for a new state penitentiary.[82]

Local leaders generally agreed on the need for a new prison, but the construction process sparked charges of corruption and factionalism. Mayor Roffignac drew criticism for the land he purchased from a Mr. Bienvenue for the new parish prison. On a local editorial page, pseudonymous author Fair-Play lamented the location designated for the new prison. Situated about two miles beyond the city center adjacent to Faubourgs Tremé and Marigny, the new jail would sit "amidst a slave population, which would aggravate the danger of any revolt among the prisoners, who might achieve incalculable mischief before sufficient force could be brought to quell them." This author feared a very immediate and potentially destabilizing synergy between disorder in the parish prison and the disordered neighborhoods just beyond it. Even one of the mayor's supporters conceded the mayor "acted hastily (and he acknowledges it himself) in sanctioning the resolve for purchasing Mr. Bienvenu's lot, in the present embarrassed state of the city finances." As across the US South, many free residents criticized the fiscal costs of the prison as well as the threat such sites of concentrated state power posed to their conceptions of settler republicanism and limited government.[83]

---

[82] Gustave Auguste de Beaumont de la Bonnière and Alexis de Tocqueville, *On the Penitentiary System in the United States and Its Application in France* (Carbondale and Edwardsville: Southern Illinois University Press, 1964), 49, 195. On slaves in the state penitentiary, see Jeff Forret, "Before Angola: Enslaved Prisoners in the Louisiana State Penitentiary," *Louisiana History* 54, no. 2 (Spring 2013): 133–171.

[83] Fair-Play, "For the *Louisiana Gazette*," *Louisiana Gazette*, May 30, 1823; Fiat Justitia, "For the *Louisiana Gazette*," *Louisiana Gazette*, May 31, 1823. The latter contributor's

FIGURE 4.1 Orleans Police Jail and Parish Prison, ca. 1864, from Marshall Dunham Photograph Album, Mss 3241, Louisiana and Lower Mississippi Valley Collections, LSU Libraries, Baton Rouge, LA.

In the 1830s, former Saint-Dominguan Joseph Pilié, the city surveyor and public works manager, became the architect charged with designing a new jail for Orleans Parish. Located near Congo Square (and therefore the execution grounds), adjacent to Faubourg Tremé at the intersection of Tremé, Orleans, St. Ann, and Marais Streets (present-day Louis Armstrong Park), the new structure held separate quarters for women, white men, black men, debtors, and non-violent offenders, as well as a separate section for those who paid for their own lodgings. Builders completed the project in 1837, which was the same year officials demolished the old police jail. Built at a cost of some $200,000, the new facility hewed to the conventions of nineteenth-century penology and racist ideology. This state-of-the-art jail segregated inmates by race, class, and sex and used architecture in an attempt to foreclose radical, multiracial communities, and politics and to impose the binary categories of the Old South.[84]

Hierarchies have histories. The politics of place inside of the New Orleans jail created and responded to shifting social categories in a cosmopolitan society. Local leaders called for the discrete categories that defined the nation – free whites, black slaves, and free blacks who increasingly became "slaves without masters" – and they paid guardsmen, wardens, jailers, architects, and contractors to classify and situate the people within those categories.[85] The prison industrial complex and mass incarceration did not develop parallel to or after slavery, but in conjunction with it. The state, private enterprises, and citizens alike have benefitted from the labor of the oppressed, slave and free, for a long time. Punishment inside the jail and on its chain gangs became one means for flattening a port city's diversity into an almost exclusively black–white binary.

From one perspective, this change-over-time story charts a familiar story: the gradual construction of racist segregation in the Deep South. In the 1830s (and well beyond), residential patterns in New Orleans were not defined by racial segregation. Within the prison, however,

---

Latin eponym means "Let justice be done." On southern white backlash against prisons, see Ayers, *Vengeance and Justice*, chapter 2.

[84] *The New Orleans Bee*, July 12, 1837. The new structure was demolished in 1895. Roulhac Toledano, Mary Louise Christovich, Betsy Swanson, and Robin Von Breton Derbes, *New Orleans Architecture Volume 6: Faubourg Tremé and the Bayou Road* (New Orleans: Pelican Publishing Company, 2003), 63; For Pilié's Saint-Dominguan origins, see Dessens, *Creole City*, 178.

[85] Ira Berlin, *Slaves without Masters: The Free Negro in the Antebellum South* (New York: Pantheon Books, 1974).

officials experimented with such segregation, a process that anticipated subsequent partitions across the twentieth-century urban landscape, whether through the vigilante violence of Jim Crow or through red-lining, block busting, and other methods of housing discrimination. In this sense, the management of free blacks and slaves in the antebellum prison incubated strategies for the management of black citizens in the post-emancipation era and even into the present.

Yet, even as penal theorists, prison wardens, and local officials constructed barriers to collaboration across physical and figurative borders, individuals and collectives contested imperial race-making at each step. They built strategic solidarities across the very lines that authorities hoped to cement. Their radical histories remind us that there is nothing timeless about segregation. Then, as now, hierarchies in the Deep South and in the Global South required constant reinforcement as well as constant contestation.

5

Atlantic Spaces

I presume that His Majesty's Government could not (if from motives of prudence alone) have intended that 500 slaves who had just obtained their freedom in the manner they had done, should be thrown abroad upon any Colony where slavery existed, without considering itself bound to meet the expense of proper Controul and Inspection, as well as of mere subsistence.

Sir Ralph Woodford to Earl Henry Bathurst, 1818

[T]ake measures for having the Settlers of both Settlements distinctly apprized that they are free to make such bargains for their labor as they may think proper & that no person has a right to appropriate their labor otherwise than in conformity with the terms for which they may have contracted to give it.

Howich to Major-General Sir Lewis Grant, 1831

The wars of a revolutionary age led to sweeping journeys for Charles-Joseph de Loppinot and his slaves. Loppinot's journeys began with the Acadian Removal, when the British expelled French residents from Nova Scotia in an event that presaged the Seven Years War (1756–1763). Most "Cajuns" (as they came to be called) who moved from Canada to southeastern Louisiana recreated their agrarian lifestyle, but strivers like Loppinot became planters. He married a wealthy widow and took possession of her property, which included slaves. Shortly thereafter, Loppinot and his slaves moved to Saint-Domingue, where he became a *grand blanc* in Jérémie who owned land valued at 676,750 francs. When revolutionaries began their uprising in 1791, the master became a runaway. Around 1792 he left his property and under British protection escaped, reportedly aided by loyal slaves who "[placed] him in a barrel, and [sent] him to Jamaica as part of a shipment of sugar." In this era of opportunistic

162

imperial loyalties, Loppinot, who had been expelled from Canada by the British, fought for five years under that empire's flag. He aimed to defeat antislavery rebels on the island, separate from the French Republic, embrace British sovereignty, and preserve his land and slaves in Saint-Domingue. When British forces withdrew in October 1798, Loppinot and other displaced French planters settled in Jamaica, where he again came into possession of people he claimed to own. He would not stay for long. To "attract wealthy French planters" to a sparsely populated Trinidad, the Spanish enacted the *Cédula de Poblacion* of 1783. That act granted to each white Catholic immigrant, male or female, who swore loyalty to Madrid thirty-two acres for each household member and half that for every slave (free blacks and mulattos could claim half the land allowances specified for white settlers). Though Trinidad had become a British crown colony in 1797, it continued to follow Spanish laws. As a result, Loppinot's large number of slaves entitled him to nearly fifteen times the amount of land typically granted to white settlers. In April 1800, two years after his arrival in Jamaica, Loppinot, his wife, and his slaves moved to Trinidad, where his slaves' existence secured land for him even as their sweat insulated him from the colony's chronic labor shortage. By 1806, Loppinot and the slaves on "La Reconnaissance," his estate in Trinidad, drew on expertise honed in Nova Scotia, Louisiana, Saint-Domingue, and Jamaica to produce cocoa and coffee for the global commodities market.[1]

---

[1] Loppinot appears in several archival sources from colonial Louisiana. On July 5, 1766, the colony of New Orleans disbursed to Loppinot, the Commander of the Artillery, for himself and eleven subordinates at the English Turn ["Detour," short for "Detour des Anglais"] the following provisions: six *livres* of bread, twelve *livres* six *onces de biscuit*, and five *livres* of lard. In February 1774, Don Carlos Loppinot sold a "bosales," or African-born, man named Telemaco to Juan Antonio Gayarré. That same year, he was also party to *Don Joseph Loppinot vs. Juan Villeneuve for the Loss of His Slave, Named Mulet, by Drowning* (1774), a unique document that demonstrates Spanish civil procedure in colonial Louisiana. Loppinot sued his neighbor for compensation for his mulatto bondman's accidental death. *Journal des dépenses de la colonie de la Nouvelle Orléans*, July 5, 1766, entry number 25, page 75, NYPL; Act of Sale, Loppinot to Gayarré, Notary Andres Almonester y Roxas, New Orleans, February 3, 1774, page 74, NANO; "The Documents in Loppinot Case, 1774," trans. Laura L. Porteous, *The Louisiana Historical Quarterly* 12, no. 1 (January 1929): 39–120; Jerome F. Lopinot, "Charles Joseph – Compte de Lopinot," Typed Manuscript (photocopy), Lopinot Family Papers, SC 49, West Indiana & Special Collections Division, Main Library, UWI.

On the Acadian Removal, see Gabriel Debien, "The Acadians in Santo Domingo: 1764–1789," *The Cajuns: Essays on Their History and Culture*, ed. and trans. Glenn R. Conrad (Lafayette, LA: Center for Louisiana Studies, University of Southwestern Louisiana, 1983), 19–78; Carl A. Brasseaux, *Acadian to Cajun: Transformation of a People, 1803–1877* (Jackson: University Press of Mississippi, 1992).

A descendant memorialized Loppinot as a "good slave master [who] treated his slaves with a kindness which existed on no other estate in Trinidad." Oral histories from his slaves characterized him as a man who christened a "hanging tree" to deter disobedience. Loppinot would likely have recognized himself in both accounts, since he considered the proper management of slaves essential to individual and imperial power. Even in 1814, as the exiled Napoleon languished on the Island of Elba, Loppinot pleaded with French officials to "preserve that important colony" – Haiti – which by that point had been an independent republic for over a decade. This scheme to reverse the Haitian Revolution was not far-fetched for a man who named his Trinidad estate "La Reconnaissance." If Loppinot could become "reacquainted" with the Louisiana planter's prosperity some 2,000 nautical miles south in Trinidad, then France could become reacquainted with imperial greatness through the re-enslavement of Haiti.[2]

Like Loppinot, blacks in the revolutionary Atlantic also crossed imperial borders in search of prosperity, but the long reach of slavery and the novel coercions of contract labor frustrated their efforts to locate meaningful freedom. This culminating chapter uses the small migration of several hundred freedom-seeking ex-slaves from the sugar plantations of southern Louisiana to the Company Villages of Trinidad after the War of 1812 to illuminate the possibilities and limits of transatlantic migration as a method for escaping the increasingly global confinements of the modern era. In April 1814 an embattled British Vice Admiral Sir Alexander Cochrane issued a proclamation that offered freedom, resettlement, and land grants to the men and their families who enlisted in the Colonial Marines to fight for the Crown. Thousands from across the Eastern Seaboard volunteered, as did their counterparts in the Gulf South, including those in Louisiana and Spanish Florida. After the January 1815 Battle

---

On the *Cédula* of 1783, see Kit Candlin, *The Last Caribbean Frontier, 1795–1815* (Houndmills: Palgrave Macmillan, 2012), 56–57, 100; Gomez, *Black Crescent*, 61–65; A. Meredith John, *The Plantation Slaves of Trinidad, 1783–1816: A Mathematical and Demographic Enquiry* (Cambridge: Cambridge University Press, 1988), 14.

[2] Lopinot, "Charles Joseph – Compte de Lopinot," 1; The jail and "hanging tree" references are taken from Archibald Chauharjasingh, *Lopinot in History* (Port of Spain: Columbus Publishers, 1982), 19, 26. "de se conserver cette importante colonie," Joseph Loppinot to Lieutenant General of Louis XVIII, June 19, 1814, Collection P164, Fonds Charles-Joseph de Loppinot, 1794–1926, Bibliothèque et Archives nationals du Québec (Previously Collection AP-G-164), Québec, Canada, photocopy in Lopinot Family Papers, SC 49, UWI. Loppinot and Lopinot are variations of the same surname.

Loppinot was not the only Frenchman who could not conceive of the Haitian Revolution. See Trouillot, *Silencing the Past*.

of New Orleans, about 300 such volunteers withdrew with British forces and settled in Trinidad.

Though virtually absent in history and memory, this demographically small migration encapsulated and anticipated the sea changes of the global nineteenth century. If by 1815 their colonial histories rendered Louisiana and Trinidad somewhat exceptional in their respective empires, the migrants' experiences in each place provide unique insight into the Atlantic-wide transition from an era of imperial competition to internal consolidation, mercantilism to free trade, and slavery to something akin to freedom.[3] In 1815, to meet industrial demand, staple-producing planters across the Americas demanded ever-increasing labor supplies just as those who advocated wage labor as the profitable and humane alternative to chattel slavery became more and more influential. In Cuba and Brazil, planters relied on the transatlantic slave trade to supply laborers. Sugar and cotton planters in the Lower Mississippi River Valley looked to Africa and then, after the 1807 criminalization of the transatlantic trade, to Maryland, Virginia, and the Carolinas. According to some estimates, between 1800 and 1809 Louisiana imported over 2,600 slaves, a number that exploded to nearly 50,000 in the next decade.[4] Trinidad, by contrast, did not have the same options. Though slave importation increased markedly in the 1790s thanks to the British trade, imperial limits on the transatlantic slave trade in 1807 and intercolonial slave trades shortly thereafter meant that the island's planters could not acquire the number of slaves needed to maximize production.[5]

---

[3] Works that focus on black migration from the Chesapeake after the War of 1812 include Alan Taylor, *The Internal Enemy: Slavery and War in Virginia, 1772–1832* (New York: W. W. Norton & Co., 2013); Harvey Amani Whitfield, *Blacks on the Border: The Black Refugees in British North America, 1815–1860* (Burlington: University of Vermont Press, 2006). Scholars who devote attention to the specific migration from Louisiana to Trinidad include Gene Allen Smith, *The Slaves' Gamble: Choosing Sides in the War of 1812* (New York: Palgrave Macmillan, 2013) and Rothman, *Slave Country*, 119–162. On the significance of small numbers, see Arjun Appadurai, *Fear of Small Numbers: An Essay on the Geography of Anger* (Durham: Duke University Press, 2006).

[4] Michael Tadman, "The Interregional Slave Trade in the History and Myth-Making of the U.S. South," in *The Chattel Principle: Internal Slave Trades in the Americas*, ed. Walter Johnson (New Haven, CT: Yale University Press, 2004), 117–142, 120. On the ways the domestic slave trade helped strengthen US national sovereignty, see Johnson, "The Racial Origins of American Sovereignty," 50–59.

[5] Because of the timing of its entry into the Atlantic plantation complex, Trinidad has become a central point of contention in debates about Britain's economic versus ideological motivations for the outlawing of the international slave trade and abolition. Trinidadian scholar and statesman Eric Williams contended that the transition from slavery to wage labor occurred after slavery became less profitable and was, therefore,

In Trinidad, as planters watered hanging trees to manage expanding slave populations, British imperial officials and formerly enslaved settlers together piloted a program for black emancipation and free labor.[6] Unlike Haiti, which in its constitution granted freedom to all blacks who migrated there, Trinidad was not "free soil" in 1815. But as British officials resettled its black veterans and their families and Africans taken from slave ships in Trinidad, they created another category of black laborers, neither slaves nor wholly free. As planters, imperial officials, and the migrants themselves wrangled over their labor and domestic arrangements on the island, they became harbingers in the international struggle over race and labor in the new global economy.[7]

The year 1815 represented a turning point in the political economy of the Atlantic World, and that shift augured a stark new context for black

---

a response to economic, not ideological pressures. Seymour Drescher and others have since contended that slavery remained profitable even as antislavery activists came to power in Britain and that, as a result, ideological motivations outweighed economic self-interest in the end of slavery. Eric Williams, *Capitalism & Slavery* (Chapel Hill: The University of North Carolina Press, 1944); David Brion Davis, *The Problem of Slavery in the Age of Revolution, 1770–1823* (Ithaca, NY: Cornell University Press, 1975); Seymour Drescher, *Abolition: A History of Slavery and Antislavery* (Cambridge: Cambridge University Press, 2009); Seymour Drescher, "The Fragmentation of Atlantic Slavery and the British Intercolonial Slave Trade," in Johnson, ed., *The Chattel Principle*, 234–255; Seymour Drescher, *Econocide: British Slavery in the Era of Abolition* (Pittsburgh, PA: University of Pittsburgh Press, 1977).

The relationship between capitalism and slavery remains a central concern in slavery studies, as scholars reject a linear progression from pre-capitalist slave systems to capitalist free labor systems to excavate the interdependence of slavery and economic liberalism. See Beckert, *The Empire of Cotton*; Johnson, *River of Dark Dreams*.

[6] These resettlements included the "prize Negroes" rescued from the transatlantic slave trade. Historian Roseanne Adderley writes that officials considered Trinidad a "large plantation colony" in which planters and administrators viewed the liberated Africans as a convenient source of labor that could replace the thousands of slaves who rejected plantation employment after emancipation ... Trinidad received fewer than 1,000 liberated Africans between 1808 and 1840, but once organized projects began to use these slave trade refugees as emigrant labor for British sugar colonies, the southern Caribbean island became a major destination for African recaptives.

Rosanne Marion Adderley, *"New Negroes from Africa": Slave Trade Abolition and Free African Settlement in the Nineteenth-Century Caribbean* (Bloomington: Indiana University Press, 2006), 9; Gomez, *Black Crescent*, chapter 2.

This maritime flight to freedom connected port cities across North America to maritime marronage networks across the Caribbean. See Ferrer, "Haiti, Free Soil, and Antislavery in the Revolutionary Atlantic," 40–66; Chinea, "Diasporic Marronage," 259–284; Rupert, "Marronage, Manumission and Maritime Trade in the Early Modern Caribbean," 361–382.

[7] Christopher Leslie Brown, *Moral Capital: Foundations of British Abolitionism* (Chapel Hill: The University of North Carolina Press, 2006).

life across the Americas. Until the early nineteenth century, indigenous nations and enslaved people manipulated imperial rivalries to secure some benefit for themselves. From the birth of the US nation, blacks looked beyond its borders for freedom. Despite George Washington's best efforts, 15,000 self-liberated blacks escaped with the British after the American Revolution.[8] And again in the War of 1812, enslaved people exploited the apertures of war, not to claim membership in the nation, but to escape it altogether.[9] By 1815, however, a devastating peace foreclosed such opportunities. With its victory in the War of 1812, the United States defended its national sovereignty from its former imperial ruler, deprived the British Empire's Native American allies of a key partner, and foiled British efforts to invigorate mercantilist policies. For the British, their triumph over Napoleon's France overshadowed their relatively minor defeat in North America. The resulting *Pax Britannica* proved a boon for both the British and their "hitchhiking" former colonists. When viewed from above, that peace fostered commerce and comity. But from below, it promised cutting-edge cruelty, as the enslaved worked ever harder in the staple-producing fields of the Americas.[10] Amid this shift, the "Merikens" became a recognizable group in Trinidad who even today commemorate their ancestors' flight from slavery to freedom, a journey

[8] Maya Jasanoff, *Liberty's Exiles: American Loyalists in the Revolutionary World* (New York: Vintage, 2011); Alan Gilbert, *Black Patriots and Loyalists: Fighting for Emancipation in the War for Independence* (Chicago: The University of Chicago Press, 2012); Taylor, *Internal Enemy*; Landers, *Atlantic Creoles in the Age of Revolutions*, chapter 1; Campbell, *Middle Passages*.

[9] Some slaves and free men of color fought on behalf of the United States hoping to secure full citizenship only to witness the hardening of racist hierarchies in the war's aftermath. In his 1911 text, *Our People, Our History*, Rodolphe Desdunes, one of the earliest historians of the free people of color in New Orleans, criticized the self-interested appeals of the US armed forces to black soldiers amid persistent racism and exclusion. In describing the betrayal of the free men of color who fought in the War of 1812, Desdunes lamented: "Oh, did we not hear those same words in 1861, in 1865, and in 1898, and shall we not hear them again and again in other tragic times?" Those dates call attention to black military participation on both sides of the US Civil War and on behalf of the U.S. in the Spanish-American War. Rodolphe Lucien Desdunes and Dorothea Olga McCants, *Our People and Our History; a Tribute to the Creole People of Color in Memory of the Great Men They Have Given Us and of the Good Works They Have Accomplished*, trans. and ed., Dorothea Olga McCants (Baton Rouge: Louisiana State University Press, 1973 [1911]), 3–9. See also Bell, *Revolution, Romanticism, and the Afro-Creole Protest Tradition in Louisiana, 1718–1868*, 51–61.

[10] On the relationship between borderlands, frontiers, and the nation-state, see Jeremy Adelman and Stephen Aron, "From Borderlands to Borders: Empires, Nation-States, and the Peoples in between in North American History," *AHR* 104 (June 1999): 814–841.

that inverted the geography of African-American freedom from Canada in the north toward the Caribbean in the south. Yet each stage of that journey captures in microcosm the predicaments of blackness, both slave and free, in an era of imperial peace. Even for its most ardent seekers, freedom would remain difficult to locate.[11]

This chapter consists of three parts. First, it revisits the place of slaves in southern households to illuminate the radical ideologies that prompted the oppressed to use wartime instabilities to escape. The patriarchal white household was the building block of American empire. When the self-liberated ex-slaves and their British allies threatened its sanctity, they symbolically threatened the entire nation. The second section examines the confined cosmopolitanism these black migrants experienced on British navy vessels and at the way station in Bermuda. On the sea as on land, these migrants confronted heterogeneous social camaraderie amid material inequality. The third section explores the migrants' experiences in Trinidad, where the self-liberated migrants, local planters, and the British Empire constructed competing visions for the new settlers. The challenges that the migrants confronted in Trinidad as they attempted to practice their own version of freedom in yet another labor-hungry place highlight the promises and limits of migration as a strategy for escaping the hierarchies of the Global South.

"ENTERED THE CITIZENS' ENCLOSURE, AND RELEASED PERFORCE HIS SLAVE"

Given the rancor of national and global politics, the early nineteenth century seemed a time for slaves, indigenous persons, citizens, and even the U.S. government to "joine neither party," as John McDonogh, Sr. counseled, but to instead "cultivate friendship on all sides."[12] In his 1796 "Farewell Address," considered the founding text of US foreign policy, George

---

[11] A foundational article on black Atlantic migrations and modernity is Tiffany Patterson and Kelley, "Unfinished Migrations." See also Rothman, *Beyond Freedom's Reach*; Grandin, *The Empire of Necessity*; Sweet, *Domingos Álvares, African Healing, and the Intellectual History of the Atlantic World*; Byrd, *Captives and Voyagers*; Campbell, *Middle Passages*; Scott, "Common Wind."

[12] John McDonogh, Sr. to John McDonogh, Jr., December 8, 1804, The John McDonogh Papers, Manuscripts Collection 30, Box 3, Folder 20, Manuscripts Department, TU.
On trade, sovereignty, and empire in this period, see Johnson, "The Racial Origins of American Sovereignty," 50–59; Eliga Gould, *Among the Powers of the Earth: The American Revolution and the Making of a New World Empire* (Cambridge, MA: Harvard University Press, 2012).

Washington exhorted the young nation "to steer clear of permanent alliances" and to protect the fragile nation's sovereignty through non-
entanglement in European affairs.[13] Eight years later, John McDonogh
Sr., who fought in the American Revolution under Washington, gave his
son, merchant John, Jr., similar advice. "It seems to be very troublesome
times at present all over the world, and much party affairs in America at this
time, and seems fomenting," the elder McDonogh warned. Times were
indeed troublesome. The factionalism of the First Party System divided the
nation from within as it negotiated its position "among the powers of the
earth." England and France remained locked in a Great War, while former
slaves and their allies created Haiti, the first black republic. President
Thomas Jefferson exploited these tensions to purchase Louisiana, which
doubled the landmass of the United States, unleashed settler-imperialists
into the Lower Mississippi River Valley, dispossessed Native Americans,
and heightened domestic tensions about the nation's future.

In the years after the American Revolution, early leaders harnessed
the domestic and economic ambitions of white settlers to forcibly dispos-
sess native people's lands and expand the young nation. Americans had
overthrown one centralized authoritarian empire – Great Britain – and
generally had neither the desire nor the power to create another. With the
Northwest Ordinance of 1787, early leaders used incentives rather than
force to secure the allegiance of white settlers in the Great Lakes region.
Those incentives included protections for private property, electoral
representation, and relative household autonomy. This imperial strategy
hinged on a reciprocal relationship between natural increase and national
increase: through biological reproduction, white households would produce new citizens and domesticate foreign territories in the process.
As incubators of the nation, patriarchal households became the foundation of US settler-imperialist expansion.[14]

The Great Lakes had a relatively small slave population; Lower
Louisiana, by contrast, was a hub of slaves, and their numbers increased

---

[13] Quoted in Jay Sexton, *The Monroe Doctrine: Empire and Nation in Nineteenth-Century America* (New York: Hill and Wang, 2011), 24. See also Felix Gilbert, *To the Farewell Address: Ideas of Early American Foreign Policy* (Princeton: Princeton University Press, 1961).

[14] On this "anticolonial colonization" model, see Sexton, *The Monroe Doctrine*, 32; Peter S. Onuf, *Statehood and Union: A History of the Northwest Ordinance* (Bloomington: Indiana University Press, 1987); D. W. Meinig, *The Shaping of America: A Geographical Perspective on 500 Years of History* (New Haven: Yale University Press, 1986), 2: 341–348.

every day. In Territorial Louisiana, the slaveholding household was more than a living space; it was an incubator for citizens, a unit of production, and a site of slave discipline. Rural slaveholding households in particular produced staple crops as they made material the paternalistic and white supremacist ideologies that normalized chattel slavery. There were exceptions to this scheme. White widows and free blacks headed households, but they generally did not enjoy the rights and perquisites that propertied white men enjoyed. And those who rejected households altogether – "vagrants" if white, suspected fugitive slaves if black – were subject to imprisonment. Households became an engine of imperial expansion even as they remained the private fiefdoms of white patriarchs.[15]

A shared commitment to the inviolability of private property united Louisiana elites across national, linguistic, and cultural differences. In an era of the Quasi-War between the US and French privateers in the Caribbean (1798–1800) and the Alien and Sedition and Naturalization Acts, Federalists doubted the loyalties of the nation's newest citizens. In 1805, De Bordes, a refugee from Jérémie who arrived to Louisiana via Jamaica, wrote a fellow refugee: "The French here are in an alternating breeze (*brise alternance*). If they join the Americans, they are traitors against France. If they remain neutral, they will be persecuted."[16] Such differences notwithstanding, the sanctity of private property was one right upon which Francophone and Anglophone citizens agreed. When Pierre-Clément Laussat, Napoleon's Colonial Prefect, announced the sale of Louisiana to the United States, he promised elite Francophiles of New Orleans that they would "enjoy the rights, advantages, and immunities of U.S. citizens" and that the new administration would "maintain and protect the enjoyment of their liberty, property, and free exercise of religion that they possessed."[17] This guarantee about private property

---

[15] On households, slavery, and empire, see Diane Mutti Burke, *On Slavery's Border: Missouri's Small-Slaveholding Households, 1815–1865* (Athens: University of Georgia Press, 2010); Rockman, *Scraping By*; Thavolia Glymph, *Out of the House of Bondage: The Transformation of the Plantation Household* (Cambridge: Cambridge University Press, 2008); Lyons, *Sex among the Rabble*; Kirsten E. Wood, *Masterful Women: Slaveholding Widows from the American Revolution through the Civil War* (Chapel Hill: The University of North Carolina Press, 2004).

[16] De Bordes to Lambert, July 22, 1805, my translation, Lambert Family Papers, MC 244, Folder 1, TU.
Rothman, *Slave Country*; Thompson, *Exiles at Home*.

[17] Pierre Clément Laussat, "Proclamation Au Nom de la République Française aux Louisianais," *Moniteur de la Louisiane*, December 3, 1803. Laussat's words parallel those of the third article of the Treaty of Cession between the United States and France.

rights hearkened to the coded language for slaves that founders embedded in the nation's constitution. White patriarchs would pledge allegiance to the nation in exchange for continued sovereignty over their private dwellings.

In the tinderbox of colonial occupation, seemingly mundane infringements on the sovereignty of private households took on imperial significance. One such event happened in New Orleans on Saturday, July 4, 1807, a day that many across the nation celebrated independence. That day, "a Citizen (a Planter)" chose to "correct" his bondwoman. What to this slave woman was the Fourth of July, a day her master attacked her so viciously that her screams soared above the hustle and bustle of the weekend waterfront? Likely fueled by masculine ideals, patriotism, and alcohol, one naval crew left the waterfront and charged onto land to rescue the distressed woman. Perhaps the American sailors thought a white woman was being abused, an all-too-common occurrence. In 1810, for example, Rebecca Johnson swore "her husband . . . is in the habit of beating this Deponent when he is in a passion," and hers was no isolated incident.[18] When the sailors arrived at the site of the beating,

---

"Transcript of Louisiana Purchase Treaty," available at Our Documents, www.ourdocuments.gov/doc.php?doc=18&page=transcript, accessed March 12, 2014.

[18] Claiborne to Madison, July 16, 1807, in *Letter Books*, IV: 129–130; Deposition, Rebecca Johnson before Mather, New Orleans, August 17, 1810, NYHS NOC Box 8, Folder 8. The night before her testimony, she claimed, another man "abused" her "and cursed her children." When her husband came home and discovered the melee, "instead of taking the part of the deponent, [he] began to be in a passion against her and finally beat her until he knocked her down." Domestic violence was endemic to urban and rural households, so it is possible the sailors thought they would rescue a white woman from physical abuse.

Johnson was not alone. Nancy Brinckman testified that John Shreider, a Dutchman, sought lodgings at her house. Their landlord-tenant relationship soured, and he verbally abused her and threatened to beat her with a stick "every time he would meet her in the streets." Magdeleine Berthold, a free woman of color, testified that she and her daughter, Adelaide, lived in the home of the city chaplain. The holy man was not above devilment. Adelaide swore he verbally and physically abused the mother and daughter "to the point of endangering their lives." Both free women, one white and the other of color, brought their claims of domestic abuse before the state, a right unavailable to enslaved women. Deposition, Nancy Brinckman before James Mather, New Orleans, August 3, 1811, NYHS NOC 8:9; Deposition, Joseph Quayes before Macarty, New Orleans, October 14, 1818 NYHS NOC 8:14; Magdeleine Berthold before Roffignac, New Orleans, March 28, 1822 NYHS NOC 9:3. See also Augustin Peyraud before Roffignac, New Orleans, October 12, 1825 NYHS NOC 9:5. On domestic violence, see Loren Schweninger, *Families in Crisis in the Old South: Divorce, Slavery, and the Law* (Chapel Hill: The University of North Carolina Press, 2012).

however, they found a patriarch beating his bondwoman and, remarkably, they set out to rescue her. According to Territorial Governor William Claiborne, "three of the young officers accompanied by a few Sailors entered the Citizens' enclosure, and released perforce his slave." The woman likely savored the unexpected respite, but her master seethed. "The Planter is of respectable standing in this society," Claiborne wrote, "and many of his acquaintances feel equally indignant with himself, at this improper interference." The planters feared this act would "produce insubordination among their slaves" who might now look above their masters to the U.S. empire for deliverance. Local planters called on Claiborne to "punish with all the severity of the Law, the actors in this Scene."[19]

Masters beat slaves all the time, but that violence unsettled only those people unaccustomed to the soundscape of slavery. When architect Levi Weeks moved from Massachusetts to Natchez, Mississippi, he discovered "some little prejudice of the Yankees that must be overcome, such as aversion to slavery and the like." The shock and indignation that these sailors experienced was not unusual. What was unusual was their decision to intervene on behalf of an enslaved woman. When they trespassed on her behalf, they pitted the sovereignty of American empire against that of slaveholding households and societies. No wonder the planters organized to voice their displeasure before the governor, and their discontent reached Secretary of State James Madison. Presumably this woman enjoyed an impermanent deliverance. Only a few years later, however, a different empire's servicemen trespassed onto the citizens' enclosures of Louisiana, and when they retreated they did not leave the slaves behind.[20]

---

[19] Claiborne informed Madison that the matter had been brought before "one of our Tribunals of Justice." Though some locals considered the sailors' intrusion part of a larger pattern of "Military Despotism," Claiborne assured Madison that "the public mind was speedily calmed, and the affair will take the course, which Law and Justice shall prescribe." Claiborne to Madison, July 16, 1807.

On enclosure, households, and colonization, see Allan Greer, "Commons and Enclosure in the Colonization of North America," *AHR* 117, no. 2 (April 2012): 365–386. On the inseparability of national and imperial power in "empire-states," see Jane Burbank and Frederick Cooper, *Empires in World History: Power and the Politics of Difference* (Princeton: Princeton University Press, 2011). On the intimate as a realm of imperial contestation, see Ann Laura Stoler, *Carnal Knowledge and Imperial Power: Race and the Intimate in Colonial Rule* (Berkeley: University of California Press, 2002).

[20] Levi W. Weeks to Ephraim Hoyt, Esq., September 27, 1812, Weeks Family Papers, MC 198, Box 1, Folder 6, TU. On seasoning for free and enslaved persons, see Conevery Bolton Valencius, *The Health of the Country: How American Settlers Understood Themselves and Their Land* (New York: Basic Books, 2002). On the sensory history of chattel slavery, see Mark M. Smith, *How Race Is Made: Slavery, Segregation, and the*

Even as Louisiana's planters defended their household sovereignty from the encroachments of US empire, the federal government struggled to safeguard its national sovereignty and commercial neutrality from its former empire. Britain's naval superiority after its 1805 victory at Trafalgar jeopardized US trade with Napoleonic France. Britain presented US merchants an ultimatum: end the profitable trade with France or risk the confiscation of goods and the impressment of American seamen into the Royal Navy. The British impressed some 10,000 US sailors, a practice that separated families and threatened commerce. In June 1812, not quite two months after Louisiana's admittance as the eighteenth state, the US Congress declared war on Great Britain.[21] As the nation fought to defend its independence from its former colonial power, a Louisiana runaway advertisement warned that an enslaved man had escaped a Lafourche Parish plantation: "It is supposed that the said negro was enticed away by an American." A state that belonged to three empires in just over one decade, and where "Americans" remained a subset of the population, would now be called upon to defend its new nation.[22]

In the face of foreign invasion, Louisiana's citizens feared an alliance between domestic enemies – Native Americans and slaves – and the British. Such an alliance had precedent, as both groups had a long history of entering strategic alliances during imperial conflicts. Native Americans used those alliances to protect their land and independence from US settler-imperialism. In the Seven Years War, native alliances were critical to Britain's victory over France. And again during the American Revolution the Mohawks allied with the British, while the Oneidas and Tuscaroras allied with the revolutionaries. Others sought neutrality, including certain groups among the Senecas, Shawnees, and Delawares.[23] Enslaved persons also weighed the advantages and risks of alliances in the Revolutionary Era. Thousands responded to colonial Virginia Governor Lord Dunmore's proclamation, which guaranteed freedom to those

---

Senses (Chapel Hill: The University of North Carolina Press, 2006); Mark M. Smith, *Listening to Nineteenth-Century America* (Chapel Hill: The University of North Carolina Press, 2001).

[21] Alan Taylor, *The Civil War of 1812: American Citizens, British Subjects, Irish Rebels, & Indian Allies* (New York: Alfred A. Knopf, 2010); Gould, *Among the Powers of the Earth*; Jon Latimer, *1812: War with America* (Cambridge, MA: Belknap Press of Harvard University Press, 2007); Henry Adams, *The War of 1812* (New York: Cooper Square Press, 1999).

[22] *Louisiana Courier*, September 20, 1813.

[23] Colin G. Calloway, *The American Revolution in Indian Country: Crisis and Diversity in Native American Communities* (Cambridge: Cambridge University Press, 1995).

enslaved persons who fought on behalf of the British Empire. Some 15,000 self-liberated veterans and other persons of African descent fled the United States and settled in Canada, England, and the British Caribbean. The black refugees who settled in Nova Scotia after 1783 formed meaningful communities and established churches, but they also confronted unequal treatment before colonial authorities and anti-black racism in everyday life. Meanwhile, leaders in Great Britain sought to establish a British settlement at Sierra Leone, an important harbor, and they planned to use free black settlers to do it. The blacks who settled in Nova Scotia became the avant-garde of a long line of "back to Africa" settlers in search of freedom. That province, however, was located within eyeshot of Bunce Island, one of Britain's largest slave trading castles. British visions of empire included both free black settlements and the international slave trade.[24]

Louisiana's citizens harbored a fear of slaves and a fear of becoming slaves. Even before the war's theater edged closer to Louisiana, officials there scrutinized the servile classes for signs of insurrection or defection to the British, and for good reason. The Haitian Revolution and the Pointe Coupée revolts of 1793 and 1795 remained fresh in public memory, as did the 1811 Deslondes Revolt.[25] In September 1813 Adjutant-General Alexander La Neuville, a free man of color, wrote Major-General Jacques Philippe Villeré: "Last night we had a small alert, according to some people an insurrection of negroes was possible during the night." La Neuville warned his commander, "The rumors (*Les bruits*) might be true or false, but in the present circumstance one must always be 'en garde.'"[26] The following year, Claiborne warned Villeré that "one of the enemy's projects is to excite the blacks (*les noirs*) to revolt and to massacre the whites (*les blancs*)."[27] Eligius Fromentin, US senator from Louisiana from 1813 to 1819, wrote Villeré: "You know how much we have to fear about the <u>domestic enemy</u>," he wrote, "and you know very well how limited is our defense in case of invasion."[28] A few days after Fromentin's frenzied

[24] Jasanoff, *Liberty's Exiles*; Byrd, *Captives and Voyagers*; Campbell, *Middle Passages*; Whitfield, *Blacks on the Border*.

[25] *Louisiana Gazette*, January 10, 1811. See also Johnson, *River of Dark Dreams*, 18–23; Daniel Rasmussen, *American Uprising: The Untold Story of America's Largest Slave Revolt* (New York: Harper, 2011).

[26] Alexander La Neuville to Jacques Phillipe Villeré, September 12, 1813, Jacques Philippe Villeré Papers, MC 14, Folder 1, HNOC.
        See also Rothman, *Slave Country*, 123; Rodriguez, "Always 'En Garde'," 399–416.

[27] Claiborne to Villeré, August 12, 1814, De La Vergne Family Papers, Box 1, Folder 31, TU.

[28] Fromentin to Villeré, October 19, 1814, Villeré Papers, MC 14, Folder 20, HNOC, emphasis original.

letter British forces under Admiral George Cockburn defeated US forces at the Battle at Bladensburg. Cockburn's men torched the nation's capitol to avenge the destruction of the Parliament Buildings of Upper Canada during the Battle of York (1813). James Madison fled the White House, and the Capitol and Library of Congress sustained severe damage. The symbolism of a destroyed national capitol was not lost on Louisiana's residents. "[W]hen the Enemy invaded our country," Jemima Smith exclaimed, "it was expected that we should become bond-men and women to the hostile Enemy[.]" She understood national defeat in the idiom she knew best – slavery.[29]

The British invaded Louisiana as diplomats in Ghent, Belgium, worked to preserve the map as it stood before the war. On December 24, 1814, as the Gulf South experienced the "hurry & confusion" of the "desperate fight," delegates a world away produced the Treaty of Ghent, a document more remarkable for what it did not address than for what it did.[30] It did not resolve the issues of trade neutrality or impressment, and it largely restored the status quo of prewar geographies: "All territory, places, and possessions whatso-ever, taken by either party from the other during the war," with a handful of exceptions, "shall be restored without delay." Britain also agreed to not carry off "any slaves or other private property" from US citizens, as they had done in the aftermath of the American Revolution. Alliances between British troops and Louisiana's slaves would make it difficult for the imperial combatants to honor their own agreement.[31]

Louisiana's slaves used the turmoil of war to map legal and illicit geographies. Military and civilian leaders impressed bondspersons to labor in defense of the slaveholding republic. Even as local leaders feared subversive assemblages, they gathered bondspersons into work gangs that dug trenches, erected batteries, and built forts. Slave owners did not protest these laboring intimacies; they profited from them through

---

[29] Jemima Smith to Moses Newton, October 17, 1815, The War of 1812 Series, MC 541, Folder 14, Manuscripts Department, TU.

[30] Lewis Moore, New Orleans, to John Moore, St. Mary Parish, December 17, 1814, Nicholls Family Papers, MC 639, Box 1, Folder 6, Manuscripts Department, TU.

[31] Treaty of Peace and Amity between His Britannic Majesty and the United States of America (Treaty of Ghent), December 24, 1814, in *Treaties and Other International Acts of the United States of America*, ed. David Hunter Miller (Washington: Government Printing Office, 1931). See also Gould, *Among the Powers of the Earth*, 174; Whitfield, *Blacks on the Border*, chapters 1 and 2.

reimbursement from the state. Other slaves remained uninvolved: "The people appear to be Don and blacks, none of whom seem anxious to become allies," a British officer complained as his unit invaded the plantations of southern Louisiana.[32] One of the few enslaved actions that suggested violent rebellion – two bondsmen fled their master, a gunpowder manufacturer and took with them some eighty pounds of the explosive – likely owed as much to their economic opportunism as to their political radicalism. Their owner suspected the men would sell the gunpowder to the highest bidder.[33] The most common form of wartime resistance was flight. The day after the Battle of New Orleans, Edward Livingston's son Lewis complained: "The greatest parts of the negroes at work in this place ran away yesterday during the battle."[34] All over the Gulf South slaves used the War of 1812 to leave their designated places.

The location of coastal Louisiana's slaves was critical military intelligence for the British, who used promises of freedom to recruit fighters across the hemisphere. Throughout the Age of Revolution, black men fought on behalf of empires to secure freedom and land for themselves and their families.[35] The second Anglo-American conflict was no exception. Blacks in the British West India Regiments fought against the United States during that war, and in April 1814 Cochrane offered freedom and land grants to those men who enlisted in the Colonial Marines as well as their families. Across Louisiana and the Gulf South, Major Edward Nicolls, a noted abolitionist, and other officers recruited slaves into their ranks. A map drawn by one such officer entitled "Sketch of the Position of the British and American forces during the Operations against New Orleans from 23rd December 1814 to January 18th, 1815" (Figure 5.1)

[32] *Louisiana Gazette*, June 2, 1815.
   The term "Don" likely referred to *Los Isleños*, or the Canary Islanders who migrated to southern Louisiana in the 1770s and 1780s, as well as other Spanish-speaking residents. See Gilbert C. Din, *The Canary Islanders of Louisiana* (Baton Rouge: Louisiana State University Press, 1988).

[33] "Runaway Negroes," *Louisiana Courier*, December 5, 1813.

[34] Lewis Livingston to Villeré, January 9, 1815, Villeré Papers, Folder 34, HNOC. See also Rothman, *Slave Country*, 148–151.

[35] Childs, *The 1812 Aponte Rebellion in Cuba and the Struggle Against Slavery*, chapter 1; Scott, "Common Wind"; Hanger, *Bounded Lives, Bounded Places*; David Patrick Geggus, "Slavery, War, and Revolution in the Greater Caribbean, 1789–1815," in *A Turbulent Time: The French Revolution and the Greater Caribbean*, eds. David Barry Gaspar and David Patrick Geggus (Bloomington: Indiana University Press, 1997), 1–50; Roger Norman Buckley, *Slaves in Red Coats: The British West India Regiments, 1795–1815* (New Haven, CT: Yale University Press, 1979).

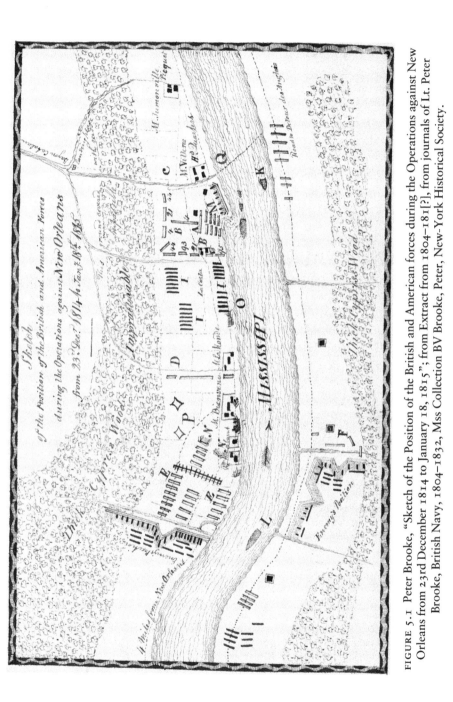

FIGURE 5.1 Peter Brooke, "Sketch of the Position of the British and American forces during the Operations against New Orleans from 23rd December 1814 to January 18, 1815"; from Extract from 1804–181[?], from journals of Lt. Peter Brooke, British Navy, 1804–1832, Mss Collection BV Brooke, Peter, New-York Historical Society.

recorded the locations of plantations on either side of the Mississippi River and just south of New Orleans.[36]

When British forces established a headquarters on the banks of the Mississippi, they considered the enslaved persons who inhabited the region's plantations as a valuable local resource.[37] Men could enlist and fight in the war effort, and many males and females had invaluable knowledge of the terrain essential to the foreign force compelled to navigate the bayous and cypress swamps. Enslaved persons could give food and other provisions to an embattled force. Finally, a slave's decision to ally with the British deprived owners of their labor.

British forces left the household of Major General Villeré particularly undone, and he and his supporters imbued the destruction with local, national, and Atlantic significance. According to Villeré's neighbor, friend, and fellow French Creole Hugues de la Vergne, on the morning of December 23, 1814 British forces surprised the plantation while the major general was on the front lines. Gabriel Villeré, his son and fellow military man, escaped to warn General Andrew Jackson of the impending threat. The Villeré women – whom de la Vergne did not name but instead referred to metaphorically as "beauty, innocence, and virtue" – also escaped.[38] As one historian notes, during the American Revolution British soldiers deployed rape as "a propaganda tool of proportions

---

[36] Peter Brooke, "Extract from 1804–181[?], from Journals of Lt. Peter Brooke, British Navy, 1804–1832," Mss Collection BV Brooke, Peter, microfilm, NYHS. On Nicolls, see Taylor, *Internal Enemy*, 340.

[37] See Dubois, *A Colony of Citizens*, 224, 230–232; Whitfield, *Blacks on the Border*, chapter 2; Jasanoff, *Liberty's Exiles*; Buckley, *Slaves in Red Coats*.

[38] Hugues Lavergne to an unnamed friend in Bordeaux, April 24, 1815, De La Vergne Family Papers, Box 1, Folder 42, TU. Villeré's plantation and the others were located downriver from Faubourg Marigny, and at least some parts of those plantations were carved from the famous heir's landholdings. In July 1808, for example, Jacques and Gabriel Villeré purchased land located "about two and a half leagues south of this city and having seven and one quarter arpents more or less, adjoining one side of the Villeré Senior's house . . . and the other side next to Mr. Julius Jumonville." In that 1808 transaction, Marigny also sold to the Villerés ten slaves. As will be discussed shortly, either three or four of them subsequently fled with the British. Act of Sale, Bernard Marigny to Jacques and Gabriel Villeré, Narcisse Broutin, Notary, New Orleans, July 2, 1808, my translation, volume 18, pages 244–246, NANO.

On gender, domesticity, and empire, see Amy S. Greenberg, *Manifest Manhood and the Antebellum American Empire* (Cambridge: Cambridge University Press, 2005); Amy Kaplan, *The Anarchy of Empire in the Making of U.S. Culture* (Cambridge, MA: Harvard University Press, 2002); Stephanie McCurry, *Masters of Small Worlds: Yeoman Households, Gender Relations, & the Political Culture of the Antebellum South Carolina Low Country* (New York: Oxford University Press, 1995); Ann Patton Malone, *Sweet Chariot: Slave Family and Household Structure in Nineteenth-Century Louisiana* (Chapel Hill: The University of North Carolina Press, 1992).

unmatched in early American history," and in the days leading up to the Battle of New Orleans US newspapers warned that British soldiers sought "beauty and booty." As American soldiers fought to protect their nation, British soldiers allegedly sought sexual libertinage and plunder. In de la Vergne's transcribed imagination, he celebrated the escape of the Villeré women and the southern, American, white women they personified.[39]

Presumably the Villeré women returned, but the fifty-three slaves who escaped did not. They and over 200 other slaves from southern Louisiana ran to the British rather than away from them. Some likely enlisted solely to exact vengeance against their masters, such as the one who "boast[ed] of having shot his" during the war.[40] Another motivation was the promise of economic and political liberty. Though he fought for the United States during the War of 1812, ex-slave Charles Ball's autobiography gives insight into blacks on both sides of the conflict. Ball wrote about the freedom seekers from the Chesapeake, but those from Louisiana likely shared their motivations: "Their heads were full of notions of liberty and happiness in some of the West India Islands." There, the migrants believed, "they would have lands given to them, and where they were to be free." Nearly two weeks after the Battle of New Orleans, a sympathetic British sailor recorded in his journal the following about the would-be migrants from Louisiana:

Above 100 slaves with their families have followed us to this place. In the Proclamation published by the Admiral, he says that the slaves as private property will not be taken away. But these people have many of them assisted us since we came and naturally dread returning to their masters. Who would not wish for liberty & what will a person not attempt to gain it. I know not what is to be done with these poor creatures but they ought every man of them to be taken away.

The slaves-turned-fighters in Louisiana left the slaveholding households of the Gulf South to become free landowners in the British Caribbean. They

---

[39] Sharon Block, *Rape & Sexual Power in Early America* (Chapel Hill: The University of North Carolina Press, 2006), 230–238; Eustace, *1812*, 206–207, 213.

[40] Ralph Woodford to Charles Bathurst, Trinidad, March 4, 1816, Letters from Sir Ralph Woodford to C. B. Bathurst, D421/X13, GRO, emphasis original; Whitfield, *Blacks on the Border*, 32.

    The literature on black political visions in the revolutionary era is vast. See C. L. R. James, *The Black Jacobins: Toussaint L'Ouverture and the San Domingo Revolution* (New York: Random House, 1938); Robinson, *Black Marxism*; Dubois, *A Colony of Citizens*.

hoped to secure as subjects in the Crown colony the rights enjoyed by citizens in Louisiana.[41]

Of course that is not how masters understood this exodus, and they and British officials offered competing accounts of the escapes. Where before the local fighting, masters considered slaves latent insurrectionists, after hostilities ended masters understood the slaves' departure, not as a political act prompted by ideology, but as a passive acquiescence to imperial seduction. In what Michel-Rolph Trouillot calls a "formula of banalization," these masters trivialized an act of political resistance to discredit and ultimately erase it.[42] "The slaves that [the British] captured," de la Vergne wrote, "became the objects of their lust and of their greed. They led them to their ships, rage, despair, and revenge in their hearts." In mid-January 1815, a plantation mistress recalled the moment a messenger ran to her "all bewildered, telling us that the English were here and that they were carrying off all of the Negroes from the plantations." The masterful woman "immediately sent the Negroes to the woods and continued [her] reading." A few days later, Villeré received a request for a detachment of men to "recover the slaves of the planters who have been seduced or forcibly carried away by the enemy." For masters, bondspersons did not voluntarily escape chattel slavery. Rather, Redcoats "seduced" feminized bondspersons away from patriarchal plantations while the men were away at the front lines.[43]

---

[41] Charles Ball, *Fifty Years in Chains: Or the Life of an American Slave* (New York: Dover Publications, 1970), 472, 473; Journal entry, January 20, 1815, Sir John Maxwell Tylden diary, 1814–1815, MssCol 3050, NYPL.
    The ex-slaves were not alone in fleeing the American nation after the War of 1812. In January 1815, Cochrane instructed Rear Admiral Hotham "to grant safe conduct for a vessel freighted by Mr. Paul Hyde de Neuville to carry French emigrants from New York to England agreeably to the directions of my Lords Commissioners of Admiralty." Some Francophone Americans allied with the British during the War of 1812 and secured passage to Europe. It is possible that some free French speakers in Louisiana did the same. Journal entry, Cochrane, January 5, 1815, Admiralty: Admirals' Journals, Sir A. F. I. Cochrane, 1813-1815, TNA ADM 50/122.

[42] Trouillot, *Silencing the Past*, 96–97.

[43] Lavergne to unnamed friend, April 24, 1815; Marie-Françoise Gérard Favrot to Louis Favrot, January 17, 1815, *The Favrot Family Papers*, V: 248–249; H. Butler to Maj. Gen. Villeré, January 21, 1815, Villeré Papers, Folder 46. De La Vergne later swore he "had seen & known personally all and everyone of the fifty-three slaves" who escaped from Villeré's plantation. Deposition, Hugues de la Vergne before Gallien Préval, New Orleans, May 19, 1821, Slave Evaluation Reports, MSS 199, Microform, HNOC (hereafter SER).

British leaders insisted that enslaved persons possessed free will, chose to leave Louisiana, and remained free. John Power, stationed at Dauphin Island in Alabama, wrote Claiborne: "All those slaves, who were not willing & who objected to return to their former masters have been embarked for the island of Bermuda to be sent from thence to Trinidad." To deepen the insult, Power noted that one British official implored the self-liberated men and women to return to their masters, "but he did not feel himself authorized to resort to force to oblige them to do so – as they threw themselves on his protection which they were entitled to having served with the British army and which they did voluntarily and without complaint." Though British officials did not recognize this same right for the slaves that British planters held in Jamaica, Barbados, or Trinidad, they strategically deployed a language of will and agency in discussing this select set of self-liberated blacks from the United States.[44]

The diverse migrants who exercised this option to leave Louisiana included African-born and American-born men. Jacques Villeré lost the most enslaved property, fifty-three bondspersons. They reportedly included "many creole negroes of the first quality and of first rate african [*sic*] negroes accustomed to the climate." Many of the thirty-nine men labored as field hands, but others possessed occupational titles: carter and cartwright, cooper, coachman, carpenter, sawyer, cook, ploughman, driver, and, of course, sugar maker. Not only were these migrants diverse in terms of skill sets, they were also linguistically, culturally, and ethnically diverse. Of the thirteen bondspersons who fled Pierre Lacoste's plantation, eight were men, including Francois, listed as "Congo," and Louis, described as Bambara. Even supposedly faithful slaves left. Marie Ursule Marin widow Chancerel's witness swore that the British had forced Louis away because of his past fidelity: "Louis at the time of the revolution of St. Domingue ... left there his friends and relations to accompany his mistress and follow her in her misfortunes." As discussed in the first

---

This narrative hearkened to the seduction literature dominant in nineteenth-century print culture. In those narratives, white women fell prey to the coercions of libertine men. On seduction, see Block, *Rape & Sexual Power*, chapter 1.

Women like Favrot mastered their plantations during the wartime absence of men. See Wood, *Masterful Women*.

[44] On notions of liberal subjecthood in the context of US chattel slavery, see Johnson, "On Agency," 113–124. For a sustained treatment of the migrants and the postwar diplomatic contests over their values, see Rashauna Johnson, "A Shudder in the Ledgers: Evaluating Louisiana's Freedom-Seekers after the War of 1812," manuscript in possession of author.

chapter, Louis had not been the only slave to accompany her from the Cul de Sac-Leogane plains of Saint-Domingue to Santiago de Cuba and then to New Orleans. Two others followed the same trajectory and landed on the New Orleans auction block. No wonder Louis had little faith in the widow's supposed fidelity to him. He left her behind in Louisiana and again migrated across imperial borders in hopes of a better result.[45]

Not every migrant from Louisiana enlisted as a Colonial Marine, but they were all fighters. Almost one in five of them were self-liberated women, a ratio that reflects the male-dominated demographics of sugar plantations as much as they did the British preference for fighters. These women presumably left under the auspices of marriage to enlisted men. Though the state did not recognize their marriages, enslaved communities imbued them with meaning through spiritual ceremonies, and some couples lived together. To make such far-flung (and presumably irreversible) journeys appealing, Cochrane encouraged nuclear families to flee together. From Antoine Phillipon's plantation, Marie ran away with her three-year-old daughter Caroline and two other men, Jean-Baptiste and Alexandre, one of whom may have been Caroline's father. Likewise, sixteen Africans who belonged to Major-General Pierre Denis De Laronde went with the British, which included twelve men, three women, and a two-year-old girl. Of course all families, let alone slave families, were not necessarily nuclear, biological, or heteronormative; any number of social relationships might have been severed or transformed through these journeys. It is equally possible that men and women entered into strategic partnerships to pass muster with British officials and secure passage from Louisiana.[46]

---

[45] Deposition, Jumonville de Villiers before Gallien Préval, New Orleans, May 18, 1821, SER; Deposition, Ducournau before Préval, New Orleans, May 24, 1821, SER; Deposition, Marie-Ursule Marin widow Chancerel before Préval, New Orleans, June 18, 1821; Deposition, Dulcide Barrow before Préval, New Orleans, June 18, 1821, SER. In 1810, Chancerel sold Pierre-Charles, a slave who had belonged to her husband, Francois Pierre Marie Chancerel, to Bernard Marigny, and in 1813 she sold "une negresse" named Evoline to a free woman of color named Minette Chiffré. Act of Sale, Dame Ursule Marin to Bernard Marigny, Michel De Armas, Notary, June 10, 1810, New Orleans, volume 3, page 84, NANO; Act of Sale, Ursule Marin to Minette Chiffré [free woman of color], Michel De Armas, Notary, New Orleans, June 10, 1810, volume 7A, page 982, NANO.

On reading between prices as methodology, see Johnson, *Soul by Soul*, 45–77. On the difficulties of assessing master-slave intimacies, see Gordon-Reed, *The Hemingses of Monticello*, 353–375. The phrase "privileged class" comes from Spillers, "Mama's Baby, Papa's Maybe," 65–81.

[46] Deposition, Antoine Philippon before Préval, New Orleans, June 1821 [exact date missing], SER; Deposition, Pierre Denis De Laronde before Préval, New Orleans, June 4,

MAP 5.1 Map of New Orleans and the Caribbean.

Female migrants also possessed valuable skills, and in a few instances the circulations required of them as part of their labor may have contributed to their decision to leave. Of the five women who fled the Lacoste plantation, two of them, Manette and Rosalie, labored as "sellers," or

1821, SER. On Cochrane's proclamation and his mandate for family-friendly migratory policies, see John McNish Weiss, *The Merikens: Free Black American Settlers in Trinidad, 1815–16* (London: McNish & Weiss, 2002), 6–7. On sugar production in the Atlantic World, see Richard Follett, *The Sugar Masters: Planters and Slaves in Louisiana's Cane World, 1820–1860* (Baton Rouge: Louisiana State University Press, 2005); Gillian McGillivray, *Blazing Cane: Sugar Communities, Class, and State Formation in Cuba, 1868–1959* (Durham: Duke University Press, 2009), chapter 1; Sidney Mintz, *Sweetness and Power: The Place of Sugar in Modern History* (New York: Penguin Books, 1986); Franklin W. Knight, *Slave Society in Cuba during the Nineteenth Century* (Madison: University of Wisconsin Press, 1970).

peddlers. As discussed in the second chapter, female peddlers circulated across the region. As they moved goods along trade routes, they also built and sustained far-flung communities of free and enslaved persons. These women's familiarity with the region beyond the plantation's borders may have primed them for a move to another part of the hemisphere. This relationship could go in both directions. Manon, the sole woman out of twenty escapees from the de Villiers plantation, was described as a thirty-five-year-old "negro" woman "cook, washer, ironer and excellent servant." Her unrelenting intimacy with her master's family may have motivated her escape. Mothers likely brought along the two infants listed among the group of fugitives, while other parents undoubtedly left children behind. Whatever the case, the gender imbalance between male and female migrants would become an intimate and imperial concern in Trinidad, and again the British Empire would look to slavery for a solution.[47]

"WHILST ON BOARD THIS SHIP"

The migrants who left Louisiana and the other states bore a heightened visibility as they entered a dynamic British maritime world. Commanders understood that these men, women, and children served as potent symbols in the United States, "where our conduct towards these Negroes is strictly watched, though for different ends both by Whites & Blacks."[48] In the event of a third conflict, the commanders hoped, an established record of favorable treatment of this set of migrants might secure future allies. On the other hand, these migrants entered a British imperial world defined by strict hierarchies of birth, status, and race, and those ideological hierarchies translated into material inequalities. During their shipboard passage from Louisiana to Trinidad, the migrants discovered that their "notions of liberty" conflicted with those of the imperial officials who "professed to be their deliverers," and these borderlands fighters steeled themselves for a second conflict.[49]

---

[47] Deposition, Pierre Lacoste before Préval, May 31, 1821, New Orleans, SER; Deposition, Jumonville de Villiers before Gallien Préval, New Orleans, May 18, 1821, SER. On domesticity and bondage, see Glymph, *Out of the House of Bondage*.

[48] Cockburn to Maj. Gen. Sir H. Torrent K.C.B., Bermuda, August 23, 1815, Despatches from Governor Sir James Cockburn (1815), TNA CO 37/73.

[49] James Monroe, January 26, 1814, reprinted in *The Times* [London], November 21, 1814, quoted in Cochrane to Monroe, March 8, 1815, reprinted in *Louisiana Gazette*, July 25, 1815 ("professed"). In that letter, Monroe accused the British of re-enslaving the

During their initial journey from Louisiana to Dauphin Island, the refugees entered the heterogeneous social world of the Royal Navy. Charles Ball found himself on one such ship off the Chesapeake coast when citizens sent him as part of a delegation charged with the uphill task of convincing the freedom-seekers to return to slavery. His experience sheds light on that of the Louisiana migrants. "I lived well whilst on board this ship, as they allowed me to share in a mess," Ball wrote. Mess sometimes reinforced the ship's hierarchies – marines did not eat with sailors, and officers did not eat with the crew – so it is significant that Ball experienced mess as a time of inclusion. Ball also engaged in yarning: "I amused myself," Ball remembered, "by talking to the sailors, and giving them an account of the way in which I had passed my life on the tobacco and cotton plantations." Ball listened as "the seamen gave many long stories of their adventures at sea, and of the battles they had been engaged in." Sailors enjoyed other pastimes, including music and dance, backgammon, and reading, but their drunkenness and promiscuity (and the attendant disease) were legendary. As during the Middle Passage, all of the migrants but especially the female ones were vulnerable to sexual assault or coercion while on the vessels.[50] Whatever their experiences on the ship and at Dauphin Island, their time there was short. By the end of March, the migrants had already left for Bermuda.[51]

As the migrants' first point of disembarkation in the British Caribbean, Bermuda quickly became a site for claims-making. The migrants from the Chesapeake, Eastern Florida, and Gulf Coast converged on the small island where they articulated their own ideas about the practice of freedom. "From the state of their minds," Cockburn complained, it was "perhaps impracticable, to reason them out of a belief once firmly adopted."[52] What

migrants in the British Caribbean. On this debate, see Matthew Mason, "The Battle of the Slaveholding Liberators: Great Britain, the United States, and Slavery in the Early Nineteenth Century," *The William and Mary Quarterly* 59, no. 3 (July 2002): 665–696.

[50] "The whole of the runaways were on board this ship, lounging about on the main deck, or leaning against the sides of the ship's bulwarks. I went amongst them, and talked to them a long time, on the subject of returning home; but found that their heads were full of notions of liberty and happiness in some of the West India islands." Ball, *Fifty Years in Chains*, 472, 474.

On ship life in the Georgian navy, see Janet Macdonald, *Feeding Nelson's Navy: The True Story of Food at Sea in the Georgian Era* (London: Chatham Publishing; Pennsylvania: Stackpole Books, 2004); N. A. M. Rodger, *The Wooden World: An Anatomy of the Georgian Navy* (Annapolis, MD: Naval Institute Press, 1986), 37–81. On the diversity of sailors, see Scott, "Common Wind"; Linebaugh and Rediker, *The Many-Headed Hydra*; Bolster, *Black Jacks*.

[51] John Power, to Claiborne, Dauphin Island, March 30, 1815, SER.

[52] Cockburn to Maj. Gen. Sir H. Torrent K.C.B., Bermuda, August 23, 1815.

leaders experienced as intransigence was in fact the migrants' determination to hold the empire accountable for promises made to its newest subjects. As across the revolutionary Atlantic, these men and women claimed material and political entitlements based on their military labor. It is not clear how much these migrants knew about the Magna Carta and the rights unevenly guaranteed to free British subjects across its empire, but they certainly articulated and insisted upon what they considered to be fair treatment.

Though united by shared wartime experiences, Marines cleaved along national lines, and Ireland Island consequently became a site in which imperial officials exploited the tensions of diaspora. In the colonial and early republican periods, birthplace became a point of cleavage between bondspersons. Sometimes, enslaved persons born in the Americas elevated their counterparts who had been recently imported from Africa because the new arrivals possessed information that linked those in diaspora to their homelands. At other times, some of those born in the Americas viewed the recently imported men and women with derision.[53] On Ireland Island, British commanders commented on (and thereby perpetuated) the alleged ethnocentrism of the American blacks vis-à-vis those from the Caribbean. Cockburn wrote of "the strong & determined prejudices of these men against the West Indian Corps, & the high ideas of superiority which they attach to themselves over the African Negroes who chiefly compose those regiments."[54] Another British observer noted, "The generality of the Negroes which compose the Colonial Battalion of Marines, are of superior mental abilities to those I have had an opportunity of noticing serving in the West India Regiments."[55] Since some of the Colonial Marines from Louisiana were themselves born in Africa or the Caribbean, it is possible that they identified more strongly with the West Indian Regiments than with the Colonial Marines from the Chesapeake.[56]

Racial wage labor defined the Bermudan economy, though the Louisiana migrants did not spend much time there. Even as British

---

[53] For competing perspectives about the meanings that those enslaved in the Americas ascribed to the fact of African birth, see Smallwood, *Saltwater Slavery*, 6–7; Gomez, *Exchanging Our Country Marks*, chapter 8.

[54] Cockburn to Maj. Gen. Sir H. Torrent K.C.B., Bermuda, August 23, 1815.

[55] A. Kinsman to Cockburn, Ireland Island, Bermuda, August 10, 1815, TNA CO 37/73.

[56] On the gradual shift from the valorization to the devaluation of African born persons in the colonial and antebellum US South, see Gomez, *Exchanging Our Country Marks*.

officials deprived the migrants of essential provisions, they exploited their lack of market freedom to pay substandard wages on a public works project at Ireland Island. In March 1815, as the Louisiana migrants arrived, Cochrane notified a lieutenant that "from 1500 to 2000 Refugee Negroes" in Bermuda were "in want of Clothing as well as Provisions."[57] The next month, he suggested the Colonial Marines garrisoned in Bermuda "perform all the work at the naval yard where there is full employment for a number of workmen for five years to come."[58] Cochrane planned to use the expertise honed in slavery to build British defenses on the cheap: "As the Corps includes a number of artificers and as the works at Ireland are still in a very incompleat [sic] state, a great saving will also accrue to Government by employing them instead of hiring white artificers."[59] Like the prisoners in the New Orleans jail, these black laborers would build the infrastructure of empire. Unlike those prisoners, these men would be paid, but they would not earn the "extravagant wages" that white laborers would have earned.[60] Because the volunteers from the Gulf Coast did not enter service under the same terms as the other marines, they did not have to work on that project. Major Nicholls "enlisted his men to serve during the American War only with a promise of land & protection at its termination, and they are all discharged."[61]

Though spared this one instance of labor exploitation, the Louisiana migrants in Bermuda had to have sensed their own vulnerability. "The slaves are to go with us," one British sailor wrote during his time in Louisiana. "They all of them show the greatest aversion to their masters and all agree in the same story of cruelty. There must be some truth in it, or they would hardly trust themselves to the chance of what we may do with them."[62] Across the British Atlantic, from Sierra Leone to Barbados, planters benefitted from the discounted labor of Africans purportedly rescued from slavery and the slave trade. Cochrane himself famously exploited ostensibly free black laborers for personal gain. In 1808 he sent from one to 200 Africans rescued from the slave trade from the Caribbean island Tortola to work on his personal estate in Trinidad. He

---

[57] Cochrane to Lieut. Gen. Sir J. C. Sherbrooke, Bermuda, March 25, 1815, TNA ADM 50/122.
[58] Cochrane, Bermuda, to Lord Viscount Melville, April 2, 1815, TNA CO 37/73.
[59] Cochrane to John W. Croker, Bermuda, April 6, 1815, TNA CO 37/73.
[60] Cochrane to Melville, April 2, 1815.
[61] A. Kinsman to Cockburn, Ireland Island, Bermuda, August 10, 1815, TNA CO 37/73, emphasis original.
[62] John Maxwell Tylden, journal entry dated January 26, 1815.

apprenticed them for fourteen years, the maximum allowable term. The magistrate reported Cochrane to British abolitionist William Wilberforce, who pressured the military man to end this practice. Nonetheless, the labor arrangement went on for five years, and the experiences of "Cochrane's Negroes" or "Cochrane's African Apprentices" foreshadowed those of other "Prize Negroes" in the British Caribbean.[63] The specter of re-enslavement loomed over every aspect of this journey, especially since some Louisiana migrants had experienced the dislocations of the Middle Passage and Haitian Revolution firsthand. Slavery was on the rise in Trinidad. These migrants had to have been suspicious of a black freedom journey that led to the British Caribbean in 1815. No wonder they insisted so forcefully on their claims. "They are particularly tenacious of promises made to them," one observer wrote.[64] "They have a great dislike to being sent to the West Indies," another complained, "and cannot divest themselves of the idea that by going there they would become Slaves."[65]

Whatever apprehensions they held, eighty-eight of the migrants who joined the diverse crew of the *HMS Levant* at Bermuda came from Louisiana, and their individual and collective names at embarkation highlight the translations and mistranslations of diaspora and empire. Some of them retained the surnames of their former masters, including Valentine and Manuel from Pierre Lacoste's plantation and Mannette, Michael (Michel), and Julie from Villeré's plantation. Some attempted to keep the names of their Louisiana masters, but British officials struggled to transcribe the French names inflected by African diasporic tongues. One British sailor wrote that the Louisiana migrants "speak bad French and worse English."[66] As a result, "Narcisse" became "Nacius," Ceasar Villeré became "Cesar Videre," and DeLassise became "Lacees." Based on the sources consulted, those are the only names that definitively connected self-liberated men and women from Louisiana's plantations to Trinidad. The rest of the migrants likely changed their names to avoid recapture and to mark their freedom. Collective naming of the group proved equally problematic. The captain of the *Levant* called them "Goree (US) Refugees," which at once associated these men, women, and children with the their ancestral (and, for a few, actual) homeland

---

[63] Campbell, *Middle Passages*; Adderley, *"New Negroes from Africa,"* 63–65.

[64] A. Kinsman to Cockburn, Ireland Island, Bermuda, August 10, 1815.

[65] Cochrane to Croker, April 6, 1815.

[66] John Maxwell Tylden, journal entry dated January 26, 1815. This phrase calls to mind the runaway advertisement for Figaro discussed in the first chapter. There his alleged owner claimed the fugitive spoke "good French and bad English."

of West Africa, the transatlantic slave trade, and, parenthetically, the nation they rejected. The administrator of the *Carron* used more conventional nomenclatures of race and gender: "List of Black Refugee Men for Passage to Trinidad."[67]

In that maritime journey, their third in four months, the migrants processed the emotions that such a whirlwind of events undoubtedly raised even as they again confronted material inequalities, this time in the food political economy aboard the ship. Even while at Bermuda, officials scrambled to feed the migrants. "Many of these men have wives and children," Cochrane wrote. "I propose allowing them the same rations as are given women & children by the Army until salt-fish and rice can be procured for them, which is a food more congenial to their former living than the usual rations."[68] On the ships, however, refugees received lower rations of food than those granted to the crew and supernumeraries, and the amount refugees received varied depending on gender and age. On the *Carron*, refugee men were "victualled at 2/3 Allowance." With a handful of exceptions, female refugees received one-half allowance, and children at one-fourth allowance. On the *Levant*, the Louisiana refugees received half the spirits given to the crew. Seven refugees, likely children, received one-fourth the standard food allowance. In the naval ship's food political economy, the differences between sailors, the black veterans, and their families came into relief, as did the gender and age hierarchies between black migrants. The *Levant* left Bermuda on May 2, 1815 and arrived in Trinidad twenty-five days later. Those hierarchies did not vanish in Trinidad.[69]

"ALLOW THE AMERICAN SETTLERS TO TAKE AS WIVES . . . THESE AFRICAN FEMALES"

In 1812, Sir Ralph Woodford cherished a simple dream: to reach his "former & original Destination" of "attending some ... Grand Duchess to her opera box" in London. Unfortunately for him, he could not find

---

[67] *Levant* Muster, ADM 37/4667, Admiralty: Ships' Musters (Series II), Ship: Levant, March 1814–November 1815, TNA; Admiralty: Ships' Musters (Series II), Ship: CARRON, July 1815–August 1816, ADM 37/5507, TNA; Woodford to Bathurst, Trinidad, March 4, 1816, GRO. See also Weiss, *The Merikens*, 54–57.

[68] Cochrane to Croker, April 6, 1815.

[69] Cochrane to Sir J. C. Sherbrooke, March 25, 1815, Cochrane's Journals, ADM 50/122, TNA; Carron Muster List, ADM 37/5507, TNA; Muster List, *Levant*, TNA, ADM 37/4667.

employment in the capital. His desire for upward mobility sent him outward to Madeira, a small island off the coast of Morocco and Portugal that briefly came under British administration during the Napoleonic Wars. From that post Woodford wrote detailed letters to his patron, Charles Bathurst. "The peasantry of the Island," Woodford wrote, "are of a very dark brown." He further assessed their bodies by gender. The men, he claimed, were of average height, "very athletic & well made," while the women he deemed "generally ugly ... with black eyes & hair." The climate, he predicted, would produce "The fruits of the West Indies and the north of Europe." Accordingly Woodford concluded "the possession of this Island as a Peace is a most desirable object." Woodford trained the homoerotic imperial gaze that he honed in Madeira at his next post, Trinidad, where one of his most important duties was to manage a diverse and expanding population. Some of those arrivistes had traded the slave spaces of Louisiana for freedom and land ownership in Trinidad. The challenges they confronted in a region that was even more cosmopolitan than the one they had just left proved harbingers of things to come in Louisiana, Trinidad, and indeed the entire world.[70]

Thanks to the patronage of Bathurst, the Secretary of War and Colonies, Woodford arrived in Trinidad in 1813 to serve as governor and to embark upon "the Situation of Registring [sic] the slaves."[71] The black migrants from the United States who came shortly thereafter entered what one historian calls the "last Caribbean frontier." Unlike Jamaica – which by 1800 was a sugar powerhouse – Trinidad's economy was far less established. During its Spanish period, the island harbored revolutionaries and self-liberated persons of African descent from nearby

---

[70] Woodford to Bathurst, Madeira, January 1, 1809, GRO; Woodford to Bathurst, Madeira, July 21, 1810, GRO. On the co-constitutive relationship between England and empire, see Catherine Hall, *Civilising Subjects: Metropole and Colony in the English Imagination 1830–1867* (Chicago: The University of Chicago Press, 2002). On the white male gaze, material hierarchies, and the "Old World" making of Atlantic racial ideologies, see Morgan, *Laboring Women*, 12–49; James Sweet, "The Iberian Roots of American Racist Thought," *The William and Mary Quarterly* 54 (January 1997): 143–166.

[71] After the British Empire outlawed the transatlantic slave trade in 1807, abolitionists turned their focus to the inter-island slave trade. In March 1812, the Order in Council established a slave registration act designed to account for, and thereby police, the movement of Trinidad's existing slave population. A handful of other colonies established similar policies before an 1819 Act of the British Parliament required slave registration across the colonies. B. W. Higman, *Slave Populations of the British Caribbean, 1807–1834* (Baltimore, MD: The Johns Hopkins University Press, 1984), chapter 2.

Venezuela and other parts of the Caribbean and South America. In 1782, Trinidad's population was estimated at a little over 2,800, a relatively small number that prompted officials in Madrid to issue the *cédula* a couple of years later. That offer of land ownership attracted settlers, and by 1789 the island's population had more than tripled to 13,104 residents: 5,170 free people (whites and free people of color); 1,483 indigenous persons; and 6,451 slaves. British officials took possession of the island in 1797, and in the first four years of British Governor Thomas Picton's administration more than 10,000 African slaves entered the island, a huge influx that was nearly four times the number of slaves imported into Louisiana between 1800 and 1809. Even still, the chronic lack of capital and labor nonetheless meant the sugar boom that planters and officials expected did not materialize. From below, poisoning conspiracies and other forms of slave resistance hindered their efforts. From above, the increasing importance of the "moral capital" that Britain derived by remaking itself into an antislavery empire hindered colonial planters' efforts to maximize staple production through slave labor.[72]

When in a letter to his patron Woodford referred to Trinidad as "my Barataria," he was even more incisive than he perhaps understood, as his reference alluded to the Spanish Empire and its former possessions, which included Louisiana and Trinidad. In Miguel de Cervantes' *Don Quixote*, which was published in the early seventeenth century, Sancho Panza, the protagonist's travel companion, briefly governs the isle of Barataria. Perhaps like Woodford, a gullible Panza accepts the position filled with utopian visions of prosperity and social ascendancy, but his actual experience is a dispiriting one. More than that, Woodford's allusion also calls attention to other similarities between Louisiana and Trinidad. In Louisiana, Barataria Bay was the storied headquarters of the Pirates Lafitte, while in Trinidad Barataria is a town located east of Port-of-Spain and Laventille and west of San Juan.[73]

The similarities between Louisiana and Trinidad did not end there. First, both societies were diverse. Woodford complained about the difficulties of managing "such a mixed & widely extended Population" in Trinidad. That population included British settlers

[72] Woodford to Bathurst, Bath, July 23, 1812, GRO; Candlin, *The Last Caribbean Frontier*, 54, chapters 3–5; Epstein, *Scandal of Colonial Rule*; Adderley, "New Negroes from Africa," 9; Brown, *Moral Capital: Foundations of British Abolitionism*.

[73] Woodford to Bathurst, Port of Spain, July 8, 1813, GRO. On Panza's utopian vision, see Myriam Yvonne Jehenson and Peter N. Dunn, *The Utopian Nexus in Don Quixote* (Nashville, TN: Vanderbilt University Press, 2006), 65–66.

("My own countrymen are, as usual abroad, among the most trouble-some"). To increase the number of British settlers, some suggested the resettlement of convicts, prostitutes, and beggars from London or the mass migration of families from the Scottish Highlands. Others advocated Chinese laborers, but it would be a few more years before Asia would supply a significant number of migrant workers to the British Caribbean. Other residents included radical republican French Creoles "banished from Grenada & other Colonies" whom Woodford suspected had not "abandoned entirely their former principles." Catholic settlers from nearby Venezuela and other South American ports also immigrated to the island.

Second, as in Louisiana, that diverse population lived in a white supre-macist slave society. The first decade of British administration in Trinidad left the island suspended between legal codes. Initially, Spanish laws remained in force, and rights such as coartación gave slaves the right to purchase and thereby free themselves. Relationships between white men and women of color allowed some free blacks to acquire freedom, prop-erty, and privilege. Free blacks, including women of color and veterans of the British West India Regiments, enjoyed certain protections under Spanish law. "Prize Negroes," or Africans rescued from the international slave trade, subsequently settled there in small numbers. Freedom did not mean the absence of coercion, however. Sir Thomas Picton's decision to torture Louisa Calderon, a free mulatto woman, prompted debates about the relationship between British civilization and the systemic violence of colonialism in the West Indies and in India. In addition, Trinidad was home to a significant slave population. Woodford claimed that life was not so bad for the island's slaves, who "on Sundays [were] better drest [sic] than their owners & make 10 or 20 Dollars by the sale of the super-abundance of vegetables from their garden grounds in the market." Though enslaved market women did sell their surplus crops for profit, the island's early civil code drew heavily on Martinique's *Code Noir* and circumscribed the rights of slaves and free persons of color. The alleged 1805 Christmas conspiracy among the enslaved of Trinidad only heigh-tened repression. For the refugees from Louisiana, at least, the destination probably looked a lot like the point of departure.[74]

In an era defined by republican revolts against European monarchs, the resettlement of the freed migrants from the United States exacerbated

[74] Woodford to Bathurst, Trinidad, March 25, 1814, GRO; Woodford to Bathurst, Port of Spain, July 8, 1813, GRO; Epstein, *Scandal of Colonial Rule*.

the schism between Trinidad's planters and the British Empire. Where planters in the British Caribbean once greeted slave ships with excitement – agents rowed buyers out to slave ships, plied them with wine and food, and coaxed them into expensive purchases – they met the arrival of freed blacks with suspicion. After all, these settlers were former slaves who had taken up arms against their masters and who would now become subsidized landowners. "I presume that His Majesty's Government could not (if from motives of prudence alone) have intended that 500 slaves who had just obtained their freedom in the manner they had done," Woodford wrote, "should be thrown abroad upon any Colony where slavery existed, without considering itself bound to meet the expense of proper Controul and Inspection, as well as of mere subsistence."[75] Woodford (whose own unpopularity with colonists coupled with financial mismanagement ultimately cost him his job) regularly reminded imperial officials of colonists' hostility toward the refugees. Bathurst and other officials acknowledged that the migrants' arrival "excited much anxiety and alarm on the part of the neighboring proprietors," but Bathurst encouraged Woodford to persist in his plans.[76] Bathurst then received a petition from the "white and free colored inhabitants of the Quarters of North and South Naparima, occasioned by the settlement of American Refugees which has been established in this neighborhood." A multiracial coalition of landowners in Trinidad took issue with the migrants' settlement. Not slaves, not wholly free, the men and, to a lesser number women and children, from the United States entered a precarious rung of local society.[77]

[75] Woodford to Harrison, Trinidad, May 5, 1818 TNA T 1/4323.
  On the arrival of slave ships into the English Caribbean, see Smallwood, *Saltwater Slavery*, 161.
  On the increasing alienation of planters from their empires and its implications for nationalism during the Age of Revolution, see Anderson, *Imagined Communities*.
  By the 1820s, the settlers' costs represented not quite 2 percent of the colony's annual revenue. See "State of the Account of Sir Ralph Woodford Bart Governor of Trinidad, of the Receipts and Disbursements of the Revenues of that Island from the 1st of January to the 31st of December 1824"; "Abstract of the State of the Account of Sir Ralph Woodford [Baronet,] Governor of Trinidad from 1st January to the 31st December 1825, Audited 9th January 1827"; Edmund Byng, Thomas Counoy, and J. Kingston, "State of the Account of Sir Ralph Woodford Bart Governor of Trinidad of the Receipt and Disbursements of the Revenue of that Island from the 1st January to the 31st December 1826," 11 June 1828; all T 1/4323 Box 1.
[76] Bathurst to Woodford, London, January 11, 1817 TNA CO 296/5.
[77] Bathurst to Woodford, London, January 17, 1817 TNA CO 296/5.

Where in Louisiana and across the United States they were enslaved, in Trinidad these men and women were freed, and they set out to turn that legal status into a meaningful experience. They relocated under the assumption that they would receive land and freedom. To make good on their promise, the British brought these migrants to the ten or twelve "Company Towns" of Naparima, Laventille, and Caroni. There they became international symbols of state-subsidized free black labor and yeoman domesticity. Though some eighty early veterans were hospitalized with ulcers and faced daunting recoveries, many others settled between eight and a dozen "Company Villages" of about eighty men each. Each man received sixteen acres of land. In the earliest years they reportedly "built themselves good Huts, and those that are industrious have a considerable quantity of land cleared." To support their efforts, Woodford requested permission from the Treasury to supply them with "mules, pigs, dogs & for the largest quantity of provisions brought to the Market, and of Fowling Pieces, European garden seeds, to which they have been accustomed in America."[78] The next year a visitor wrote of the 650 or so residents: "[Woodford] has appointed them land to cultivate, and allowed them rations until it be made sufficient support."[79] In 1817 Woodford again requested permission from the Treasury to use the colony's funds to supply a ration to the women and children who lived in Naparima, as the later waves of arrivals arrived during a drought and had "not been established long enough to possess the resource of plantains in the dry season."[80]

Migrants also recreated, melded, and transformed African diasporic cultural and spiritual systems in Trinidad. The first group of migrants consisted of African-born and American-born settlers. "Of the last 500 that arrived in the Colony, eighty are Africans, who are by much the most industrious. The Rest are Virginians, intelligent but prone to idleness." Some of them asked for "beads and clothes of which they appear to be very fond."[81] Beads certainly held aesthetic appeal, but, in addition, they

---

[78] "Extract of a letter from Governor Sir Ralph Woodford to Lord Bathurst dated Trinidad 31 July 1814," TNA T 1/4323. On the slavery, health, and the body in slavery and freedom, see Jim Downs, *Sick from Freedom: African-American Illness and Suffering during the Civil War and Reconstruction* (New York: Oxford University Press, 2012).

[79] Woodford to Bathurst, March 4, 1816, GRO.

[80] Woodford to Bathurst, Trinidad, August 13, 1817 TNA T 1/4323; Gomez, *Black Crescent*, 64.

[81] "Extract of a letter from Governor Sir RW to Lord Bathurst dated Trinidad 31 July 1814."

also held religious significance across the African diaspora. Perhaps this request was for rosary beads, as many enslaved persons in Louisiana were practicing Catholics. In Islam, prayer beads, like prayer mats, veils and head coverings, and dietary laws, were an important aspect of religious devotion. Most of the Colonial Marines absconded from Virginia and the Carolinas, both regions where Africans from the Senegambia in particular were known to have practiced the Islamic faith. The same holds for Louisiana, an area that received a significant influx of African-born peoples in the final years of Spanish rule. Trinidad became home to an organized and upwardly mobile black Muslim population in the nineteenth century. It is wholly possible, therefore, that the Colonial Marines who requested the beads were either Catholics or Muslims who hoped to practice their faith in yet another land.[82]

The migrants also likely continued in or converted to various strains of Protestantism in Trinidad. The Louisiana migrants likely represented a diverse faith community, as the majority of the enslaved population was African-born, and Catholicism was the dominant religion in local society. By contrast, thanks to the Great Awakening of the mid-1700s and subsequent conversions between 1790 and 1830, the Chesapeake blacks were predominately Baptist and Methodist despite the retrenchment of white church leaders from antislavery positions. As such, they became part of a black Baptist Atlantic that stretched from Canada to the Eastern Seaboard, Sierra Leone to Jamaica. Due to the dominance of the Baptist faith in the larger community, then, some Louisiana migrants perhaps converted to Protestantism in Trinidad. "The Establishment of an English Church and an officiating minister is greatly wanted by these Refugees," Woodford wrote in 1814.[83]

---

[82] On Islam in the US South and Caribbean, see Gomez, *Exchanging Our Country Marks*, chapter 4; Gomez, *Black Crescent*, chapter 2. On sartorial performance in the African diaspora, see White, "'Wearing Three or Four Handkerchiefs Around His Collar, and Elsewhere About Him': Slaves' Constructions of Masculinity and Ethnicity in French Colonial New Orleans," in *Dialogues of Dispersal*, eds. Sandra Gunning, Tera Hunter, and Michele Mitchell (Malden, MA: Blackwell Publishing, 2004), 132–153; Shane White and Graham J. White, *Stylin': African American Expressive Culture from Its Beginnings to the Zoot Suit* (Ithaca, NY: Cornell University Press, 1998).

[83] "Extract of a letter from Governor Sir RW to Lord Bathurst dated Trinidad 31 July 1814." On black Christianity in the United States, see Gomez, *Exchanging Our Country Marks*, chapter 9; Sylvia R. Frey, *Water from the Rock: Black Resistance in a Revolutionary Age* (Princeton: Princeton University Press, 1991); Sylvia R. Frey and Betty Wood, *Come Shouting to Zion: African American Protestantism in the American South and British Caribbean to 1830* (Chapel Hill: The University of North Carolina Press, 1998);

Yet faith also became a point of separation that created distance between the "Meriken" settlers and their enslaved neighbors. Even as Woodford lobbied for a Baptist church for these settlers, his patron Bathurst in London sought to restrict the contagion of that faith among Trinidad's slaves. He expressed to Woodford a concern about Baptist missionaries who performed baptisms and burials and taught doctrines that undermined those of the Church of England and the Catholic Church. Bathurst reminded Woodford to "prohibit any missionary from preaching to the Slaves, unless he shall previous find himself to a strict observance of" that rule. Baptists, with their anti-hierarchical teachings, destabilized the colonies and the empire.[84]

Trinidad's landholders also feared commingling between the overwhelmingly male migrants and women, whether slave or free, in surrounding households, which prompted officials to activate imperial networks to obtain sexual partners for these men. Though the preference for enslaved male laborers resulted in so-called gender imbalances across the Atlantic plantation world, some British authors and enslaved people themselves advocated monogamous, heterosexual marriages and partnerships for bondspersons. But in the context of chattel slavery, planters' demand for enslaved women's productive and reproductive labor took precedence over

Margaret Washington Creel, *"A Peculiar People"*: *Slave Religion and Community-Culture among the Gullahs* (New York: New York University Press, 1988); Stuckey, *Slave Culture*, chapter 1; Albert J. Raboteau, *Slave Religion: The "Invisible Institution" in the Antebellum South* (New York: Oxford University Press, 1978).

"Some of these blacks had obtained a little knowledge of the Gospel while in America," two officials from London Missionary Society reported, an account later reprinted in a host of periodicals. British abolitionist Thomas Clarkson, whose Society for Effecting the Abolition of the Slave Trade worked towards its 1807 criminalization, cited these settler communities as exemplars of the promise of supervised black emancipation. "Trinidad," *The Religious Intelligencer . . . Containing the Principal Transactions of the Various Bible and Missionary Societies, with Particular Accounts of Revivals of Religion*, April 25, 1818, 758, www.proquest.com, accessed March 4, 2010; "Extract from a Late Pamphlet, Written by the Celebrated Thomas Clarkson," *Genius of Universal Emancipation*, April 1, 1824, 158, www.proquest.com, accessed March 4, 2010.

On the spiritual survivals of the black soldiers resettled in the Company Towns, see Maureen Warner-Lewis, *Trinidad Yoruba: From Mother Tongue to Memory* (Kingston: The Press, University of the West Indies, 1997); Lorna McDaniel, "Memory Spirituals of the Liberated American Soldiers in Trinidad's 'Company Villages,'" *Caribbean Quarterly* 40, no. 1 (March 1994): 38–58. Whitfield suggests that some of the settlers who fled the Georgia and South Carolina Sea Islands were Muslims. See Whitfield, *Blacks on the Border*, 29; Gomez, *Black Crescent*.

[84] Bathurst to Woodford, London, November 8, 1817, February 5, 1818, and June 23, 1818, all TNA CO 296/5.

On the Baptist War in Jamaica, see Brown, *The Reaper's Garden*, 232–246.

the civilizing imperatives of bourgeois domesticity. Due to the intersecting oppressions that women experienced under chattel slavery, the class- and faith-based ideologies of bourgeois domesticity were not necessarily available or even desirable to them. But as small numbers of liberated black men and, to a lesser extent, women began to settle across the British Caribbean in the early 1800s, the imperial state cultivated bourgeois norms of masculinity and femininity among them as part of the transition from slaves to imperial subjects. In this incubatory era (and subsequently, on a far larger scale, during the apprenticeship period), British officials used specific policies to encourage liberated men to become husbands and providers and to coax freedwomen to become wives, mothers, and homemakers. The performance of compulsory heteronormative gender roles became a key marker of these settlers' path to Englishness.[85]

Despite the landholders' many complaints about the migrants, one of the few that Bathurst took seriously involved the sexual availability of women for the veterans: "But the inadequacy of the Females as compared with the other parts of the Establishment has induced me to take measures for supplying that deficiency." Bathurst set out to find sexual partners for these men and in the process became an imperial matchmaker. He ordered a commander at Barbados "to send down to Trinidad by the first opportunity a considerable number of females" taken from a French slaver headed from Africa to the Caribbean. Upon their arrival, Bathurst ordered, "allow the American Settlers to take as Wives such as these African Females as may prefer such a marriage to being apprenticed as servants in the usual manner." Bathurst gave these African-born "prize" women taken from the transatlantic slave trade the circumscribed choice of either years of labor as apprentices or marriage to a complete stranger. Even if this situation were preferable to apprenticeship, it tied these women's labor and sexuality to men they did not know and, due to language barriers, with whom they likely could not communicate. They also became vulnerable to domestic abuse. On the other hand, as historian Rosanne Adderley points out, their position as women allowed them the option of a choice, as men in the same situation could only enter into apprenticeship. Whatever the case, within a few months time, forty-two of the fifty-three African women were married and seven more were engaged.

---

[85] Paton, *No Bond but the Law*, 53–56; Adderley, *"New Negroes from Africa,"* chapter 4; Barbara Bush, *Slave Women in Caribbean Society, 1650–1838* (Kingston: Heinemann Publishers, 1990), 98–103. See also Mimi Sheller, *Democracy from below: Erotic Agency and Caribbean Freedom* (Durham: Duke University Press, 2012).

Only the four youngest women had not entered into these partnerships. A few years later Woodford's successor requested reimbursement for the "the expenses of the sixty African females sent here from Antigua for the settlers."[86] The resettlement of these women accomplished the biopolitical engineering that Bathurst intended: in roughly two years, the free black population had grown to 396 men, 180 women, and 300 children for a total population of 876.[87]

The promise of liberty and economic independence attracted settlers to Trinidad, but they did not all enjoy the daily grind. That number included Governor Woodford. "When this Island is brought into a habit of <u>order</u> & attention to the Laws," he wrote, "I hope I may be translated back to the <u>Old World</u> again."[88] Some self-liberated settlers agreed. Free labor did not mean an absence of coercion, which the black migrants learned firsthand. Some of them labored under the supervision of a planter named Joseph Mitchell, who also worked as Commandant of Naparima, "a large and populous quarter inhabited by French colored rich Proprietors who required an active Superintendence." After what Woodford considered adequate supervision of the first 60 refugees, he appointed Mitchell to a salaried position as superintendent to the American Negroes, a position that came with two servants.[89]

What officials and landowners considered a public safety measure the migrants experienced as nearly the same surveillance and labor exploitation that they had hoped to leave behind in the US South. Nearly two decades after their initial settlement, Trinidad's then Governor Major-General Sir Lewis Grant decided that the "control" that the elder Mitchell inflicted on the migrants might have been necessary initially, but that in subsequent years the governor "observed that a great degree of oppression" now defined their treatment. The migrants were "considerably disgusted" at their labor arrangements: "They were called upon to work on the Plantation of the Superintendent, and, if they received any wages at all,

---

[86] Ibid.; R. Mitchell to Woodford, North Naparima, Trinidad, August 5, 1817 TNA T 1/ 4323; Aretas William Young to George Harrison, Trinidad, April 19, 1821 TNA T 1/ 4323.

 For other references to liberated African women as wives for the refugees, see Bathurst to Woodford, London, July 6, 1820 TNA CO 296/5.

[87] Woodford to Bathurst, Trinidad, June 8, 1823 TNA T 1/4323; Adderley, *"New Negroes from Africa,"* chapter 4.

[88] Woodford to Bathurst, March 25, 1814, GRO, emphasis original.

[89] "Extract of a letter from Governor Sir RW to Lord Bathurst dated Trinidad 31 July 1814"; Woodford to George Harrison, Trinidad, May 5, 1818 TNA T 1/4323 Box 1.

they were paid at a low rate and in 'Truck' charged at an exorbitant price." Mitchell and other nearby planters colluded to extract cheap labor from the settlers, and "all manners of possible difficulties were put in the way of the Refugees" when they attempted to earn money outside of that exploitive system.[90] In short, the superintendent – whose salary was deducted from the veterans' pension funds – exploited their labor, paid them in non-standard currency, limited their purchasing power and ability to save, and thereby ensured their continued exploitation.[91]

Dissatisfaction with such labor arrangements motivated some migrants to again escape into the Atlantic World. Within two years of their arrival, one or two migrants from the United States applied "to return to the Country of the Indians from which they had been brought." They might have referred to the Great Lakes region, Spanish Florida, or the Gulf Coast, but they deemed their experiences in native nations far superior to those on the Caribbean frontier. Woodford also fielded requests from settlers who wanted to go to "neighbouring Colonies[,] to Bermuda and to England."[92] Bathurst rejected their requests. For their own comfort, the paternalist averred, he would prevent their migration to neighboring British colonies or to England. At a time when colonizationists in London exported black Londoners to Sierra Leone, the last thing Bathurst wanted was more black settlers in England. He did, however, authorize their return to the American Indian nations. These peripatetic migrants, however, were a determined group. Some of them undoubtedly found their way back to the high seas.[93]

Those who remained were subject to labor exploitation right through the eve of British emancipation. In 1831, after he received word of the

---

[90] Grant to Howich, London, August 26, 1831 TNA T 1/4323 Box 2.
[91] On the relationship between chattel slavery and wage labor in the nineteenth-century Caribbean and US South, see Mary Turner, ed., *From Chattel Slaves to Wage Slaves: The Dynamics of Labour Bargaining in the Americas* (London: James Currey, 1995).
[92] Woodford to Secretary of State, July 31, 1817, Trinidad, TNA, CO 295/44.
  The black refugees' relationship to the Indian populations might have taken any number of forms, from enslavement to kinship. Perhaps the migrants missed the culture and community that defined his or her previous life or grew weary of the policies that governed them in Trinidad. On kinship, community, and conflict at the intersection of Native American and African American histories, see Barbara Krauthamer, *Black Slaves, Indian Masters: Slavery, Emancipation, and Citizenship in the Native American South* (Chapel Hill: The University of North Carolina Press, 2013); Celia E. Naylor, *African Cherokees in Indian Territory: From Chattel to Citizens* (Chapel Hill: The University of North Carolina Press, 2008); Tiya Miles, *Ties That Bind: The Story of an Afro-Cherokee Family in Slavery and Freedom* (Berkeley: University of California Press, 2005).
[93] Bathurst to Woodford, London, November 8, 1817 TNA CO 296/5.

exploitive conditions under which the veterans labored, Lord Goodrich instructed Grant to instruct the "American Negro" and West India Regiment settlements "that they are free to make such bargains for their labor as they may think proper & that no person has a right to appropriate their labor otherwise than in conformity with the terms for which they may have contracted to give it."[94] In theory, the right to bargain over one's wages and to enter into a labor contract was the antithesis of slavery. Yet as many workers the world over would soon learn, the transition from bondage to contract did not guarantee an elevated quality of life. In postemancipation societies across the Americas, even bold efforts at collective bargaining did not reverse the systemic concentration of wealth and power that defined the late nineteenth century. Even with a dramatic decision to abandon the plantations of Louisiana and the US South, enlistment in the British armed forces, maritime journeys from the Gulf South to Trinidad, and the passage of two decades, these "Merikens," though assuredly privileged relative to the island's slaves, remained vulnerable before planter power.[95]

"A FREE PORT TO ALL NATIONS"

"The only chance [Trinidad] has is of being made a commercial Entrepôt and[,] what I fear is out of the question," Woodford predicted in 1814, "a free port to all nations."[96] As his own empire fought to prevent free trade between the United States and Napoleonic France, Woodford rightly noted that a liberal economic policy would meet resistance from above. But after 1815, Woodford must have felt vindicated as he witnessed a shift in British commerce. "The Commissioners of Victualling having contracted with Mr. John Marryat for the supply of 770 Barrels of American Flour for the use of the Troops in Trinidad," Bathurst wrote to Woodford. "I am to request that you will take measures to prevent any difficulty in the admission of this Flour free of

---

94 Howich to Grant, September 6, 1831 TNA T 1/4323 Box 2.
95 Demetrius L. Eudell, *The Political Languages of Emancipation in the British Caribbean and the U.S. South* (Chapel Hill: The University of North Carolina Press, 2002); Frederick Cooper, Thomas C. Holt, and Rebecca J. Scott, *Beyond Slavery: Explorations of Race, Labor, and Citizenship in Postemancipation Societies* (Chapel Hill: The University of North Carolina Press, 2000); Amy Dru Stanley, "The Legend of Contract Freedom," in *From Bondage to Contract: Wage Labor, Marriage, and the Market in the Age of Slave Emancipation* (New York: Cambridge University Press, 1998), 1–59.
96 Woodford to Bathurst, Trinidad, March 25, 1814 GRO.

Colonial Duties." Four years after the Treaty of Ghent and three years after Napoleon's defeat, British imperial officials entered into a contract with an American merchant, and they agreed to import duty-free staples from its former colony and adversary.[97]

Perhaps a couple hundred refugees made it from the greater New Orleans area to Trinidad, and the number might have been far smaller. But even the larger emigration of several thousand blacks after the War of 1812 did not weaken either empire. On the contrary, both the United States and Britain flourished in the peace that followed. In the United States, patriotism in Louisiana and across the country ran high; the "Era of Good Feelings" (temporarily) supplanted partisan bickering; and Native Americans lost their major imperial ally, which allowed American settler-imperialism to encroach on ever increasing acres of land. Across the Atlantic World, a century of war gave way to the *Pax Brittanica*. US merchants pursued free trade opportunities, and both states established commercial ties that would eventually allow for imperialistic free trade in South America and Asia.[98]

Arguably, these migrants journeyed from slavery to freedom. They did not trek north to Canada, which would later become famous as the terminus of the Underground Railroad. Instead, they sailed south to British Trinidad. There, they enjoyed privileged status relative to the slaves, if not total control over their labor. Their vulnerability to planter power prevented them from becoming the Jeffersonian yeoman farmers they might have hoped to become. Their challenges as "free" blacks who lacked a meaningful market freedom over their labor presaged the difficulties that emancipated persons confronted in the British Caribbean in the 1830s and the United States in the 1860s.

If from afar those settlers represented an uneven experiment in black freedom and wage labor, then the blacks who poured into Louisiana after

---

[97] Bathurst to Woodford, London, October 9, 1819 TNA CO 296/5.

[98] The foundational article here is John Gallagher and Ronald Robinson, "The Imperialism of Free Trade," *The Economic History Review* 6, no. 1 (1953): 1–15. The rise of capitalism after the War of 1812 also reshaped the United States. As J. C. A. Stagg writes:

> As a result [of wartime mobilization], after the war, many of the hallmarks of a "culture of capitalism" – a heightened sense of individuality, the increasing importance of the consumption of material goods, and extensive geographical and social mobility – became more firmly entrenched than ever, all at the expense of older notions of communal republican virtue. In these ways the conflict could be seen as a decisive moment in the emergence of the United States as a modern capitalist society.

See Stagg, *War of 1812*, 7.

the War of 1812 weathered the apotheosis of chattel slavery. The first decades of the nineteenth century witnessed the explosion of King Cotton in the Lower Mississippi River Valley. Between 1800 and 1809, Louisiana imported over 2,600 slaves. In the following decade, that number soared to over 47,000 arrivals, mainly from the Chesapeake. In the next two decades, the number of imports skyrocketed again to an additional 100,000 slaves. "In the years 1820–1860," one historian writes, "a sevenfold increase in the Valley's slave population produced a fortyfold increase in its production of cotton."[99] As British imperial officials experimented with wage labor on an island of plantations, the oligarchic planters of Louisiana bet their future on bound black bodies suspended between infinite rows of white cotton that, once picked, fed the textile mills of industrial England and the northern United States.[100]

After 1815, Louisiana and Trinidad existed within a single Atlantic space of capital and labor that confined the possibilities of all people of African descent, both slave and free. Slave and wage labor were both linked to the interconnected structures of capital that rewrote the individual and collective destinies of people across the Global South. Nonetheless, like capital, black freedom dreams also crossed the lines of empire and nation. In an era of wartime patriotism, a time when racialized conceptions of citizenship excluded slaves and free blacks from the body politic, these migrants linked fates with a competing empire, and once resettled they continued to fight for their own freedom – if not necessarily for that of the island's slaves. Their lives reflected and produced the diverse, diasporic communities for which both Louisiana and Trinidad remain known even as they highlighted the burdens of blackness in each site.[101] The exceptionality of their small story illuminates the stark contours of bondage in the Americas, but their willingness to fight the owners who enslaved them, the planters who exploited them, and the imperial deliverers who selectively supported them reminds us that liberation is not a destination; it is a demand.[102]

---

[99] Johnson, *River of Dark Dreams*, 256. See also Tadman, "Interregional Slave Trade," 120.

[100] Johnson, *River of Dark Dreams*; Beckert, *The Empire of Cotton*; Rothman, *Slave Country*, chapter 5; Johnson, *Soul by Soul*; Johnson, ed., *The Chattel Principle*; Deyle, *Carry Me Back*.

[101] John Weiss maintains a website and gatherings in commemoration of the Meriken migration. www.mcnishandweiss.co.uk/JWhistoryindex.html, accessed November 29, 2012.

[102] David Theo Goldberg, *The Racial State* (Malden, MA: Blackwell Publishing, 2002).

Conclusion

Modern Spaces

Some things you forget. Other things you never do. But it's not. Places, places are still there. If a house burns down, it's gone, but the place – the picture of it – stays, and not just in my memory, but out there, in the world.
Toni Morrison, Beloved

By compulsion and by choice, slaves traversed the streets and streams of greater New Orleans and its Atlantic passageways. *Slavery's Metropolis* set out to track the political, economic, and social transformations of a revolutionary age through the literal and figurative place of those slaves. And their varied and contingent geographies at the turn of the nineteenth century reveal the malleability of modern power. This book has argued that, in contrast to the relatively fixed borders and boundaries long (though now decreasingly) associated with the plantation south, local leaders in New Orleans required a form of cosmopolitanism in their slaves. Such enslaved participation in local and international journeys and heterogeneous assemblages could be constitutive of masters' power. Nonetheless, bondage in an emergent port city offered enslaved persons of African descent opportunities to participate as real-time actors in the Atlantic assemblages that crowded the city's hovels and highways. Enslaved persons in New Orleans also used their positions in that port city to build communities, earn money, launch daring international escapes, resist to the point of revolt, and simply survive. Those bondspersons carved their own geographies that, in the most vivid examples, brought them to some version of freedom in adjacent empires.

Even as people of African descent created and appropriated space for themselves, however, those in power sought not simply to limit slave mobility, but to figure out how to best exploit it. For them, the challenge of modernity was not how to end slavery, but how to capitalize on the degraded position of slaves. This insight is old hat for historians of the slave trades, as scholars of the Middle Passage and domestic slave trades have long been attentive to the fundamental roles of labor and migration in black Atlantic experiences. However, this book insists that such motion did not necessarily end once the purchaser bought his or her new human property. That act of sale could be one moment in an even longer, dynamic trajectory of bondage. Some slaves had to interact with a global population every day, and some had to undertake local, regional, and even international journeys. Whether as immigrants from an antislavery revolution who became enslaved at the early republic's border, peddlers in the streets, inmates in a jail, or laborers on chain gangs, these slaves did not have the luxury of provincialism. Multiracial gatherings and international journeys were not by definition subversive of the slave system. Sometimes far-flung travels and mixed assemblies offered respites and escapes from the burdens of chattel slavery; at other times, they were themselves the burden.

This book offers several contributions to our understanding of modern slavery. First, it reminds us that the coercions of slavery did not work in one way. The most characteristic sights and sites of slavery – shackles, slave pens, enclosed plantations – call attention to the rigid geographies of slavery. But those bounded plantations existed to supply staple crops for a global market. The need to circulate those commodities across rural landscapes and through ports created a germ of black movement even in contexts that seemed most prohibitive. Beyond that, slaves themselves labored in a carceral landscape that included interdependent plantations and port cities. To be sure, most slaves labored on rural plantations, but like the goods they grew these slaves' value stemmed from their embedment in urban and rural, regional and Atlantic geographies.

It is far too convenient to dismiss the history of human bondage and its shameful sadisms to the backwaters of rural society. But from the Louisiana Purchase in 1803 until the 1830s, slaves made up one-third of the urban population of New Orleans, a city that at its inception had Parisian pretensions and became the fifth largest city in the United States. Not all of them lived quarantined behind a cordon sanitaire or hidden behind an evil master's property fences. They were real-time, living, breathing people who covered the urban landscape. A heterogeneous port city could be a capital of slaves, and local officials and bondspersons themselves contested the structures for managing such a mobile and interconnected servile population. As present-day activists who fight against human trafficking point out, slavery as an institution functions even in places that seem to revel in flouting conventional lines of authority.

The number of slaves in motion on the urban landscape forces a re-evaluation of the vaunted New Orleans exceptionalism. Historians of colonial Louisiana long labored in the shadow of historian Frank Tannenbaum's dichotomy between a static, binary racial system in the United States and a more fluid one in Latin America.[1] However, comparative perspectives that consider the extent to which New Orleans belonged to a distilled version of the US South *or* the Caribbean and Latin America elide the many ways the city functioned as an entangled crossroads for all of those spaces. And slaves, their migrations, and networks made it a crossroads. As we continue to decenter the thirteen colonies in North American history, we also shake up the contours of norms and exceptions. Certainly, much of colonial New Orleans history did not hew to the norms that defined much of British colonial North America. That city witnessed successive Old World and New World imperial administrations, practiced Catholicism rather than Protestantism, and was home to a sizable and politically engaged free black population, among other characteristics. Even after the Louisiana Purchase, many Americans imagined New Orleans as an internal colony of sorts, a city central to the nation yet also distinct from distilled versions of the "real" south. The phrase "except in Louisiana" has become an important one in broader histories of the US South, and this formulation offers certain advantages. The city was (and remains) unique, and we need tools to explain its rich heritage.

Too much of a focus on New Orleans and its cultural uniqueness, however, obscures the concrete ways that circuits of capital, communication, and migration simultaneously rooted that city firmly within a larger American expansionist project and Atlantic plantation complex. New Orleans had much in common with other port cities even as it attracted hordes of settlers from across continental areas more conventionally defined as American. New Orleans was no exception in the early modern world; it was an exaggeration. Yet to situate it only within a circum-Caribbean context, for example, elides the ways that developments along the Eastern Seaboard or in London also affected the course of New Orleans history.

In addition, this book reveals that the legal and illegal motions of slaves in the port city connected them to regional and international

---

[1] Tannenbaum, *Slave and Citizen.*

networks of slaves and free people that broke down overly neat dichotomies between plantation and urban space. The geographies of slavery were expansive, contingent, and constantly contested. To be sure, the majority of slaves lived and labored in a carceral landscape defined by plantations, but for many others their labors required a more elastic system of boundaries that encompassed yet extended beyond fences and dogs. On the one hand, this ability to structure the place of slaves in space through ideological and physical boundaries is evidence of the disquieting genius of modern power. The ability to circulate across the landscape, which under other conditions might seem a perquisite of the privileged, under the weight of chattel slavery became forced labor. But even under those conditions, slaves could create communities that brought people in the heart of the city into simultaneous if fractured communities with their counterparts in rural areas. As such, urban assemblages produced slave communities that encompassed regional and Atlantic geographies.

Lastly, and perhaps most hauntingly, this work reminds us that integration and travel are no substitute for antiracism and meaningful equality, and, in fact, they can have the opposite effect of heightening socioeconomic chasms. Some celebrate movement and multicultural community as part of the linear narrative of progress in modern American and Atlantic history. According to this perspective, cutting-edge transportation and communication technologies offered financial profit, freedom from parochial constraints of a given society, and opportunities for self-fashioning. Thomas Jefferson and his yeoman settler-imperialists looked outward for a geographic antidote to the hierarchies of class, gender, and nation that foreclosed their possibilities along the Eastern Seaboard. In black Atlantic history, the association between movement and freedom is apotheosized in the Underground Railroad of the nineteenth century and the Great Migration of the twentieth. From Renaissance man Martin Delany's path-breaking novel _Blake_ to Randall Robinson's _Quitting America_, we celebrate the liberatory potential of transnational escape and activism. Yet the theme that repeatedly emerges in this work is the dreadful reality that integration or physical relocation alone is not enough to broaden life possibilities. Freedom and equality are acts of will, not accidents of geography.[2]

---

[2] Martin Robison Delany, _Blake; or, the Huts of America, a Novel_ (Boston: Beacon Press, 1970); Isabel Wilkerson, _The Warmth of Other Suns: The Epic Story of America's Great_

New Orleans history after the revolutionary era reveals as much. By the 1820s and 1830s, Anglo-Americans on the southwestern frontier clamored for increasing amounts of land to transform into cotton fields. At the same time, global diasporas converged on the slave country. Streams of German, Irish, Italian, and Jewish immigrants fled the traumas of Europe to try their luck in the planter's paradise. Slavery continued to expand as did the hunger for land. New Orleans became a staging ground for the US–Mexican War (1846–1848), William Walker's filibustering efforts in Nicaragua, and imagined planter exoduses to Cuba and Brazil. All of these efforts were designed to preserve and expand chattel slavery even as the institution fell out of favor in the British Empire and the northern United States. By the 1850s, even as European immigrants poured into New Orleans, some free people of color left for Haiti to escape the racism in the Deep South.[3]

After the Civil War, the spaces of New Orleans again became sites of contestation. During Reconstruction, former slaves and free people of color extended their struggles for political and economic rights. As freed blacks negotiated fair wage contracts, southern elites looked to Cuba for Chinese, or "coolie," laborers who they hoped would work for exploitive wages. White men established secret organizations such as the Ku Klux Klan and Carnival krewes that used the spectacle of street parades to instill terror in blacks and recent European immigrants. Despite the best efforts of southern blacks and their allies, Reconstruction haltingly gave way to the Redemption, and state and local officials again used laws to regulate space to police hierarchies of race, gender, class, and sexuality. In New Orleans, local officials created Storyville, a defined area in racially and culturally mixed Faubourg Tremé, to quarantine prostitution. The controversial plan sought to keep the sex workers, both white and black women, confined within that red-light district and outside of other, more respectable neighborhoods. And in 1890, Louisiana passed the Separate Car Act, which mandated that rail companies in Louisiana maintain separate accommodations for white and non-white passengers. A group of activists, including Homer Plessy, and the East Louisiana Railroad Company allied to fight this legislation. In *Plessy* v. *Ferguson* (1896), the US Supreme Court upheld states' right to mandate race-based

---

Migration (New York: Random House, 2010); Randall Robinson, *Quitting America: The Departure of a Black Man from His Native Land* (New York: Dutton Adult, 2004).

[3] Matthew Pratt Guterl, *American Mediterranean: Southern Slaveholders in the Age of Emancipation* (Cambridge, MA: Harvard University Press, 2008).

segregation. At the dawn of the American century, the same New Orleans neighborhood that gave jazz to the world gave Jim Crow to the nation.[4]

Even today, the spaces of New Orleans remain contested. On the one hand, the city, its impressive, imposing mansions along St. Charles Avenue and the quaint cottages (and alcohol-soaked alleyways) of the Vieux Carré appeal to streams of visitors each year. Their distinctive architecture and eclectic residents past and present captivate historians, filmmakers, novelists, and residents alike. Every year, millions flock to the Crescent City to see the past performed in ghost tours, to scribble three Xs on Marie Laveau's tomb, and to join in the cultural celebrations. It would seem that the city and its past are extraordinarily visible. However, beyond the saccharine southern charm, the place of black people in those streets, in history and memory, remains invisible. Slave quarters are now "mother-in-law suites" and carriage houses that match their mansions. The houses have been painted, but the places are still there. And the places of our enslaved ancestors in those places are still there. The pained histories that their bruised, black feet pressed into the sidewalks of New Orleans offer a cautionary tale to those who even today, especially today, would convince us that racist immigration and citizenship policies, free market liberalism, hedonistic pleasure, carceral landscapes, and bloody wars of empire offer guaranteed paths toward freedom for all.

[4] The seminal text on Reconstruction remains W. E. B. Du Bois, *Black Reconstruction in America: An Essay toward a History of the Part which Black Folk Played in the Attempt to Reconstruct Democracy in America, 1860–1880* (New York: Oxford University Press, [1935] 2007). On "coolie" labor, see Moon-Ho Jung, *Coolies and Cane: Race, Labor, and Sugar in the Age of Emancipation* (Baltimore, MD: The Johns Hopkins University Press, 2006); Rebecca J. Scott, *Degrees of Freedom: Louisiana and Cuba after Slavery* (Cambridge, MA: The Belknap Press of Harvard University Press, 2005); John C. Rodrigue, *Reconstruction in the Cane Fields: From Slavery to Free Labor in Louisiana's Sugar Parishes 1862–1880* (Baton Rouge: Louisiana State University Press, 2001). On Carnival krewes, see James Gill, *Lords of Misrule: Mardi Gras and the Politics of Race in New Orleans* (Jackson: University Press of Mississippi, 1997).

Selected Bibliography

PUBLISHED PRIMARY SOURCES

Alliot, Paul. *Louisiana under the Rule of Spain, France, and the United States, 1785–1807*, trans. James Alexander Robertson, 2 vols. Cleveland, OH: The Arthur H. Clark Company, 1911.

Andrews, Jr., Johnnie, ed. *Mobile County Wills, 1807–1837; Abstracts of Will Book I of Mobile County, Alabama*. Prichard, AL: Bienville Historical Society, 1988.

Ball, Charles. *Fifty Years in Chains: Or the Life of an American Slave*. New York: Dover Publications, 1970.

Berquin-Duvallon, Pierre Louis, and John Davis. *Travels in Louisiana and the Floridas, in the Year, 1802: Giving a Correct Picture of Those Countries*. New York: Printed by and for I. Riley & Co., 1806.

Bradley, Jared William. *Interim Appointment: W. C. C. Claiborne Letter Book, 1804–1805*. Baton Rouge: Louisiana State University Press, 2002.

Clayton, Ronnie, ed. *Mother Wit: The Ex-slave Narratives of the Louisiana Writers' Project*. New York: Peter Lang Publishing, Inc., 1990.

Conrad, Glenn R. *The German Coast: Abstracts of the Civil Records of St. Charles and St. John the Baptist Parishes, 1804–1812*. Lafayette, LA: University of Southwestern Louisiana, 1981.

"The Documents in Loppinot Case, 1774," trans. Laura L. Porteous, *The Louisiana Historical Quarterly* 12, no. 1 (January 1929): 39–120.

Equiano, Olaudah. *The Interesting Narrative of the Life of Olaudah Equiano, or Gustavus Vassa, the African*, 2 vols. (London: Printed for and Sold by the Author, 1789).

Flint, Timothy, and James Flint. *Recollections of the Last Ten Years, Passed in Occasional Residences and Journeyings in the Valley of the Mississippi, from Pittsburg and the Missouri to the Gulf of Mexico, and from Florida to the Spanish Frontier: In a Series of Letters to the Rev. James Flint, of Salem, Massachusetts*. Boston: Cummings, Hilliard, and Co., 1826.

Foster, Elborg, and Robert Foster, eds. and trans. *Sugar and Slavery, Family and Race: The Letters and Diary of Pierre Dessalles, Planter in Martinique, 1808–1856.* Baltimore, MD: The Johns Hopkins University Press, 1996.

Laussat, Pierre-Clément de. *Memoirs of My Life to My Son during the Years 1803 and after, Which I Spent in Public Service in Louisiana as Commissioner of the French Government for the Retrocession to France of That Colony and for its Transfer to the United States.* Baton Rouge: Louisiana State University Press, 2003.

Livingston, Edward. *Letter from Edward Livingston, Esq. to Roberts Vaux, on the Advantages of the Pennsylvania System of Prison Discipline.* Philadelphia: Jesper Harding, 1828.

A System of Penal Law for the State of Louisiana. Philadelphia, PA: James Kay, Jun. & Co., 1833.

Miller, David Hunter, ed. *Treaties and Other International Acts of the United States of America.* Washington: Government Printing Office, 1931.

Moreau Lislet, Louis. *A General Digest of the Acts of the Legislature of Louisiana.* New Orleans, LA: Benjamin Levy, 1828.

Náñez Falcón, Guillermo, and Wilbur E. Meneray, eds. *The Favrot Family Papers: A Documentary Chronicle of Early Louisiana,* 5 vols. New Orleans, LA: Howard Tilton Memorial Library, 1988.

Northup, Solomon. *Twelve Years a Slave,* eds. Sue Eakin and Joseph Logsdon. Baton Rouge: Louisiana State University Press, 1968.

Nugent, Maria. *Lady Nugent's Journal of Her Residence in Jamaica from 1801 to 1805,* ed. Philip Wright. Kingston, Jamaica: Institute of Jamaica, 1966.

Pitot, James, and Robert D. Bush. *Observations on the Colony of Louisiana, from 1796 to 1802.* Baton Rouge: Published for the Historic New Orleans Collection by the Louisiana State University Press, 1979.

Police Code, or Collection of the Ordinances of Police Made by the City Council of New Orleans. New Orleans, LA: J. Renard, Printer of the Corporation, 1808.

Robin, C. C., and Stuart O. Landry. *Voyage to Louisiana, 1803–1805.* New Orleans, LA: Pelican Pub. Co., 1966.

Rowland, Dunbar, ed. *Official Letter Books of W.C.C. Claiborne, 1801–1816.* Jackson: State Department of Archives and History, 1917.

Stoddard, Amos. *Sketches, Historical and Descriptive of Louisiana* (Philadelphia, PA: Matthew Carey, 1812; reprinted New York: AMS Press, 1973).

Walker, David. *Appeal in Four Articles; Together with a Preamble, to the Coloured Citizens of the World, but in Particular, and Very Expressly to Those of the United States of America.* Boston: David Walker, 1829.

Woods, Earl C., and Charles E. Nolan. *Sacramental Records of the Roman Catholic Church of the Archdiocese of New Orleans.* New Orleans, LA: Archdiocese of New Orleans, 1987.

NEWSPAPERS

Courrier de la Louisiane (Louisiana Courier)
Daily Orleanian
El Misisipi
L'Ami des Lois
Lanterne Magique
L'Echo du Commerce
Louisiana Gazette
Mobile Gazette
Moniteur de la Louisiane
New Orleans Bee
New Orleans Daily Chronicle
New Orleans Daily Crescent
New York Times
The Telegraphe
The Union

LEGAL CASES

Superior Court of the Territory of Orleans

Adèle v. *Beauregard*, 1 Mart. (o.s.) 183. New Orleans, Fall 1810.
Dormenon's Case, 1 Mart. (o.s.) 129. New Orleans, Spring 1810.
Ramozay et al. v. *The Mayor &c. of New Orleans*, 1 Mart. (o.s.) 241.
New Orleans.

Superior Court of Louisiana

Tonnelier v. *Maurin's Ex'r.* 2 Mart. (o.s.) 206. New Orleans, Spring
1812.

Supreme Court of Louisiana

Bertoli v. *The Citizens' Bank*, 1 La.Ann. 119. New Orleans, May,
1846.
Chardon's Heirs v. *Bongue*, La.Rptr 458. New Orleans, May 1836.
Delery v. *Mornet*, 11 Mart. (o.s.) 4. New Orleans, February 1822.
Montillet v. *Shiff*, 4 Mart. (n.s.) 83. New Orleans, July 1825.
Prudence v. *Bermodi*, No. 1888, 1 La. 234. New Orleans, April, 1830.

SECONDARY SOURCES

Adams, Henry. *The War of 1812*. New York: Cooper Square Press, 1999.

Adderley, Rosanne. *"New Negroes from Africa": Slave Trade Abolition and Free African Settlement in the Nineteenth-Century Caribbean*. Bloomington: Indiana University Press, 2006.

Adelman, Jeremy. *Sovereignty and Revolution in the Iberian Atlantic*. Princeton: Princeton University Press, 2006.

Adelman, Jeremy, and Stephen Aron. "From Borderlands to Borders: Empires, Nation-States, and the Peoples in between in North American History." *American History Review* 104 (June 1999): 814–841.

Agnew, John A. "Space and Place." In *The Handbook of Geographical Knowledge*, edited by John A. Agnew and David N. Livingstone, 316–330. London: Sage Publications, 2011.

Alexander, Michelle. *The New Jim Crow: Mass Incarceration in the Age of Colorblindness*. New York: New Press, 2010.

Allende, Isabel. *Island Beneath the Sea*. New York: Harper Collins Publishers, 2011.

Anderson, Benedict. *Imagined Communities: Reflections on the Origin and Spread of Nationalism*. London: Verso, 1983.

Appadurai, Arjun. *The Social Life of Things: Commodities in Cultural Perspective*. Cambridge: Cambridge University Press, 1986.

Fear of Small Numbers: An Essay on the Geography of Anger. Durham: Duke University Press, 2006.

Appiah, Kwame. Anthony. *Cosmopolitanism: Ethics in a World of Strangers*. New York: W. W. Norton & Co., 2006.

Aptheker, Herbert. *American Negro Slave Revolts*. New York: International Publishers, 1983.

Ayers, Edward L. *Vengeance and Justice: Crime and Punishment in the 19th Century American South*. New York: Oxford University Press, 1984.

Bald, Vivek. *Bengali Harlem and the Lost Histories of South Asian America*. Cambridge, MA: Harvard University Press, 2013.

Baptist, Edward E. "'Cuffy,' 'Fancy Maids,' and 'One-Eyed Men': Rape, Commodification, and the Domestic Slave Trade in the United States," *AHR* 106 (December 2001): 1619–1650.

The Half Has Never Been Told: Slavery and the Making of American Capitalism. New York: Basic Books, 2014.

Bardaglio, Peter. "'Shamefull Matches': The Regulation of Interracial Sex and Marriage in the South before 1900." In *Sex, Love, Race: Crossing Boundaries in North American History*, edited by Martha Hodes, 112–138. New York: New York University Press, 1999.

Beattie, Peter M. "'Born under the Cruel Rigor of Captivity, the Supplicant Left It Unexpectedly by Committing a Crime': Categorizing and Punishing Slave Convicts in Brazil, 1830–1897," *The Americas* 66, no. 1 (July 2009): 11–55.

Beckert, Sven. *Empire of Cotton: A Global History*. New York: Knopf, 2014.

Bell, Caryn Cossé. *Revolution, Romanticism, and the Afro-Creole Protest Tradition in Louisiana, 1718–1868.* Baton Rouge: Louisiana State University Press, 1997.

Benton, Lauren A. *A Search for Sovereignty: Law and Geography in European Empires, 1400–1900.* Cambridge: Cambridge University Press, 2010.

Berger, Dan. *Captive Nation: Black Prison Organizing in the Civil Rights Era.* Chapel Hill: The University of North Carolina Press, 2014.

Berlin, Ira. *Slaves without Masters: The Free Negro in the Antebellum South.* New York: Pantheon Books, 1974.

   Generations of Captivity: A History of African-American Slaves. Cambridge, MA: Belknap Press of Harvard University Press, 2003.

Blackmar, Elizabeth. *Manhattan for Rent, 1785–1850.* Ithaca, NY: Cornell University Press, 1989.

Blair, Cynthia M. *I've Got to Make My Livin': Black Women's Sex Work in Turn-of-the-Century Chicago.* Chicago: The University of Chicago Press, 2010.

Blassingame, John W. *The Slave Community: Plantation Life in the Antebellum South.* New York: Oxford University Press, 1972.

   Black New Orleans, 1860–1880. Chicago: University of Chicago Press, 1973.

   "Using the Testimony of Ex-Slaves: Approaches and Problems." *The Journal of Southern History* 41 (November 1975): 473–492.

Block, Sharon. *Rape and Sexual Power in Early America.* Chapel Hill: The University of North Carolina Press, 2006.

Bolster, W. Jeffrey. *Black Jacks: African American Seamen in the Age of Sail.* Cambridge, MA: Harvard University Press, 1997.

Bontemps, Alex. *The Punished Self: Surviving Slavery in the Colonial South.* Ithaca, NY: Cornell University Press, 2001.

Brasseaux, Carl A. *Acadian to Cajun: Transformation of a People, 1803–1877.* Jackson: University of Mississippi Press, 1992.

Brasseaux, Carl A., Glenn R. Conrad, and David Cheramie, eds. *The Road to Louisiana: The Saint-Domingue Refugees, 1792–1809.* Lafayette, LA: Center for Louisiana Studies, University of Southwestern Louisiana, 1992.

Bristol, Douglas W. *Knights of the Razor: Black Barbers in Slavery and Freedom.* Baltimore, MD: The Johns Hopkins University Press, 2009.

Brown, Christopher Leslie. *Moral Capital: Foundations of British Abolitionism.* Chapel Hill: The University of North Carolina Press, 2006.

Brown, Kate. "Gridded Lives: Why Kazakhstan and Montana Are Nearly the Same Place." *AHR* 106 (February 2001): 17–48.

Brown, Vincent. "Slave Revolt in Jamaica, 1760–1761: A Cartographic Perspective." http://revolt.axismaps.com.

   The Reaper's Garden: Death and Power in the World of Atlantic Slavery. Cambridge, MA: Harvard University Press, 2008.

   "Social Death and Political Life in the Study of Slavery." *AHR* 114, no. 5 (December 2009): 1231–1249.

Buchanan, Thomas C. *Black Life on the Mississippi: Slaves, Free Blacks, and the Western Steamboat World.* Chapel Hill: The University of North Carolina Press, 2004.

Buck-Morss, Susan. "Hegel and Haiti." *Critical Inquiry* 26 (Summer 2000): 821–865.

Buckley, Roger Norman. *Slaves in Red Coats: The British West India Regiments, 1795–1815*. New Haven: Yale University Press, 1979.

Burke, Diane Mutti. *On Slavery's Border: Missouri's Small-Slaveholding Households, 1815–1865*. Athens: University of Georgia Press, 2010.

Bush, Barbara. *Slave Women in Caribbean Society, 1650–1838*. Kingston, Jamaica: Heinemann Publishers, 1990.

Butler, Judith. *Gender Trouble: Feminism and the Subversion of Identity*. New York: Routledge, 1990.

Bodies that Matter. London: Routledge, 1993.

Byrd, Alexander X. *Captives and Voyagers: Black Migrants Across the Eighteenth-Century British Atlantic World*. Baton Rouge: Louisiana State University Press, 2008.

Calloway, Colin G. *The American Revolution in Indian Country: Crisis and Diversity in Native American Communities*. Cambridge: Cambridge University Press, 1995.

Camp, Stephanie. *Closer to Freedom: Enslaved Women and Everyday Resistance in the Plantation South*. Chapel Hill: The University of North Carolina Press, 2004.

Campanella, Richard. *Bienville's Dilemma: A Historical Geography of New Orleans*. Lafayette, LA: University of Louisiana at Lafayette, 2008.

Campbell, James T. *Middle Passages: African American Journeys to Africa, 1787–2005*. New York: Penguin Press, 2006.

Candlin, Kit. *The Last Caribbean Frontier, 1795–1815*. Houndmills: Palgrave Macmillan, 2012.

Carby, Hazel V. *Race Men*. Cambridge, MA: Harvard University Press, 1998.

Carretta, Vincent. *Equiano, the African: Biography of a Self-Made Man*. Athens: University of Georgia Press, 2005.

Phillis Wheatley: Biography of a Genius in Bondage. Athens: The University of Georgia Press, 2011.

Castellanos, Henry C. *New Orleans as It Was: Episodes of Louisiana Life*. New Orleans, LA: The L. Graham Co., Ltd., 1905.

Cauna, Jacques. "93–24 LABATUT (St-Domingue et Martinique, 18°)." *Généalogie et Histoire de la Caraïbe* Bulletin 63 (Septembre 1994): 1149–1150.

ed. *Toussaint Louverture Et L'indépendance D'haïti: Témoignages Pour Un Bicentenaire*. Hommes Et Sociétés. Paris: Société française d'histoire d'outre-mer, 2004.

Cecelski, David S. *The Waterman's Song: Slavery and Freedom in Maritime North Carolina*. Chapel Hill: The University of North Carolina Press, 2001.

Chalhoub, Sidney. "Illegal Enslavement and the Precariousness of Freedom in Nineteenth-Century Brazil." In *Assumed Identities: The Meanings of Race in the Atlantic World*, edited by John D. Garrigus and Christopher Morris, 88–115. College Station: Published for the University of Texas at Arlington by Texas A&M University Press, 2010.

Chase, John Churchill. *Frenchmen, Desire, Good Children ... and Other Streets of New Orleans!* Gretna, LA: Pelican, [1949] 2010.

Chauharjasingh, Archibald. *Lopinot in History.* National Cultural Council. Port of Spain, Trinidad: Columbus Publishers, 1982.

Chauncey, George. *Gay New York: Gender, Urban Culture, and the Makings of the Gay Male World, 1890–1940.* New York: Basic Books, 1994.

Childs, Matt D. *The 1812 Aponte Rebellion in Cuba and the Struggle against Atlantic Slavery.* Chapel Hill: The University of North Carolina Press, 2006.

Chinea, Jorge L. "Diasporic Marronage: Some Colonial and Intercolonial Repercussions of Overland and Waterborne Slave Flight, with Special Reference to the Caribbean Archipelago." *Revista Brasileira do Caribe* 10, no. 19 (July–December 2009): 259–284.

Clark, Emily. *Masterless Mistresses: The New Orleans Ursulines and the Development of a New World Society, 1727–1834.* Chapel Hill: The University of North Carolina Press, 2007.

The Strange History of the American Quadroon: Free Women of Color in the Revolutionary Atlantic World. Chapel Hill: The University of North Carolina Press, 2013.

Clark, Gracia. *Onions Are My Husband: Survival and Accumulation by West African Market Women.* Chicago: University of Chicago Press, 1994.

Clark, John Garretson. *New Orleans 1718–1812: An Economic History.* New Orleans, LA: Pelican Publishing Company, 1982.

Conrad, Glenn R. ed. *The Cajuns: Essays on Their History and Culture.* Lafayette, LA: Center for Louisiana Studies, University of Southwestern Louisiana, 1983.

Cooper, Fred, and Jane Burbank. *Empires in World History: Power and the Politics of Difference.* Princeton: Princeton University Press, 2011.

Cooper, Frederick, Thomas C. Holt, and Rebecca J. Scott. *Beyond Slavery: Explorations of Race, Labor, and Citizenship in Postemancipation Societies.* Chapel Hill: The University of North Carolina Press, 2000.

Craton, Michael. *Testing the Chains: Resistance to Slavery in the British West Indies.* Ithaca, NY: Cornell University Press, 1982.

Creel, Margaret Washington. *"A Peculiar People": Slave Religion and Community-Culture among the Gullahs.* New York: New York University Press, 1988.

Crenshaw, Kimberlé. "Mapping the Margins: Intersectionality, Identity Politics, and Violence Against Women of Color." *Stanford Law Review* 43, no. 6 (July 1991): 1241–1299.

Crutcher, Jr., Michael E. *Tremé: Race and Place in a New Orleans Neighborhood.* Athens: University of Georgia Press, 2010.

Cummins, Light T. "Oliver Pollock's Plantations: An Early Anglo Landowner on the Lower Mississippi, 1769–1824." *Louisiana History* 29, no. 1 (Winter 1988): 35–48.

Davis, David Brion. *The Problem of Slavery in the Age of Revolution, 1770–1823.* Ithaca, NY: Cornell University Press, 1975.

Davis, Thadious M. *Games of Property: Law, Race, Gender, and Faulkner's Go Down, Moses.* Durham: Duke University Press, 2003.

Southscapes: Geographies of Race, Region, and Literature. Chapel Hill: The University of North Carolina Press, 2011.

Davis, Thomas J. *A Rumor of Revolt: The "Great Negro Plot" in Colonial New York*. New York: Free Press, 1985.

Dawdy, Shannon Lee. *Building the Devil's Empire: French Colonial New Orleans*. Chicago: University of Chicago Press, 2008.

Dayan, Colin (Joan). *Haiti, History, and the Gods*. Berkeley: University of California Press, 1995.

De Certeau, Michel. *The Practice of Everyday Life*, trans. Steven F. Rendall. Berkeley: University of California Press, 1984.

Debien, Gabriel, and Philip Wright. *Les colons de Saint-Domingue passés à la Jamaïque: 1792–1835*. Basse-Terre: Archives Départementales, 1975.

Deggs, Mary Bernard, Virginia Meacham Gould, and Charles E. Nolan. *No Cross, No Crown: Black Nuns in Nineteenth-Century New Orleans*. Bloomington: Indiana University Press, 2001.

Delany, Martin Robison. *Blake; or, the Huts of America, a Novel*. Boston: Beacon Press, 1970.

Desdunes, Rodolphe Lucien, and Dorothea Olga McCants. *Our People and Our History: Fifty Creole Portraits*. Baton Rouge: Louisiana State University Press, 1973.

Dessens, Nathalie. *From Saint-Domingue to New Orleans: Migration and Influences*. Gainesville: University Press of Florida, 2007.

Creole City: A Chronicle of Early New Orleans. Gainesville: University Press of Florida, 2015.

Deyle, Steven. *Carry Me Back: The Domestic Slave Trade in American Life*. New York: Oxford University Press, 2005.

Din, Gilbert C. *Spaniards, Planters, and Slaves: The Spanish Regulation of Slavery in Louisiana, 1763–1803*. College Station: Texas A&M University Press, 1999.

Diner, Hasia R. *The Jews of the United States, 1654 to 2000*. Berkeley: University of California Press, 2006.

Domínguez, Virginia R. *White by Definition: Social Classification in Creole Louisiana*. New Brunswick, NJ: Rutgers University Press, 1986.

Downs, Jim. *Sick from Freedom: African-American Illness and Suffering during the Civil War and Reconstruction*. New York: Oxford University Press, 2012.

Drescher, Seymour. *Econocide: British Slavery in the Era of Abolition*. Pittsburgh: University of Pittsburgh Press, 1977.

"The Fragmentation of Atlantic Slavery and the British Intercolonial Slave Trade." In *The Chattel Principle: Internal Slave Trades in the Americas*, edited by Walter Johnson, 234–255. New Haven: Yale University Press, 2004.

Abolition: A History of Slavery and Antislavery. Cambridge: Cambridge University Press, 2009.

Dreyfus, Hubert L., Paul Rabinow, and Michel Foucault. *Michel Foucault, Beyond Structuralism and Hermeneutics*. 2nd edition. Chicago: University of Chicago Press, 1983.

Du Bois, W. E. B. *The Suppression of the African Slave Trade to the United States of America, 1638–1870.* New York: Oxford University Press, [1896] 2007.

Black Reconstruction in America: An Essay toward a History of the Part Which Black Folk Played in the Attempt to Reconstruct Democracy in America, 1860–1880. New York: Oxford University Press, [1935] 2007.

Dubois, Laurent. *Avengers of the New World: The Story of the Haitian Revolution.* Cambridge, MA: The Belknap Press of Harvard University Press, 2004.

A Colony of Citizens: Revolution and Slave Emancipation in the French Caribbean, 1787–1804. Chapel Hill: The University of North Carolina Press, 2004.

"The Haitian Revolution and the Sale of Louisiana." *Southern Quarterly* 44, no. 3 (2007): 18–41.

Ellison, Ralph. *Invisible Man.* New York: Random House, 1952.

Eltis, David, and David Richardson. *Atlas of the Transatlantic Slave Trade.* New Haven: Yale University Press, 2010.

Epstein, James. *Scandal of Colonial Rule: Power and Subversion in the British Atlantic during the Age of Revolution.* Cambridge: Cambridge University Press, 2012.

Eudell, Demetrius L. *The Political Languages of Emancipation in the British Caribbean and the U.S. South.* Chapel Hill: The University of North Carolina Press, 2002.

Eustace, Nicole. *1812: War and the Passions of Patriotism.* Philadelphia: University of Pennsylvania Press, 2012.

Evans, Freddi Williams. *Congo Square: African Roots in New Orleans.* Lafayette, LA: University of Louisiana at Lafayette Press, 2011.

Eze, Emmanuel C. *Achieving Our Humanity: The Idea of the Postracial Future.* New York: Routledge, 2001.

Fabian, Ann. *Card Sharps, Dream Books, and Bucket Shops: Gambling in 19th-Century America.* Ithaca, NY: Cornell University Press, 1990.

Fabian, Johannes. *Time and the Other: How Anthropology Makes Its Objects.* New York: Columbia University Press, 1983.

Ferrer, Ada. "Haiti, Free Soil, and Antislavery in the Revolutionary Atlantic." *AHR* 117, no. 1 (February 2012): 40–66.

Freedom's Mirror: Cuba and Haiti in the Age of Revolution. New York: Cambridge University Press, 2014.

Fett, Sharla M. *Working Cures: Healing, Health, and Power on Southern Slave Plantations.* Chapel Hill: The University of North Carolina Press, 2002.

Fick, Carolyn E. *The Making of Haiti: The Saint Domingue Revolution from Below.* Knoxville: University of Tennessee Press, 1990.

Fields, Barbara. "Slavery, Race, and Ideology in the United States of America." *New Left Review* 181 (1990): 95–118.

Fink, Leon. *Sweatshops at Sea: Merchant Seamen in the World's First Globalized Industry, From 1812 to the Present.* Chapel Hill: The University of North Carolina, 2011.

Fisher, Sybille. *Modernity Disavowed: Haiti and the Cultures of Slavery in the Age of Revolution.* Durham: Duke University Press, 2004.

Fiske, John. "Surveilling the City: Whiteness, the Black Man and Democratic Totalitarianism." *Theory, Culture & Society* 15, no. 2 (May 1998): 67–88.

Follett, Richard. *The Sugar Masters: Planters and Slaves in Louisiana's Cane World, 1820-1860.* Baton Rouge: Louisiana State University Press, 2005.

Foner, Laura. "The Free People of Color in Louisiana and St. Domingue: A Comparative Portrait of Two Three-Caste Slave Societies." *Journal of Social History* 3 (Summer 1970): 406–430.

Forret, Jeff. "Before Angola: Enslaved Prisoners in the Louisiana State Penitentiary." *Louisiana History* 54, no. 2 (Spring 2013): 133–171.

Fortier, Alcée. *A History of Louisiana.* 4 vols. Paris: Groupil & Co., 1904.

Louisiana; Comprising Sketches of Counties, Towns, Events, Institutions, and Persons, Arranged in Cyclopedic Form. Atlanta: Southern Historical Association, 1909.

Foucault, Michel. *Discipline and Punish: The Birth of the Prison*, trans. Alan Sheridan. New York: Pantheon Books, 1979.

Frey, Sylvia. *Water from the Rock: Black Resistance in a Revolutionary Age.* Princeton: Princeton University Press, 1991.

Frey, Sylvia, and Betty Wood. *Come Shouting to Zion: African American Protestantism in the American South and British Caribbean to 1830.* Chapel Hill: The University of North Carolina Press, 1998.

Gallagher, John, and Ronald Robinson. "The Imperialism of Free Trade." *The Economic History Review* 6, no. 1 (1953): 1–15.

Garraway, Doris. *The Libertine Colony: Creolization in the Early French Caribbean.* Durham: Duke University Press, 2005.

Tree of Liberty: Cultural Legacies of the Haitian Revolution in the Atlantic World. Charlottesville: University of Virginia Press, 2008.

Gaspar, David Barry. *Bondmen and Rebels: A Study of Master-Slave Relations in Antigua.* Baltimore, MD: The Johns Hopkins University Press, 1985.

Gaspar, David Barry, and Darlene Clark Hine. *More Than Chattel: Black Women and Slavery in the Americas Blacks in the Diaspora.* Bloomington: Indiana University Press, 1996.

Gaspar, David Barry, and David Patrick Geggus, eds. *A Turbulent Time: The French Revolution in the Greater Caribbean.* Bloomington: Indiana University Press, 1997.

Geertz, Clifford. "What Is a Country If It Is Not a Nation?" *Brown Journal of World Affairs* 4 (1997): 235–247.

Geggus, David, ed. *The Impact of the Haitian Revolution in the Atlantic World.* Columbia: University of South Carolina, 2001.

Germany, Kent. *New Orleans after the Promises: Poverty, Citizenship, and the Search for the Great Society.* Athens: University of Georgia Press, 2007.

"The Politics of Poverty and History: Racial Inequality and the Long Prelude to Katrina." *Journal of American History* 94, no. 3 (December 2007): 743–751.

Ghachem, Malick W. *The Old Regime and the Haitian Revolution.* Cambridge: Cambridge University Press, 2012.

Gilbert, Felix. *To the Farewell Address: Ideas of Early American Foreign Policy.* Princeton: Princeton University Press, 1961.

Gilfoyle, Timothy J. *City of Eros: New York City, Prostitution, and the Commercialization of Sex, 1790–1920*. New York: W. W. Norton & Co., 1992.

Gilroy, Paul. *The Black Atlantic: Modernity and Double Consciousness*. Cambridge, MA: Harvard University Press, 1993.

Glenn, Myra C. *Campaigns Against Corporal Punishment: Prisoners, Sailors, Women, and Children in Antebellum America*. Albany: State University of New York Press, 1984.

Glymph, Thavolia. *Out of the House of Bondage: The Transformation of the Plantation Household*. Cambridge: Cambridge University Press, 2008.

Gomez, Michael A. *Exchanging Our Country Marks: The Transformation of African Identities in the Colonial and Antebellum South*. Chapel Hill: The University of North Carolina Press, 1998.

Black Crescent: The Experience and Legacy of African Muslims in the Americas. New York: Cambridge University Press, 2005.

Gonzalez-Quijano, Lola. *Capitale de L'Amour: Filles et Lieux de Plaisir à Paris au XIXᵉ Siècle*. Paris: Vendémiaire, 2015.

Gordon-Reed, Annette. *The Hemingses of Monticello: An American Family*. New York: W. W. Norton & Co., 2008.

Gotham, Kevin Fox. *Authentic New Orleans: Tourism, Culture, and Race in the Big Easy*. New York: New York University Press, 2007.

Gould, Eliga. "Entangled Histories, Entangled Worlds: The English-Speaking Atlantic as a Spanish Periphery." *AHR* 112, no. 3 (June 2007): 764–786.

Among the Powers of the Earth: The American Revolution and the Making of a New World Empire. Cambridge, MA: Harvard University Press, 2012.

Gould, Virginia Meacham. *Chained to the Rock of Adversity: To Be Free, Black and Female in the Old South*. Athens: University of Georgia Press, 1998.

Grandin, Greg. *The Empire of Necessity: Slavery, Freedom, and Deception in the New World*. New York: Metropolitan Books, 2014.

Greenberg, Amy. *Manifest Manhood and Antebellum American Empire*. Princeton: Princeton University Press, 1998.

Greer, Allan. "Commons and Enclosure in the Colonization of North America." *American Historical Review* 117, no. 2 (April 2012): 365–386.

Grigsby, Darcy Grimaldo. *Extremities: Painting Empire in Post-Revolutionary France*. New Haven: Yale University Press, 2002.

Gross, Ariela Julie. *Double Character: Slavery and Mastery in the Antebellum Southern Courtroom*. Princeton: Princeton University Press, 2000.

Gruesz, Kirsten Silva. *Ambassadors of Culture: The Transamerican Origins of Latino Writing*. Princeton: Princeton University Press, 2002.

Guterl, Matthew Pratt. *American Mediterranean: Southern Slaveholders in the Age of Emancipation*. Cambridge, MA: Harvard University Press, 2008.

Halberstam, Jack. *Female Masculinity*. Durham: Duke University Press, 1998.

Hall, Catherine. *Civilising Subjects: Metropole and Colony in the English Imagination 1830-1867*. Chicago: The University of Chicago Press, 2002.

Hall, Gwendolyn Midlo. *Africans in Colonial Louisiana: The Development of Afro-Creole Culture in the Eighteenth Century*. Baton Rouge: Louisiana State University Press, 1992.

Databases for the Study of Afro-Louisiana History and Genealogy, 1699–1860. Baton Rouge: Louisiana State University Press, 2000.

Slavery and African Ethnicities in the Americas: Restoring the Links. Chapel Hill: The University of North Carolina Press, 2005.

Hanger, Kimberly S. *Bounded Lives, Bounded Places: Free Black Society in Colonial New Orleans, 1769–1803.* Durham: Duke University Press, 1997.

Harding, Rachel E. *A Refuge in Thunder: Candomblé and Alternative Spaces of Blackness.* Bloomington: Indiana University Press, 2000.

Harris, Cheryl. "Whiteness as Property." *Harvard Law Review* 106, no. 8 (1993): 1707–1791.

Harris, Leslie M. *In the Shadow of Slavery: African Americans in New York City, 1626–1863.* Chicago: University of Chicago Press, 2003.

Hartman, Saidiya V. *Scenes of Subjection: Terror, Slavery, and Self-Making in Nineteenth-Century America.* New York: Oxford University Press, 1997.

Lose Your Mother: A Journey Along the Atlantic Slave Route. New York: Farrar, Straus and Giroux, 2007

"Venus in Two Acts." *Small Axe,* 26 (June 2008): 1–14.

Harvey, David. *Spaces of Capital: Towards a Critical Geography.* New York: Routledge, 2001.

Higginbotham, Evelyn Brooks. "African-American Women's History and the Metalanguage of Race." *Signs* 17, no. 2 (1992): 251–274.

Righteous Discontent: The Women's Movement in the Black Baptist Church, 1880–1920. Cambridge, MA: Harvard University Press, 1993.

Higman, B. W. *Slave Populations of the British Caribbean, 1807–1843.* Baltimore, MD: The Johns Hopkins University Press, 1984.

Hindus, Michael Stephen. *Prison and Plantation: Crime, Justice, and Authority in Massachusetts and South Carolina, 1767–1878.* Chapel Hill: The University of North Carolina Press, 1980.

Hinks, Peter P. *To Awaken My Afflicted Brethren: David Walker and the Problem of Antebellum Slave Resistance.* University Park, PA: Pennsylvania State University Press, 1997.

Hirsch, Adam Jay. *The Rise of the Penitentiary: Prisons and Punishment in Early America.* New Haven: Yale University Press, 1992.

Hobbs, Allyson. *A Chosen Exile: A History of Racial Passing in American Life.* Cambridge, MA: Harvard University Press, 2014.

Hodges, Graham Russell. *Root and Branch: African Americans in New York and East Jersey, 1613–1863.* Chapel Hill: The University of North Carolina Press, 1999.

Hodges, Graham Russell, and Alan Edward Brown. *"Pretends to Be Free": Runaway Slave Advertisements from Colonial and Revolutionary New York and New Jersey.* New York: Garland Pub, 1994.

Holt, Thomas C. *The Problem of Freedom: Race, Labor, and Politics in Jamaica and Britain, 1832–1938.* Baltimore, MD: The Johns Hopkins University Press, 1992.

"Marking: Race, Race-Making, and the Writing of History." *AHR* 100 (February 1995): 1–20.

Hooks, Bell. *Talking Back: Thinking Feminist, Thinking Black.* Boston: South End Press, 1989.

Howell, Philip. *Geographies of Regulation: Policing Prostitution in Nineteenth-Century Britain and the Empire.* Cambridge: Cambridge University Press, 2009.

Hunt, Alfred N. *Haiti's Influence on Antebellum America: Slumbering Volcano in the Caribbean.* Baton Rouge: Louisiana State University Press, 1988.

Hylton, Kevin. "'Race', Sport and Leisure: Lessons from Critical Race Theory." *Leisure Studies* 24, no. 1 (January 2005): 81–98.

Ingersoll, Thomas N. "Free Blacks in a Slave Society: New Orleans, 1718–1812." *The William and Mary Quarterly* 48 (April 1991): 173–200.

Mammon and Manon in Early New Orleans: The First Slave Society in the Deep South, 1718–1819. Knoxville: University of Tennessee Press, 1999.

James, C. L. R. *Black Jacobins.* New York: Dial Press, 1938.

Jefferson, Thomas. *Notes on the State of Virginia.* London: John Stockdale, 1787.

Jehenson, Myriam Yvonne, and Peter N. Dunn. *The Utopian Nexus in Don Quixote.* Nashville, TN: Vanderbilt University Press, 2006.

John, A. Meredith. *The Plantation Slaves of Trinidad, 1783–1816.* Cambridge: Cambridge University Press, 1989.

Johnson, Jerah and Louisiana Landmarks Society. *Congo Square in New Orleans.* New Orleans, LA: Samuel Wilson, Jr. Publications Fund of the Louisiana Landmarks Society, 1995.

Johnson, Sara E. *The Fear of French Negroes: Transcolonial Collaboration in the Revolutionary Americas.* Berkeley: University of California Press, 2012.

Johnson, Walter. *Soul by Soul: Life Inside the Antebellum Slave Market.* Cambridge, MA: Harvard University Press, 1999.

"On Agency." *Journal of Social History* 37, no. 1 (Fall 2003): 113–124.

ed. *The Chattel Principle: Internal Slave Trades in the Americas.* New Haven: Yale University Press, 2004.

"The Racial Origins of American Sovereignty." *Raritan* 31, no. 3 (Winter 2012): 50–59.

River of Dark Dreams: Slavery and Empire in the Cotton Kingdom. Cambridge, MA: Harvard University Press, 2013.

Johnston, Norman. *Forms of Constraint: A History of Prison Architecture.* Urbana: University of Illinois Press, 2000.

Jones, Arthur. *Pierre Toussaint.* 1st edition. New York; London: Doubleday, 2003.

Jones, Martha S. "Time, Space, and Jurisdiction in Atlantic World Slavery: The Volunbrun Household in Gradual Emancipation New York." *Law and History Review* 29, no. 4 (November 2011): 1031–1060.

Jung, Moon-Ho. *Coolies and Cane: Race, Labor, and Sugar in the Age of Emancipation.* Baltimore, MD: The Johns Hopkins University Press, 2006.

Kastor, Peter J. *The Nation's Crucible: The Louisiana Purchase and the Creation of America.* New Haven: Yale University Press, 2004.

Kaye, Anthony E. *Joining Places: Slave Neighborhoods in the Old South.* Chapel Hill: The University of North Carolina Press, 2007.

Kelman, Ari. *A River and Its City: The Nature of Landscape in New Orleans.* Berkeley: University of California Press, 2003.

Kennedy, Roger G. *Mr. Jefferson's Lost Cause: Land, Farmers, Slavery, and the Louisiana Purchase.* New York: Oxford University Press, 2003.

Knight, Franklin W. *Slave Society in Cuba during the Nineteenth Century.* Madison, WI: University of Wisconsin Press, 1970.

Knight, Frederick C. *Working the Diaspora: The Impact of African Labor on the Anglo-American World, 1650–1850.* New York: New York University Press, 2010.

Korn, Bertram Wallace. *The Early Jews of New Orleans.* Waltham, MA: American Jewish Historical Society, 1969.

Krauthamer, Barbara. *Black Slaves, Indian Masters: Slavery, Emancipation, and Citizenship in the Native American South.* Chapel Hill: The University of North Carolina Press, 2013.

Lachance, Paul F. "The 1809 Immigration of Saint-Domingue Refugees to New Orleans: Reception, Integration, and Impact." *Louisiana History* 29, no. 2 (Spring 1988): 109–141.

"The Formation of a Three-Caste Society: Evidence from Wills in Antebellum New Orleans." *Social Science History* 18 (Summer 1994): 211–242.

Landau, Emily. *Spectacular Wickedness: Sex, Race, and Memory in Storyville, New Orleans.* Baton Rouge: Louisiana State University Press, 2013.

Landers, Jane. *Atlantic Creoles in the Age of Revolutions.* Cambridge, MA: Harvard University Press, 2010.

Latimer, Jon. *1812: War with America.* Cambridge, MA: Belknap Press of Harvard University Press, 2007.

Le Glaunec, Jean-Pierre. "Slave Migrations and Slave Control in Spanish and Early American New Orleans." In *Empires of the Imagination: The Transatlantic Histories of the Louisiana Purchase*, edited by Peter J. Kastor and François Weil, 204–238. Charlottesville: University of Virginia Press, 2009.

L'armée Indigène: La Défaite de Napoléon en Haïti. Montréal: Lux Editeur, 2014.

"*Un Nègre nommè* [sic] *Lubin ne connaissant pas Sa Nation*': The Small World of Louisiana Slavery." In *Louisiana: Crossroads of the Atlantic World*, edited by Cécile Vidal, 103–122. Philadelphia: University of Pennsylvania Press, 2014.

Lepore, Jill. *New York Burning: Liberty, Slavery and Conspiracy in Eighteenth-Century Manhattan.* New York: Knopf, 2005.

Lewis, Peirce F. *New Orleans: The Making of an Urban Landscape.* Sante Fe, NM: Center for American Places in Association with the University of Virginia Press, 2003.

Li, Stephanie. *Something Akin to Freedom: The Choice of Bondage in Narratives by African American Women.* Albany: State University of New York Press, 2010.

Linebaugh, Peter, and Marcus Rediker. *The Many-Headed Hydra: Sailors, Slaves, Commoners, and the Hidden History of the Revolutionary Atlantic.* Boston: Beacon Press, 2000.

Long, Alecia P. *The Great Southern Babylon: Sex, Race, and Respectability in New Orleans, 1865–1920*. Baton Rouge: Louisiana State University Press, 2004.

Lott, Eric. *Love and Theft: Blackface Minstrelsy and the American Working Class*. New York: Oxford University Press, 1993.

Lyons, Clare A. *Sex among the Rabble: An Intimate History of Gender and Power in the Age of Revolution, Philadelphia, 1730–1830*. Chapel Hill: The University of North Carolina Press, 2006.

Macdonald, Janet. *Feeding Nelson's Navy: The True Story of Food at Sea in the Georgian Era*. London: Chatham Publishing; Pennsylvania: Stackpole Books, 2004.

Malone, Ann Patton. *Sweet Chariot: Slave Family and Household Structure in Nineteenth-Century Louisiana*. Chapel Hill: The University of North Carolina Press, 1992.

Marler, Scott P. *The Merchants' Capital: New Orleans and the Political Economy of the Nineteenth-Century South*. New York: Cambridge University Press, 2013.

Mason, Matthew. "The Battle of the Slaveholding Liberators: Great Britain, the United States, and Slavery in the Early Nineteenth Century." *The William and Mary Quarterly* 59, no. 3 (July 2002): 665–696.

Matory, J. Lorand. *Black Atlantic Religion: Tradition, Transnationalism, and Matriarchy in the Afro-Brazilian Candomble*. Princeton: Princeton University Press, 2005.

McCurry, Stephanie. *Masters of Small Worlds: Yeoman Households, Gender Relations, and the Political Culture of the Antebellum South Carolina Low Country*. New York: Oxford University Press, 1995.

McDaniel, Lorna. "Memory Spirituals of the Liberated American Soldiers in Trinidad's 'Company Villages.'" *Caribbean Quarterly* 40, no. 1 (March 1994): 38–58.

McDonald, Roderick A. *The Economy and Material Culture of Slaves: Goods and Chattels on the Sugar Plantations of Jamaica and Louisiana*. Baton Rouge: Louisiana State University Press, 1993.

McDowell, Linda. *Gender, Identity and Place: Understanding Feminist Geographies*. Cambridge: Polity Press, 1999.

McDowell, Linda, and Joanne P. Sharp. *Space, Gender, Knowledge: Feminist Readings*. London: Arnold, 1997.

McGillivray, Gillian. *Blazing Cane: Sugar Communities, Class, and State Formation in Cuba, 1868–1959*. Durham: Duke University Press, 2009.

McKay, Jim, Michael A. Messner, and Donald F. Sabo. *Masculinities, Gender Relations, and Sport*. Thousand Oaks, CA: Sage Publications, 2000.

McKittrick, Katherine. *Demonic Grounds: Black Women and the Cartographies of Struggle*. Minneapolis: University of Minnesota Press, 2006.

McLaurin, Melton. *Celia, A Slave*. Athens: University of Georgia Press, 1991.

McLennan, Rebecca M. *The Crisis of Imprisonment: Protest, Politics, and the Making of the American Penal State, 1776–1941*. Cambridge: Cambridge University Press, 2008.

Meinig, D. W. *The Shaping of America: A Geographical Perspective on 500 Years of History*. New Haven: Yale University Press, 1986–2004.

Melish, Joanne Pope. *Disowning Slavery: Gradual Emancipation and "Race" in New England, 1780–1860*. Ithaca, NY: Cornell University Press, 1998.

Meranze, Michael. *Laboratories of Virtue: Punishment, Revolution, and Authority in Philadelphia, 1760–1835*. Chapel Hill: The University of North Carolina Press, 1996.

Miles, Tiya. *Ties That Bind: The Story of an Afro-Cherokee Family in Slavery and Freedom*. Berkeley: University of California Press, 2005.

Mintz, Sidney. *Sweetness and Power: The Place of Sugar in Modern History*. New York: Penguin Books, 1986.

Mitchell, Mary Niall. "'Rosebloom and Pure White,' or so It Seemed." *American Quarterly* 54, no. 3 (2002): 369–410.

Raising Freedom's Child: Black Children and Visions of the Future after Slavery. New York: New York University Press, 2008.

Mitchell, Michele. *Righteous Propagation: African Americans and the Politics of Racial Destiny after Reconstruction*. Chapel Hill: The University of North Carolina Press, 2004.

Mitchell, Reid. *All on a Mardi Gras Day: Episodes in the History of New Orleans Carnival*. Cambridge, MA: Harvard University Press, 1995.

Morgan, Jennifer. *Laboring Women: Reproduction and Gender in New World Slavery*. Philadelphia: University of Pennsylvania Press, 2004.

Morrison, Toni. *Playing in the Dark: Whiteness and the Literary Imagination*. Cambridge, MA: Harvard University Press, 1992.

Naylor, Celia E. *African Cherokees in Indian Territory: From Chattel to Citizens*. Chapel Hill: The University of North Carolina Press, 2008.

Neu, Irene D. "Edmond Jean Forstall and Louisiana Banking." *Explorations in Economic History* 7 (Summer 1970): 383–398.

"My Nineteenth-Century Network: Erastus Corning, Benjamin Ingham, Edmond Forstall." Presidential Address, Indiana University, reprinted in *Business and Economic History* 14 (1985), available at www.hnet.org/~business/bhcweb/publications/BEHprint/vo14/p0001-p0016.pdf, accessed January 26, 2010.

Onuf, Peter S. *Statehood and Union: A History of the Northwest Ordinance*. Bloomington: Indiana University Press, 1987.

Painter, Nell Irvin. *Sojourner Truth: A Life, a Symbol*. 1st edition. New York: W. W. Norton & Co., 1996.

Southern History Across the Color Line. Chapel Hill: The University of North Carolina Press, 2002.

Paton, Diana. *No Bond but the Law: Punishment, Race, and Gender in Jamaican State Formation, 1780–1870*. Durham: Duke University Press, 2004.

Patterson, Tiffany Ruby, and Robin D. G. Kelley. "Unfinished Migrations: Reflections on the African Diaspora and the Making of the Modern World." *African Studies Review* 43, no. 1 (April 2000): 11–45.

Peabody, Sue. *"There Are No Slaves in France": The Political Culture of Race and Slavery in the Ancien Régime*. New York: Oxford University Press, 1996.

Penningroth, Dylan C. *The Claims of Kinfolk: African American Property and Community in the Nineteenth-Century South*. Chapel Hill: The University of North Carolina Press, 2003.

Porteous, Laura L., trans. "The Documents in Loppinot Case, 1774." *The Louisiana Historical Quarterly* 12, no. 1 (January 1929): 39–120.

Powell, Lawrence N. *The Accidental City: Improvising New Orleans*. Cambridge, MA: Harvard University Press, 2012.

Pronger, Brian. *The Arena of Masculinity: Sports, Homosexuality, and the Meaning of Sex*. New York: St. Martin's, 1990.

Puar, Jasbir K. *Terrorist Assemblages: Homonationalism in Queer Times*. Durham: Duke University Press, 2007.

Purdue, Theda. "Cherokee Women and the Trail of Tears." *Journal of Women's History* 1, no. 1 (Spring 1989): 14–30.

Putnam, Lara. "To Study the Fragments/Whole: Microhistory and the Atlantic World." *Journal of Social History* 39, no. 3 (Spring 2006): 615–630.

  Radical Moves: Caribbean Migrants and the Politics of Race in the Jazz Age. Chapel Hill: The University of North Carolina Press, 2013.

Rasmussen, Daniel. *American Uprising: The Untold Story of America's Largest Slave Revolt*. New York: Harper, 2011.

Rediker, Marcus Buford. *The Slave Ship: A Human History*. New York: Viking, 2007.

Rightor, Henry, ed. *Standard History of New Orleans, Louisiana*. Chicago: The Lewis Publishing Company, 1900.

Roach, Joseph. *Cities of the Dead: Circum-Atlantic Performance*. New York: Columbia University Press, 1996.

Robinson, Cedric J. *Black Marxism: The Making of the Black Radical Tradition*. Chapel Hill: The University of North Carolina Press, 1983.

Robinson, Randall. *Quitting America: The Departure of a Black Man from His Native Land*. New York: Dutton Adult, 2004.

Rockman, Seth. *Scraping By: Wage Labor, Slavery, and Survival in Early Baltimore*. Baltimore, MD: The Johns Hopkins University Press, 2009.

Rodger, N. A. M. *The Wooden World: An Anatomy of the Georgian Navy*. Annapolis, MD: Naval Institute Press, 1986.

Rodrigue, John C. *Reconstruction in the Cane Fields: From Slavery to Free Labor in Louisiana's Sugar Parishes 1862–1880*. Baton Rouge: Louisiana State University Press, 2001.

Rodriguez, Junius P. "Always 'En Garde': The Effects of Slave Insurrection upon the Louisiana Mentality, 1811–1815." *Louisiana History*, 33 (1992): 399–416.

Rorabaugh W. J. *The Alcoholic Republic, an American Tradition*. New York: Oxford University Press, 1979.

Rose, Gillian. *Feminism and Geography: The Limits of Geographical Knowledge*. Oxford, UK: Polity Press, 1993.

Rothman, Adam. *Slave Country: American Expansion and the Origins of the Deep South*. Cambridge, MA: Harvard University Press, 2005.

  Beyond Freedom's Reach: A Kidnapping in the Twilight of Slavery. Cambridge, MA: Harvard University Press, 2015.

Rothman, David J. *The Discovery of the Asylum; Social Order and Disorder in the New Republic*. Boston: Little, Brown, 1971.

Rothman, Joshua D. *Notorious in the Neighborhood: Sex and Families Across the Color Line in Virginia, 1787–1861*. Chapel Hill: The University of North Carolina Press, 2003.

    Flush Times and Fever Dreams: A Story of Capitalism and Slavery in the Age of Jackson. Athens: University of Georgia Press, 2012.

Rupert, Linda M. "Marronage, Manumission and Maritime Trade in the Early Modern Caribbean." *Slavery & Abolition* 30, no. 3 (2009): 361–382.

Said, Edward W. *Orientalism*. New York: Pantheon Books, 1978.

Saxton, Alexander. *The Rise and Fall of the White Republic: Class Politics and Mass Culture in Nineteenth-Century America*. London; New York: Verso, 1990.

Scarry, Elaine. *The Body in Pain: The Making and Unmaking of the World*. New York: Oxford University Press, 1985.

Schafer, Judith Kelleher. *Slavery, the Civil Law, and the Supreme Court of Louisiana*. Baton Rouge: Louisiana State University Press, 1997.

    Becoming Free, Remaining Free: Manumission and Enslavement in New Orleans, 1846–1862. Baton Rouge: Louisiana State University Press, 2003.

    Brothels, Depravity, and Abandoned Women: Illegal Sex in Antebellum New Orleans. Baton Rouge: Louisiana State University Press, 2009.

Schama, Simon. *Rough Crossings: Britain, the Slaves and the American Revolution*. New York: Harper Collins, 2006.

Schmidt-Nowara, Chris. "*This Rotting Corpse*": Spain between the Black Atlantic and the Black Legend." *Arizona Journal of Hispanic Cultural Studies* 5, no. 1 (2001): 149–160.

Schweninger, Loren. *Families in Crisis in the Old South: Divorce, Slavery, and the Law*. Chapel Hill: The University of North Carolina Press, 2012.

Scott, James C. *Seeing Like a State: How Certain Schemes to Improve the Human Condition Have Failed*. New Haven: Yale University Press, 1998.

Scott, Julius S. "The Common Wind: Currents of Afro-American Communication in the Era of the Haitian Revolution." Ph.D. diss, Duke University, 1986.

Scott, Rebecca J. *Degrees of Freedom: Louisiana and Cuba after Slavery*. Cambridge, MA: The Belknap Press of Harvard University Press, 2005.

    "Paper Thin: Freedom and Re-Enslavement in the Diaspora of the Haitian Revolution." *Law and History Review* 29, no. 4 (2011): 1061–1087.

Scott, Rebecca J., and Jean M. Hébrard. *Freedom Papers: An Atlantic Odyssey in the Age of Emancipation*. Cambridge, MA: Harvard University Press, 2012.

Scully, Pamela, and Diana Paton, eds. *Gender and Slave Emancipation in the Atlantic World*. Durham: Duke University Press, 2005.

Semple, Janet. *Bentham's Prison: A Study of the Panopticon Penitentiary*. Oxford: Clarendon Press, 1993.

Sexton, Jay. *The Monroe Doctrine: Empire and Nation in Nineteenth-Century America*. New York: Hill and Wang, 2011.

Shah, Nayan. *Stranger Intimacy: Contesting Race, Sexuality, and the Law in the North American West*. Berkeley: University of California Press, 2011.

Sheller, Mimi. *Democracy from Below: Erotic Agency and Caribbean Freedom*. Durham: Duke University Press, 2012.

Shugg, Roger W. *Origins of Class Struggle in Louisiana; a Social History of White Farmers and Laborers during Slavery and after, 1840–1875.* Baton Rouge: Louisiana State University Press, 1939.

Smallwood, Stephanie. *Saltwater Slavery: A Middle Passage from Africa to American Diaspora.* Cambridge, MA: Harvard University Press, 2007.

Smith, Gene Allen. *The Slaves' Gamble: Choosing Sides in the War of 1812.* New York: Palgrave Macmillan, 2013.

Smith, Mark M. *Listening to Nineteenth-Century America.* Chapel Hill: The University of North Carolina Press, 2001.

    How Race Is Made: Slavery, Segregation, and the Senses. Chapel Hill: The University of North Carolina Press, 2006.

Souther, J. Mark. *New Orleans on Parade: Tourism and the Transformation of the Crescent City.* Baton Rouge: Louisiana State University Press, 2006.

Spear, Jennifer M. *Race, Sex, and Social Order in Early New Orleans.* Baltimore, MD: The Johns Hopkins University Press, 2009.

Spieler, Miranda Frances. *Empire and Underworld: Captivity in French Guiana.* Cambridge, MA: Harvard University Press, 2012.

Spillers, Hortense. "Mama's Baby, Papa's Maybe: An American Grammar Book." *Diacritics* 17 (Summer 1987): 65–81.

Stanley, Amy Dru. *From Bondage to Contract: Wage Labor, Marriage, and the Market in the Age of Slave Emancipation.* New York: Cambridge University Press, 1998.

Stansell, Christine. *City of Women: Sex and Class in New York, 1789–1860.* Urbana: University of Illinois Press, 1982.

Stolcke, Verena. *Marriage, Class and Colour in Nineteenth-Century Cuba; a Study of Racial Attitudes and Sexual Values in a Slave Society.* London; New York: Cambridge University Press, 1974.

Stoler, Ann Laura. *Carnal Knowledge and Imperial Power: Race and the Intimate in Colonial Rule.* Berkeley: University of California Press, 2002.

    ed. *Haunted by Empire: Geographies of Intimacy in North American History.* Durham: Duke University Press, 2006.

Stuckey, Sterling. *Slave Culture: Nationalist Theory and the Foundations of Black America.* New York: Oxford University Press, 1987.

Sublette, Ned. *The World That Made New Orleans: From Spanish Silver to Congo Square.* Chicago: Lawrence Hill Books: Distributed by Independent Publishers Group, 2008.

Sweet, James H. "The Iberian Roots of American Racist Thought." *The William and Mary Quarterly* 54 (January 1997): 143–166.

    Recreating Africa: Culture, Kinship, and Religion in the African-Portuguese World, 1441–1770. Chapel Hill: The University of North Carolina Press, 2003.

    Domingos Álvares, African Healing, and the Intellectual History of the Atlantic World. Chapel Hill: The University of North Carolina Press, 2011.

Tannenbaum, Frank. *Slave and Citizen: The Negro in the Americas.* New York: A.A. Knopf, 1946.

Tarry, Ellen. *The Other Toussaint: A Modern Biography of Pierre Toussaint, a Post-Revolutionary Black.* Boston: St. Paul Editions, 1981.

Taylor, Alan. *The Internal Enemy: Slavery and War in Virginia, 1772–1832.* New York: W. W. Norton & Co., 2013.

Taylor, Clyde. *The Mask of Art: Breaking the Aesthetic Contract – Film and Literature.* Bloomington: Indiana University Press, 1998.

Thompson, Katrina. *Ring Shout, Wheel About: The Racial Politics of Music and Dance in North American Slavery.* Urbana: University of Illinois Press, 2014.

Thompson, Robert Farris. *Flash of the Spirit: African and Afro-American Art and Philosophy.* New York: Random House, 1983.

Thompson, Shirley Elizabeth. *Exiles at Home: The Struggle to Become American in Creole New Orleans.* Cambridge, MA: Harvard University Press, 2009.

Thompson, Thomas Marshall. "National Newspaper and Legislative Reactions to Louisiana's Deslondes Slave Revolt of 1811." *Louisiana History,* 33 (1992): 5–29.

Thornton, John K. "'I am the Subject of the King of Congo': African Political Ideology and the Haitian Revolution." *Journal of World History* 4, no. 2 (1993): 181–214.

Africa and Africans in the Making of the Atlantic World, 1400–1800. 2nd edition. Cambridge: Cambridge University Press, [1992] 1998.

Thrasher, Albert. *"On to New Orleans!": Louisiana's Heroic 1811 Slave Revolt.* New Orleans, LA: Cypress Press, 1996.

Tinker, Edward Laroque. *Louisiana's Earliest Poet: Julien Poydras and the Paeans to Galvez.* New York: New York Public Library, 1933.

Toledano, Roulhac, Mary Louise Christovich, Betsy Swanson, and Robin Von Breton Derbes. *New Orleans Architecture Volume 6: Faubourg Tremé and the Bayou Road.* New Orleans, LA: Pelican Publishing Company, 2003.

Toledano, Roulhac and National Trust for Historic Preservation in the United States. *The National Trust Guide to New Orleans.* New York: John Wiley, 1996.

Trouillot, Michel-Rolph. *Silencing the Past: Power and the Production of History.* Boston: Beacon, 1995.

Turner, Mary, ed. *From Chattel Slaves to Wage Slaves: The Dynamics of Labour Bargaining in the Americas.* London: James Currey, 1995.

Twinam, Ann. *Public Lives, Private Secrets: Gender, Honor, Sexuality, and Illegitimacy in Colonial Spanish America.* Stanford, CA: Stanford University Press, 1999.

Upton, Dell. *Another City: Urban Life and Urban Spaces in the New American Republic.* New Haven: Yale University Press, 2008.

Usner, Daniel H. *Indians, Settlers, and Slaves in a Frontier Exchange Economy: The Lower Mississippi River Valley Before 1783.* Chapel Hill: The University of North Carolina Press, 1992.

Valencius, Conevery Bolton. *The Health of the Country: How American Settlers Understood Themselves and Their Land.* New York: Basic Books, 2002.

Vidal, Cécile, ed. *Louisiana: Crossroads of the Atlantic World.* Philadelphia: University of Pennsylvania Press, 2014.

Wagner, Bryan. *Disturbing the Peace: Black Culture and the Police Power after Slavery.* Cambridge, MA: Harvard University Press, 2009.

Waldstreicher, David. "Reading the Runaways: Self-Fashioning, Print Culture, and Confidence in Slavery in the Eighteenth-Century Mid-Atlantic." *The William and Mary Quarterly* 56, no. 2 (April 1999): 243–272.

Walker, Clarence. *Deromanticizing Black History: Critical Essays and Reappraisals*. Knoxville: University of Tennessee Press, 1991.

Walker, Daniel. *No More, No More: Slavery and Cultural Resistance in Havana and New Orleans*. Minneapolis: University of Minnesota Press, 2004.

Walker, James W. St. G. *The Black Loyalists: The Search for a Promised Land in Nova Scotia and Sierra Leone, 1783–1870*. Toronto: University of Toronto Press, 1993.

Warner-Lewis, Maureen. *Trinidad Yoruba: From Mother Tongue to Memory*. Kingston, Jamaica: The Press, University of the West Indies, 1997.

Webster, Pnina. "Vernacular Cosmopolitanism." *Theory, Culture & Society* 23, nos. 2–3 (May 2006): 496–498.

Weiss, John McNish. *The Merikens: Free Black American Settlers in Trinidad, 1815–16*. London: McNish & Weiss, 2002.

White, Ashli. "The Limits of Fear: The Saint Dominguan Challenge to Slave Trade Abolition in the United States." *Early American Studies* 2, no. 2 (Fall 2004): 362–397.

Encountering Revolution: Haiti and the Making of the Early Republic. Baltimore, MD: The Johns Hopkins University Press, 2010.

White, Deborah Gray. *Ar'n't I a Woman? Female Slaves in the Plantation South*. Rev. edition. New York: W. W. Norton & Co., [1985] 1999.

White, Shane, and Graham J. White. *Stylin': African American Expressive Culture from Its Beginnings to the Zoot Suit*. Ithaca, NY: Cornell University Press, 1998.

Whitfield, Harvey Amani. *Blacks on the Border: The Black Refugees in British North America, 1815–1860*. Burlington: University of Vermont Press, 2006.

Wilkerson, Isabel. *The Warmth of Other Suns: The Epic Story of America's Great Migration*. New York: Random House, 2010.

Williams, Eric. *Capitalism and Slavery*. Chapel Hill: The University of North Carolina Press, 1944.

History of the People of Trinidad and Tobago. London: Andre Deutsch, 1962.

Wilson, Jr., Samuel, and Leonard Victor Huber. *The Cabildo on Jackson Square*. New Orleans, LA: Pelican Publishing Company, 1988.

Wong, Edlie L. *Neither Fugitive nor Free: Atlantic Slavery, Freedom Suits, and the Legal Culture of Travel*. New York: New York University Press, 2009.

Wood, Gordon S. *Empire of Liberty: A History of the Early Republic, 1789–1815*. Oxford: Oxford University Press, 2009.

Wood, Kirsten E. *Masterful Women: Slaveholding Widows from the American Revolution through the Civil War*. Chapel Hill: The University of North Carolina Press, 2004.

Wood, Peter H. *Black Majority: Negroes in Colonial South Carolina from 1670 through the Stono Rebellion*. New York: Norton & Co., 1975.

Yarema, Allan. *The American Colonization Society: An Avenue to Freedom?* Lanham, MD: University Press of American, 2006.

Index

Figures are indicated by italics